MOMENTS
OF
TRANSCENDENCE

Also edited by Dov Peretz Elkins and published by Jason Aronson Inc.

Moments of Transcendence: Inspirational Readings for Rosh Hashanah

MOMENTS
OF
TRANSCENDENCE
Inspirational Readings for
Yom Kippur

Edited by
DOV PERETZ ELKINS

JASON ARONSON INC.
Northvale, New Jersey
London

This book was set in 10 point Schneidler by Lind Graphics of Upper Saddle River, New Jersey, and printed by Haddon Craftsmen of Scranton, Pennsylvania.

Library of Congress Cataloging-in-Publication Data

Moments of transcendence : inspirational readings for Yom Kippur / edited by Dov Peretz Elkins
    p. cm.
  Includes index.
  ISBN 0-87668-504-1
  1. Yom Kippur – Meditations. I. Elkins, Dov Peretz.
BM695.A8M66 1992
296.4'32 – dc20   92-9303

Manufactured in the United States of America. Jason Aronson Inc. offers books and cassettes. For information and catalog write to Jason Aronson Inc., 230 Livingston Street, Northvale, New Jersey 07647.

Dedicated
with respect and affection
to
Rabbi Sidney Greenberg
Mentor, Model, Teacher, and Friend

CONTENTS

5 HEAR, O ISRAEL 111

14 NEXT YEAR IN JERUSALEM   249

INTRODUCTION

The modern worshiper often finds him/herself at a loss to penetrate the meaning of the medieval poems collected in the High Holy Day prayer book, the Mahzor. Inspiration comes from the rabbi's sermon, the beautiful music of the cantor or the choir, and the penetrating blast of the shofar.

Unfortunately, the profound message of the Day of Atonement, Yom Kippur, of the importance of avoiding the sins of racism and exploitation, being insensitive to the ubiquitous abject poverty of our cities, to the homelessness and the ecological devastation, the sins of neglecting the aged, the addicted, and the diseased – little of this gets through to the heart and soul of the worshiper who is mesmerized by the rhythm of the music or the cadence of the sermon – or, alternatively, prefers to sleep (literally or otherwise) through the entire experience.

The inclusions in this volume are designed to afford today's participant in holy day services a modern midrash to make contemporary the themes of sin, repentance, personal and social change, societal justice, forgiveness, spiritual growth, living with joy and hope and ecstasy, commitment to higher ideals, becoming our truest and most authentic selves, deepening our capacity to love, and savoring the divine gift of life.

In ancient times Yom Kippur was a deeply dramatic experience. When the Kohen Gadol (high priest) entered the Holy of Holies (only on that day was he permitted to do so) and pronounced the ineffable name of God, which he was permitted to enunciate at no other time, the heightened sense of drama and religious excitement was at the highest pitch of spiritual fervor. Yom Kippur worship today needs to find new ways to connect the worshiper with the liturgy and the singular meaning of the day – if not to reach the same high pitch of drama, at least to make the worship experience become more emotional, more engaging, more filled with religious energy.

The intense drama of the biblical Temple no longer extant, this anthology of modern midrash is crafted to bind the heart and soul of the reader to the ancient and medieval prayers through contemporary commentaries, embellishments, and elaborations on its central themes.

If through reading these selections the reader is enabled to build a bridge between the words and worlds of our ancestors and the meanings, themes, and ideas that constitute the central spiritual agenda of the private and public life of the modern Jew, then the purpose of this anthology will have been well accomplished.

Shalom, Shalom – La-rachok ve-lakarov
amar Adonai, ure-fativ.

"Shalom, Shalom –
Shalom to those who are far off,
Shalom to those who are near,"
saith the Lord –
"And I shall heal them."

–Isaiah 57:19
Haftarah for Yom Kippur

1

KOL NIDRE – OUR VOWS, OUR PROMISES

The Court

In this spirit, 800 years ago, Rabbi Meir of Rothenberg transformed his congregation into a legal body on Yom Kippur. So too do we come together on this night, as a legal community, transforming our sanctuary into a court for the Jewish soul.

We understand the gravity with which we Jews approach the act of absolving a vow, yet we know that our failures cannot be simply left as a chain dragging us down. Yom Kippur is a day when –

> Rebuke leads to repentance
> Reproach leads to re-evaluation
> Regret leads to repair
> Remorse leads to renewal
> Retreat leads to revival
> Renunciation leads to rebirth.

So in the words of Rabbi Meir:

By the authority of the heavenly tribunal, and of the court below, with divine sanction and with the sanction of this holy community, we declare this congregation a lawful gathering which welcomes all transgressors into its midst.

So we turn to those around us
As did our ancestors
And those before them
So many – so often –
So long ago.
And beg –
Implore –
Seek –
Not absolution so we can saunter forth
And break anew
But understanding
And the right to start again.

–Rabbi Allen S. Maller

❈❈❈❈❈❈❈❈❈❈❈❈❈❈

A Meditation before Kol Nidre

Eternal God, who calls us to repentance, we are grateful for the opportunity to answer Your call, to forsake our sins, and to turn to You with all our hearts.

Yet we know that repentance is difficult. We know that there have been times when we resolved to mend our ways and did not succeed.

Even the admission that we have done wrong does not come easily. Our pride is as tall as the mountains; our vanity is as wide as the sea; and excuses abound.

But before You there are no secrets. To You all stands revealed. Our pettiness and our greed, our selfishness and our weakness, our running to do evil and our limping to do good – all these are known to You. On this night of atonement, we yearn to become better than we have been. For You, O Lord, have given us the great gift of atonement, enabling individuals and communities to return to You and do Your will.

Open our hearts to the call of this sacred night, so that the words of our prayers may remain with us to renew us and refine us. May our deeds make us worthy to hear Your divine assurance, *"Salahti –* I have forgiven."

–Author unknown

※※※※※※※※※※※※※※※

Introduction to Kol Nidre

It has been said: For transgressions against God, the Day of Atonement atones; but for transgressions between one human being and another, the Day of Atonement does not atone unless they have first been reconciled.

> Once more Atonement Day has come,
> All pretence gone, with naked heart,
> revealed to the hiding self,
> we stand on holy ground,
> between the day that was
> and the one that must be,
> and we tremble.
> At what did we aim?
> How did we stumble?
> What did we take, what did we give?
> To what were we blind?
> Last year's confession came easy to the lips;
> Will this one come from deeper than the skin?
> Say then: Why are these paths strewn with promises
> like fallen leaves?
> Say then: When shall our lust be for wisdom?
> Say now, "Our dream shall be of a kiss
> that mates compassion to the just."
> O Hope of Israel:
> In our weakness, give us strength;
> in our blindness be our guide;
> when we falter, hold our hand.
> Make consistent our impulse for good;
> let us know the joy of walking in your ways.
>
> Light dawns for the righteous, and
> gladness for the upright in heart.

A whisper of wings; heaven and earth embrace; promises are remembered. Saint and sinner alike commune with the Most High. We are at one.

Heart of all life, from this Day of Atonement to the next – may we reach it in peace – all Israel makes these vows: to turn from sin and wrongdoing, and to walk in the way of Your Law, the path of justice and right; help us to keep these vows made with open hearts. We have come to seek pardon and forgiveness.

–Author unknown

✺✺✺✺✺✺✺✺✺✺✺✺✺

To Raise the Fallen

At the beginning of the Atonement service the most venerable men in the congregation solemnly repeat from the *Almemor:* "With the permission of the Court of High, and with the permission of the Congregation below, we declare it permitted to pray with hardened transgressors." Why this custom? In some communities of the Middle Ages there were persons who, by their conduct, had placed themselves outside the pale of Judaism; cowardly apostates, for example, who sold their souls; informers, who broadcast false accusations against their brethren; insubordinates, outcasts, criminals. Throughout the year those never sought spiritual fellowship with their brethren. On Yom Kippur, however, they would steal into some corner of the synagogue and join the worshippers in prayer. The Rabbis thereupon instituted this solemn declaration, in order to proclaim in most unmistakable terms that, no matter what a man's mode of life – slanderer, apostate, outcast – he is still a brother. "*We* have transgressed, *we* have dealt treacherously, *we* have robbed," do we pray. We associate ourselves with the most forlorn souls that sin in darkness, because we recognize that society – we ourselves – are largely responsible for their actions. Many a time has our evil example misled others, become a stumbling-block in the way of the blind. And all our Yom Kippur vows to rise to a higher life are useless, unless we endeavor to raise others who have fallen.

–Rabbi Joseph H. Hertz

✺✺✺✺✺✺✺✺✺✺✺✺✺

Pardoned

Rabbi Levi Yitzchak once said Kol Nidre with such a passion, with many tears and great emotion, that, in the middle, he felt exhausted. He stopped the prayer and proclaimed, "Ribbono shel Olam, I have no more strength to continue. Now, YOU say: Salachti kid-varekha! 'I have pardoned them, as you have asked.'"

–Rabbi Simcha Kling

❊❊❊❊❊❊❊❊❊❊❊❊❊❊❊❊

Kol Nidre – Once a Time for Joy?

Many beautiful legends have grown up around the figure of Reb Levi Yitzchak of Berditchev, known affectionately as *Der Derbaremdiger* – as the compassionate one. The most touching one is about a Kol Nidre night in his "cloise." His weary flock and disciples had gathered for this awesome service. Behind them was a year of hunger, privation and torment at the hands of their gentile neighbors. The maggid or the *mochee-ach* – the exhorter – was invited to preach. As was the wont of maggidim in those days, he lashed out at the congregants, recounting their sins and their backsliding, described the terrible punishments awaiting them and exhorted them to repent. The crying and the weeping of the congregants reached a high pitch. At that moment Reb Levi Yitzchak ascended the pulpit in anger, shoved the exhorter aside, pounded the pulpit, called for silence, and shouted, "Stop your scolding. These are God's holy children. This is a time for rejoicing." He ordered the Sifrei Torah to be taken out of the Ark and together with his Hasidim danced in joy.

This legend is an echo of the Midrash that the second tablets were brought down from Sinai by Moses on Yom Kippur. . . .

It is the custom in many synagogues to introduce the Kol Nidre service with the hakofot of the Torah to the accompaniment of the chant *or zarua la-Zadik oole-yishray lev simcha* ["Light is sown for the righteous, and joy for the upright of heart"].

Some day, we pray, the awe of Yom Kippur will be joined to the joy of Simchat Torah. Amen.

> – Rabbi Benjamin Z. Kreitman
> *The Rabbis Speak* (ed. Teplitz)

❊❊❊❊❊❊❊❊❊❊❊❊❊❊❊❊

All Vows

All vows, promises, and commitments made in Your Presence
Since last Yom Kippur and in the years before,
May we be given strength to keep them.

Our marriage vows – may they endure
Through dark days and through dull days,
Through fatigue and through anger.
May our love prove strong enough, and our faith deep enough,
to last.

Our vows to ourselves, commitments to good health,
May we take our own lives seriously enough to heed them,
Keeping our promises in the way we eat and drink,
The way we work and rest,
And the things that get us angry.

The promises we made to study and to worship –
We meant them when we made them,
But so many things get in the way.
This time, may we be strong enough to let our better selves
   prevail.

Promises made by boys and girls, who stood on this pulpit,
Who glimpsed what life as Jews might hold in store for them,
May their idealism and their vision be with them through all their days.

Commitments made to parents and to friends,
Pledges to charity, and other good intentions, –
Help us to become as noble, compassionate, and generous,
As we saw ourselves to be at those moments.

Dear God, we meant in all seriousness the promises we made
To You, to each other, and to ourselves,
Even as we mean the vows we speak tonight.
They were our reaching toward You, as plants toward the light.

May You reach down to us as we reach up toward You,
And give us strength and self-respect, fidelity and vision,
To grow to be the people we have sworn to be.

All vows, commitments, obligations,
Promises we make
From this Yom Kippur day until the next –
May we be strong enough to keep them.

> –Rabbi Harold S. Kushner
> *For Modern Minds and Hearts* (ed. Karp)
> Copyright © 1971, Media Judaica

Promises

The English artist Jonathan Swift once made the cynical observation that "promises and piecrusts are made to be broken." Swift had probably seen ample evidence of fractured promises, and so have we.

But however casually we may sometimes treat the plighted word, deep down we do feel, as we have been taught, that a man's word should indeed be his bond, and that a person who cannot be trusted to honor a promise cannot be trusted at all. Our noblest instincts endorse the biblical teaching: "When a man vows a vow . . . he shall not break his word; he shall do according to all that proceeds out of his mouth" (Numbers 30:3).

Judaism took this teaching so seriously that the most sacred day of the Jewish year, the Day of Atonement, is ushered in with a prayer that deals with promises and vows. That prayer, Kol Nidre, dramatically reminds us that promises are not piecrusts.

Among the best-known lines of Robert Frost are: "The woods are lovely, dark and deep. /But I have promises to keep,/ And miles to go before I sleep./ . . ." Frost was once asked what promises he had in mind when he wrote those lines. The poet replied, "Oh, promises to myself and promises to my ancestors."

All of us, like the poet, have promises to keep to ourselves. And I am not thinking only of promises we put into words or write out over our signatures. Some of the most sacred promises are made without words in the silent sanctuary of the soul. There are the promises we have made to ourselves: to surrender a destructive habit, to abandon some shabby and unworthy practice, to effect a reconciliation with a friend or relative, to become more attentive parents and more devoted mates, to give more things of the spirit. How many of these promises have we treated like piecrusts?

There are other unspoken promises to ourselves. We are each endowed at birth with all sorts of magnificent potentialities. There is within us a capacity for idealism, a yearning for truth and beauty and nobility, a sensitivity to the needs and dreams of other people.

In the hopeful dawn of youth, we feel these stirrings inside us and we promise to bring them to life. And yet so often, as the years pass by, we permit these promises to be swept under the rug of expediency. We chalk them up to immaturity and we go on to live "more realistically." Then there comes a moment of honest self-confrontation when we take stock of the unkept promises and we are moved to confess, as did F. Scott Fitzgerald when he wrote, "I have been only a mediocre steward of my talent."

We have promises to keep and miles to go before we sleep.

–Rabbi Sidney Greenberg
Say Yes to Life
Copyright © 1982, Crown Publishers

✠✠✠✠✠✠✠✠✠✠✠✠✠✠✠

Modern Kol Nidre Tale

Where is Yossele?

When the American forces reached the Buchenwald death camp, they opened the gates of the camp wide and liberated the inmates. The prisoners left the camp and dispersed, each going his way.

Reb Leizer of Czenstochow was one of the freed inmates. At the gate he paused. "Where? Where should I go?" He knew that everyone else in his family had been murdered. All of them came with him to the camp, and he saw them led to the crematoria for burning.

Only one hope remained. As all of the people of the town were being herded together for shipment to the death camp, he was able to smuggle his little son Yossele out of the ghetto and into the "Aryan" section of town. "Who knows?" said Reb Leizer to himself, "Perhaps the child is still alive, still alive." He would go looking for him. But how? Where?

Reb Leizer went back to Czenstochow, disguised as a beggar. Lest the Czenstochow gentiles recognize him, he put on peasant's clothes and a cap with a low brim down to his eyes. He wandered about the streets and the market-places, and every time he saw a boy about Yossele's age, he would stop and look at him closely. Perhaps this was his son.

He began asking guardedly, "Did anybody know the Leizer family, or what happened to it?" People told him that the family had left the town in the death trains, everyone except the little boy, whom someone took to the monastery. Which monastery? No one knew.

"The boy is alive," decided Reb Leizer. "I will save him."

He went from one monastery to the next, inquiring about his son. The monks denied ever seeing him. No Jewish child, they claimed, had ever crossed the threshold of a monastery. Reb Leizer knew they were lying, but what could he do?

He went and bought an organ. Among the tunes he put into it was the melody of Kol Nidre. Reb Leizer strapped the organ to his back and began making the rounds of the streets and yards. Wherever he saw children playing he would set the organ down on its legs and begin turning the handle. Immediately he would be surrounded by children. As the children stood listening, he would watch their faces closely – particularly when the organ ground out the tune of Kol Nidre. Did any child's face change or show some emotion – fear, perhaps, or sadness and longing?

One day, as the organ was sounding the Kol Nidre tune, a villager came close and asked: "This sad melody you're playing – how did you come to it? Isn't it one of the songs of the cursed Zhids?" "This is a tune I brought from Siberia," replied Reb Leizer, "All the songs there are sad." This seemed to satisfy the peasant, and he went away.

Thus did Reb Leizer wander from village to village, from one monastery to the next. Whenever he saw a child show some emotion as the Kol Nidre melody was played, he knew that the child was Jewish. As all the other children scattered, he would follow this child, talk to him, and tell him that the war was over and he could go back to his own people.

For a full year Reb Leizer and his organ made the rounds of the monasteries. He was able to save scores of Jewish children and restore them to their faith. But Yossele was not among them. In the meantime, Reb Leizer roused suspicions. The monks drove him away, and he could no longer come near a monastery.

Reb Leizer knew that his journey was at an end. He raised his eyes to the heavens and said, "Master of the world, my wife and children went up to heaven in smoke, and I have been wandering among the monasteries to find Yossele, in vain. From now on, O Master of the world, I am allowing you the good deed of caring for Yossele. Keep him in Your sight. Safeguard him along with all the Jewish children for whom there is none to care."

Reb Leizer took his organ and buried it in the ruins of a destroyed synagogue and he went to Israel. People from that district in Poland say that at times they hear the tunes of a hand organ coming out of the earth, and among the tunes is the melody of Kol Nidre.

– Author unknown

※※※※※※※※※※※※※※

Living Lines

Merely to Have Survived

Merely to have survived is not an index of excellence,
Nor, given the way things go,
Even of low cunning.
Yet we have seen the wicked in great power.
And spreading himself like a green bay tree.
And the good as if they had never been;
Their voices are blown away on the winter wind.
And again we wander in the wilderness
For our transgressions
Which are confessed in the daily papers.

※※※※※※※※※※※※※※

Bridging the Gap of a Split Image

The mystic hold which Kol Nidre has over us may be the result of our awareness that under the pressures of life, there will be times when our deeds may not be consistent with our principles and when our achievements may not square with the promises inherent in us.

Kol Nidre prompts us to try harder to bring integrity into our decisions. The intent of Kol Nidre may be compared to that of the range finder on a camera. Looking through a range finder the photographer will see a split image–a forehead over here and a chin over there. By turning the focus ring, he brings the split image into alignment. Kol Nidre serves as the mechanism of focus.

If you are not familiar with a camera, let me suggest a TV set. Without fine tuning, facial color may be transposed on the scenery, the color of the necktie on the chin, or the color of the lipstick on the dress. Only by fine tuning can you bring the color, brightness, and image into alignment. Kol Nidre is like the fine tuner on the TV set.

In the channels of living, each person projects dreams, hopes and aspirations. We make promises; we express resolves. There are promises inherent in our family relationships, in the position we occupy in the marketplace and in the community. But somehow life blurs the promise and fogs the resolve. The promises inherent in us fade away, sometimes because of something we have done, and sometimes because of something done to us. In either case, it is all too easy to reach a point where we capitulate to a sense of failure and say, "I am sorry. I can't make it. It is not worth it; it can't be done." Life is out of focus.

Too much of life is out of focus. There is a distance between what we are and what we could be, a gap between where we are and where we wanted to be. Kol Nidre comes to help us bridge that gap.

–Rabbi Stanley Rabinowitz

※※※※※※※※※※※※※※

The Courtroom of Our Souls

We gather tonight ten days into the New Year. It is Yom Kippur. We have come to pray, to praise, to turn inward, and to reevaluate our lives and our deeds. We have come to hear Kol Nidre. As its stirring sounds draw near we think back to years gone by.

We sat then in other sanctuaries, at the side of parents or grandparents now grown old or long since gone. We gazed up at them and dimly sensed the meaning of a Jewish soul. Indeed, the piercing possibilities of this day are not this single day's alone, rather they are built upon the years of "Kol Nidres" that reach beyond memory and from tradition's sturdy root for today's ever flowing branch.

> Kol Nidre is a paradox
> Because life itself is a paradox.
> Kol Nidre, the most moving moment
> Of the most sacred day –
> Is not a prayer at all, it is
> A legal formula nullifying and canceling
> All our vows.
> Not those between people,
> Only those between a person and God.
> Yet the name of God is not even mentioned
> During the Kol Nidre.
>
> But this is the greatest paradox of all:
> Is Kol Nidre for the vows of the past year
> Or for the vows of the year to come?
> For vows we made
> That we betrayed,
> Or future vows
> To be made in vain?
> The answer lies in the human paradox:
> We need to vow
> To swear commitment
> To future hopes, to higher ideals.
> Knowing that our reach exceeds our grasp
> And that some of our vows will be made in vain –
> nevertheless we pray:
>
> > All vows, promises, and commitments we made
> > since last Yom Kippur and in the years before –
> > May we be given strength to keep them.
>
> But even as we vow, next time . . .
> We are conscious how last time . . .
> We failed.

The guilt of our failures weighs heavily.
We sinned, we transgressed, we failed.
It hurts so much, we fear to admit it.
We chastise ourselves secretly
Disparaging our efforts repeatedly,
For the more committed we were to the ideal
The greater is the guilt we feel.

Yet how can we hope to renew
When in our guilt we despair?
Thus the vows unrealized of the past
Prevent vows idealized of rebirth.

Can a year really be new
After all that we have been through?
It is a cycle that takes us nowhere
Until past guilt for human failure is
Disavowed by Kol Nidre.

There are broken vows that threaten to destroy the individual. There are vows betrayed, whereby an individual gives up something of abiding value. The Kol Nidre focuses attention upon the essential nature of self-respect and self-healing. Kol Nidre reminds us that there are abiding values of the utmost importance to each of us, that sometimes we cannot maintain faithfulness to these values, and that we are not isolated and alone in this very human situation.

It is Yom Kippur and we come, we transgressors, to confront ourselves in the courtroom of our souls. We hear Kol Nidre, the ancient legal formula, freeing us from unfulfilled vows so that we can start anew – wiser and perhaps stronger.

–Rabbi Allen S. Maller

XXXXXXXXXXXXXXX

The Stranger Within

"And all the Congregation of the people Israel shall be forgiven, as well as the stranger who dwells among them. For all the people Israel acted in error."

This is the first line we read after Kol Nidre. The stranger who lived with the Israelites and shared their way of life was entitled to the gift of forgiveness too. Yet tradition interpreted the verse differently. Say the Rabbis, the verse refers not only to strangers within the communities but to strangers within us. Alien forces of destruction and despair who are very much a part of us and whom we wish were not.

That alien is sin in tradition. The unwelcome stranger we let into our lives who makes us be other than what we want to be. The more familiar this stranger becomes, the more dangerous he becomes, for with time we fail to recognize his capacity to cause alienation in our relationships with God, each other and ourselves.

Yom Kippur is the reminder that we cannot be at peace, we cannot be the people we truly want to be until the stranger who alienates is banished from our lives. This is a task we accomplish not by hating ourselves or others, but relearning the dreams and values that make us who we are and leave no room for the stranger.

—Rabbi James S. Rosen

※※※※※※※※※※※※※※

Deeds Are Prayers

The great Rabbi Israel Salanter was missing from his synagogue on the Eve of Atonement, the Kol Nidre, the holiest night of the Jewish calendar. The elders of the synagogue went out searching for him and they found him. There are two versions: one, he was taking care of a wounded calf, the other, he was helping some sick child. And they said to him, "Rabbi, why aren't you in the synagogue?" He said, "Do you see what I'm doing?" "But Rabbi, it's your duty to be in the synagogue praying." He said, "I am praying. Every act of kindness is a prayer – a prayer that walks, moves, breathes and lives."

—Rabbi William B. Silverman

※※※※※※※※※※※※※※

Three Types of Jews

As we recite the "Shehechiyanu" blessing on Kol Nidre night, thanking God for keeping us alive, sustaining us, and helping us to arrive at this day, we may transfer the thought to those who have come to shul Kol Nidre Eve.

There are those Jews who are "shehechiyanu" – who live their Judaism but do not participate or support others in the process. There are those who are "v'kimanu"–they support and sustain "Yiddishkeit" but do not integrate the ideals they support into their own lives. And finally, there are those who are "v'higianu"–they are merely arrived at shul, at their Judaism, simply having gone along for the ride. We might even say that there is a little of each of these qualities in all of us.

We pray that the rejuvenating experience that is Yom Kippur will help us to combine these qualities of "Shehechiyanu, V'kimanu, V'higianu" to produce more complete Jewish individuals, "ki l'chol haam bishgaga"–"for the entire nation has fallen short of the mark."

–Joseph S. Ozarowski

❈❈❈❈❈❈❈❈❈❈❈❈❈

On This Night of Atonement

O God of forgiveness,
on this night of atonement we come before You,
haunted by memories of duties unperformed,
of promptings disobeyed, of beckonings ignored.

We confess
that there were opportunities for kindness and service
which we allowed to pass by in the year just ended.

We are ashamed
of sins committed with evil intent,
as well as of follies committed unwittingly,
or even with good intentions.

Make us honest enough to recognize our transgressions,
big enough to admit them, strong enough to forsake them.

Humble us by showing us what we are;
exalt us with a vision of what we may yet grow to be.

Keep us ever mindful of our dependence upon You,
and help us to understand Your need of us.

United with You in holy partnership,
may we dedicate our lives to Your law of love.

Help us to create homes filled with joy and harmony,
and to labor for peace among communities and nations.

On this sacred night, grant us atonement,
and help us to find serenity within ourselves.

Kindle within us the fires of faith;
and set aglow our courage to live the words we pray.

–Rabbi Sidney Greenberg
Contemporary Prayers and Readings for the High Holidays, Sabbaths, and Special Occasions
Copyright © 1972, Media Judaica

No More Hide and Seek

Robert Fulghum, American writer, newspaper columnist and former Unitarian minister, published a book intriguingly entitled: *All I Really Need To Know I Learned In Kindergarten,* in which he derives profound life lessons from the world of childhood and everyday, commonplace occurrences. I share with you briefly, part of Fulghum's commentary on the children's game *Hide-and-Seek.* He writes:

> Did you have a kid in your neighborhood who always hid so good, nobody could find him? We did. After a while, we would give up on him and go off, leaving him to rot wherever he was. Sooner or later he would show up, all mad because we didn't keep looking for him . . .
>
> As I write this, the neighborhood game goes on, and there is a kid under a pile of leaves in the yard just under my window. He has been there a long time now, and everybody else is found and they are about to give up on him . . . I considered going out and telling them where he is hiding . . . Finally, I just yelled "Get found, kid!" out of the window. And scared him so bad he started crying and ran home to tell his mother. It's real hard to know how to be helpful sometimes.
>
> A man I know found out last year he had terminal cancer. He was a doctor. And knew about dying, and he didn't want to make his family and friends suffer through that with him. So he kept his secret. And died. Everybody said how brave he was to bear his suffering in silence and not tell everybody . . . But privately, his family and friends said how angry they were that he didn't need them, didn't trust their strength. And it hurt that he didn't say good-bye.

Robert Fulghum concludes:

> He hid too well. Getting found would have kept him in the game. *Hide-and-seek,* grown-up style. Wanting to hide. Needing to be sought. Confused about being found. "I don't want anybody to know." "What will people think?"

Hiding is something that we do well. Too well at times. We hide from each other, we hide from our families, our friends. And we hide from our people. We hide from God. Tonight, Yom Kippur, the culmination of the Ten Days of Repentance, begins. And *teshuvah,* repentance (more correctly, return) is just that—return from our hiding places, return from where we have hidden from each other, from tradition, from God.

                                                            —Rabbi Philip S. Scheim

✠✠✠✠✠✠✠✠✠✠✠✠✠✠

"Get Up!"

O Lord, sometimes I feel rotten inside.
Empty—phony.
And no one else knows how bad I feel.
They think I am fine . . . doing well . . . successful even.
But I know all the times I have failed.
The people I disappointed . . . the mitsvot I avoided.

What hope can I have for the new year,
I shouldn't even make new promises
Seeing how my efforts in the past . . . failed.
Last Rosh Hashanah's resolutions soon faded away.
My bad habits . . . remain unbroken.
My good intentions . . . remain unrealized
I can make no new vows . . . I can make no new efforts
I give up.

And then, during the Kol Nidre, I heard your plea,
    "Get up!
    I only commanded one day for afflicting your soul.
    I gave you ten days for repentance,
    For turning over a new leaf in the Book of Life.
    Now you will have fifty weeks . . . to be renewed.
    Even if you don't have faith in yourself
    I have faith in you.
    Get up off the floor and get up quickly
    Falling isn't the worst sin,
    Staying on the floor is."

                                                            —Rabbi Allen S. Maller

✖✖✖✖✖✖✖✖✖✖✖✖✖✖✖✖

Jewish Existence – Mystery and Miracle

It is on Passover, at the Seder table, that our children ask us, *Mah nishtannah halaylah hazeh mikkol haleilot,* "Why is this night different from all other nights?" That question we might, with even greater justice, ask ourselves tonight. For Kol Nidre Eve is unique among all the nights of the year in making every Jew conscious of his Jewish existence, and reminding him of his share in the life of his people. Even the most estranged of our brothers, if he possesses the tiniest spark of loyalty to his people and his God, wishes to be in the synagogue on the night of the Sabbath of Sabbaths.

Every aspect of the Day is designed to heighten our sense of awe and wonder at the pathos and the glory of Jewish survival. Every member of the congregation draped in the Tallit, the white curtain on the Holy Ark, the white robes worn by the rabbi and the cantor – all speak to the sensitive spirit.

Above all it is the Kol Nidre prayer that stirs the heart of even the most indifferent Jew. Christians as well as Jews have been deeply moved by this outstanding prayer in our liturgy. The famous German general Helmuth von Moltke loved to have the Kol Nidre melody played for him by the well-known violinist, Joachim. The best-known setting of the Kol Nidre is that of Max Bruch, himself a non-Jew. No more beautiful tribute to the Kol Nidre has ever been written than that of the gifted German poet and dramatist, Nikolai Lenau:

"Closer to my heart than 'the Marseillaise' is a third melody, which is entirely enveloped in sorrow. It is a night-song of those seeking repentance, broken children of men who regret their sins. This prayer of grief is called *Kol Nidre.*

"I heard it many years ago in my native town. The eve of Yom Kippur had arrived. I hid myself in a corner of the synagogue, so that the pious Jews might not be distressed by the presence of a Gentile lad. Big, thick wax candles were aflame. The people stood with heads bent low in broad, snow-white garments which looked like shrouds.

"Suddenly the cantor, with a deeply earnest, heartrending melody, rich in awe and supplication, began to sing. I had to struggle with a rare feeling of emotion. Feverishly I sighed. Hot, burning tears pouring from one's eyes cast a wondrous spell and at the same time purified. I fled into the night and came home. In that unforgettable hour, no black speck defiled my soul.

"Who had created this melody? The old people do not know. They have received this song from inheritance from their ancestors. Such grief-stricken songs, it seems to me, are never created by individuals. Yes, it is a mysterious melody which undoubtedly has surged up from hundreds of souls" (translated from the German).

Lenau was right. The plaintive notes of entreaty in the Kol Nidre speak of man's weakness and sin, and the soaring crescendo expresses the strength of man's faith in God's love and forgiveness.

So much for the music of the Kol Nidre. What of its words? Like so many other manifestations of the Jewish spirit, the Kol Nidre has been slandered and maligned through time. It has been argued by anti-Semites that its purpose has been to free the Jew from the obligation to honor any commitments to other men into which he has entered.

Only the ignorant and the malicious could believe this, for one of the great Biblical commandments is, *motza' sephatekha tishmor,* "Thou shalt keep the utterance of thy lips" (*Deuteronomy* 23:24). So high is the honor of the plighted word in Judaism that in Talmudic law a witness in a law suit did not normally need to take an oath, because he could be relied upon to testify truthfully without it.

The intent and meaning of the Kol Nidre belong to an altogether different dimension of human experience. The Kol Nidre asks for the abrogation, not of the oaths which we take in our every-day business affairs, but of those oaths and promises which we made in the presence of God that involve no other human being except ourselves. Whether out of fear or anger, or because of passion, hatred, or a lust for vengeance, we may have made some promise to ourselves unworthy of being fulfilled. When the eve of Yom Kippur is ushered in, we wish to free ourselves from this incubus of unworthiness, which weighs upon our conscience. Hence we pronounce the Kol Nidre, and ask for God's forgiveness.

How did the Kol Nidre originate? The mysterious and solemn introduction intoned by the rabbi before the Kol Nidre, which originates in the dim past, has suggested one answer. The formula reads: *Biyeshivah shel ma'alah, uviyeshivah shel mattah, 'al da'at hamakom ve'al da'at hakahal, 'anu mattirin lehitpallel 'im ha'abharyanim,* "With the permission of the Court on High, and the permission of the Court on earth, with the consent of God and the approval of this congregation, we hereby declare it lawful to worship with the transgressors."

Who are these "transgressors"? Scholars have suggested that this refers to one of the many periods in Jewish history when Jews were threatened with massacre or expulsion, or the expropriation of their property, unless they adopted the dominant faith of the particular country in which they lived. In spite of these perils, many Jews clung bravely to their faith and their religion, and paid a heavy price for their loyalty. But others were too weak or the temptations were too strong, and so they adopted the faith of the majority. Throughout the year they professed alien rites and pronounced alien prayers.

Came Yom Kippur eve, and the moment of truth had arrived when their whole being cried out for the forgiveness of the God of Israel, and for fellowship with the household of Israel. And so in stealth and trembling they made their way to the synagogues, and the rabbis gave permission for them to enter, using the formula which we have already quoted. When these penitents intoned the Kol Nidre, they were asking to be forgiven for all the unworthy vows of loyalty to alien creeds, which they had spoken out of their weakness, because of their inability to resist the threats or the blandishments invoked against them.

Where did the Kol Nidre arise? The traditional explanation sees its origin in Spain, where thousands of crypto-Jews, or Marranos, professed Christianity outwardly while seeking to remain loyal to the God of Israel. Some scholars have traced the Kol Nidre further back to Babylonia, where the fanatical sect of fire worshippers compelled Jews to accept their faith, and where there were also untold numbers who lived outwardly as Zoroastrians and inwardly as Jews.

Probably the origin of the words of the Kol Nidre, like that of its moving melody, will remain forever sealed. Precisely for this reason, the Kol Nidre will continue to be the matchless and eternal expression of the miracle of Jewish survival, a miracle which is also a mystery, deepened by two thousand years of exile and persecution, of spoliation, and massacre.

–Rabbi Robert Gordis
Leave a Little to God

※※※※※※※※※※※※※※※※

Most Dramatic Moment

The most dramatic moment on Yom Kippur, a day full of impressive experiences, is the chanting of the "Kol Nidre" at the Evening Service inaugurating this holiest day of the Jewish year. The text of this prayer, a formula which annuls vows or resolutions made to God which might be unwittingly or unavoidably broken, probably dates to the fifth century – it was certainly widely known and accepted by the year 1000. It was instituted by the Rabbinic authorities as a safeguard against blasphemy – the desecration of God's Name by the breaking of a solemn oath. It was felt that in the spiritual intensity of the High Holy Days, many individuals made vows and resolutions which they eventually were unable to keep. The Kol Nidre released them from such obligations, rather than leaving the vows standing and unfulfilled. It has always been understood that this annulment applied only to vows made before God, and in no way affected a commitment or oath made to one's fellow man. However, anti-Semites have traditionally pointed to the Kol Nidre as proof that Jews were untrustworthy in their dealings. Ironically, the ceaseless persecutions of the Middle Ages gave the Kol Nidre new meaning. In times and places where Jews were forced to accept Christianity publicly, or pay homage to church images or prelates, the significance of this annulment became even greater.

The memories of such sufferings imbued the Kol Nidre with strong emotional overtones, and in the course of time, the plaintive but powerful notes of the chant sparked hosts of personal memories in the hearts of generations. So deeply ingrained in the Jewish consciousness was the love of the Kol Nidre that recurring efforts to remove it from the liturgy, by Rabbinic authorities sensitive to its common misinterpretation, were always overridden by its popular hold on the people. In our Reform liturgy, while the English paraphrase focuses on the proper positive implications of the prayer, the ancient Aramaic text, with its beloved traditional melody, has been retained. The chanting of the Kol Nidre, as the congregation stands in reverence before the open Ark, is truly one of the most exalting moments of the High Holy Days.

–Temple Emanu-El Bulletin, New York

❈❈❈❈❈❈❈❈❈❈❈❈❈❈❈

Meditation for Kol Nidre Eve

Like all other animals we eat to live.
Like some other animals we eat because
we enjoy the taste. Unlike any other
animal, human societies vary in proclaiming
what is fit to eat. On this Yom Kippur
Day Jews do not eat at all, to physically
remind ourselves that

"Mankind does not live by bread
alone, but that mankind lives by
everything that God says." (Deut. 8:3)

"This is the fast that I desire . . . to
share your bread with the hungry, to
take the wretched poor into your home,
and when you see the naked, to clothe
them." (Isaiah 58:7)

"Better a dry crust of bread than
a house full of feasting with strife."
(Proverbs 17:1)

May we who constantly face the temptations
to over consume, learn the virtue of
moderation and self denial.

May we spend less on ourselves and
our families, and give more to charity
and education.

Oh God, may those who fast today realize
the value of self discipline throughout
the next year.

And may those who still struggle
to fast, avoid the consequences of
overindulgence in the year to come.

—Rabbi Allen S. Maller

2

SIN

The Sins of Good People

Perhaps the single most striking element in the long and complex ritual of Yom Kippur is the *'Al Het* prayer, the Great Confessional. Here, in alphabetical form, forty-four transgressions are listed under the formula, *'Al het shehata'nu lephanekha,* "For the sins that we have committed before Thee–for all these forgive us, pardon us, grant us atonement."

This alphabetical catalogue of sins has often raised the derision of the cynical and the irreverent: "Who can possibly commit this long list of transgressions? One would need to be a genius at sin to be guilty of them all!" But, as is so often the case, the cynic is more naive than wise. He fails to note that the *'Al Het* is couched in the plural: "For the sins which *we* have committed before Thee." Each Jew is called upon to confess not merely the sins which he has committed as an individual, but the collective sins of society in which he is involved. Beyond the sins of which we are guilty are the sins for which we are responsible–the manifold sins of commission, omission, and permission, which are rampant in our society.

The use of the plural in the *'Al Het* should remind us of the passage in the Holiness Code in *Leviticus* (chapter 19). This important Sedrah contains the Golden Rule, "Thou shalt love thy neighbor as thyself" (v. 18). It includes another great and neglected injunction: *Lo ta'amod 'al dam re'ekha,* "Thou shalt not stand idly by the blood of thy neighbor" (v. 16). This forgotten commandment sheds a lurid light upon the major sin of the twentieth century. In our lifetime Hitler and his associates were guilty of mass murder, but the free nations, their statesmen, their religious leaders and the masses, were guilty of indifference, silence, and acquiescence in this monstrous sin. As Edmund Burke declared two centuries ago, "For evil to triumph, it is only necessary for good men to remain silent."

This moral weakness of "standing idly by" applies not only to nations but also to individuals who are concerned, not with major issues, but with so-called minor problems. In his *Reminiscences,* Justice Frankfurter asks why men who have position and, by speaking out publicly could turn on the currents of reason and decency, remain silent: "What is it that makes so many men timid creatures? I can give myself some answers. People want to avoid unpleasantness. Life is hard enough even if you've got a bank account. Life is hard enough as it is, why take on something extra? 'Why go out on a limb?' as the phrase runs. 'Why stick your neck out?' that other lovable invitation to do nothing! Even people who are economically independent are not socially independent. They may have money in the bank, but that isn't all they want. They want to be asked to dinner at certain houses. They want to run for office. They want to get a degree from some college or university. They don't want to make trouble for their wives. They have silly wives with social interests or ambitions. Or if they get into public controversies their boy in prep school will be a marked character. 'Oh, it's your Dad who says this.' " The plural in the *'Al het* confessional is designed to make us conscious of our collective responsibility.

–Rabbi Robert Gordis
Leave a Little to God

❋❋❋❋❋❋❋❋❋❋❋❋❋

True Soul-Searching Has Nothing to Do with Sins

When I was a child, a wise, older man used to visit my school and decided to look in on the classroom where we were studying. Peeking over one of our shoulders, he noticed that we happened to be learning the idea of self-evaluation.

He was a warm and humorous man, and he said, "You know, when Yom Kippur, the Day of Atonement, comes around, you have to make an account of yourself, so you do a lot of soul-searching. But what is that? How do you do it?"

He waited, but we were too timid to reply. So he smiled and said, "Well, I'll tell you what it isn't. Imagine today is Yom Kippur, the Day of Atonement. It's been ten days since Rosh Hashanah, the Jewish New Year, ten days known as the Days of Repentance. Our thoughts have been getting holier and holier, more serious with each passing day, as we've tried to become better.

"Finally, Yom Kippur has arrived. We put on white garments, we dress like angels, we think like angels, we act like angels. We don't eat, we don't drink, we don't sleep. We don't wear leather shoes. It's Yom Kippur, the holiest day of the year.

"Everybody gets together in the holiest place in town, the synagogue. Then, together as a community, we spend the entire day thinking about sins. We think about what sins we committed last January, what sins we committed last February, last March, and on and on. We do this because we want to make an account, search our souls. We want to ask the Master of the Universe to forgive any sins we might have committed against Him throughout the entire year.

"So we dredge them up. We think hard to remember every sin we committed in the course of this year. Here we are, the entire community, sitting around on the holiest day of the year, in the holiest place in town, wallowing in unholy memories! And by doing this we are supposed to become holy? This is how we are going to become refined? This is how we are supposed to make things better?

"That is certainly not soul-searching. That's degrading. It's not nice any day of the year, and certainly not on the Day of Atonement. What, then, does it mean to regret our sins?

"Not by dredging up sins, not by spending the holiest day of the year thinking about unholy, sinful memories. Proper soul-searching, true soul-searching, has nothing to do with sins, nothing to do with misdeeds, nothing to do with ugly memories. It has to do with a relationship.

"What it means to take stock of yourself and do an account of your soul, to search your soul, is to consider where your relationship stands. It does not mean to consider the sins you have committed. If you have sinned, then the sin is that you have violated your relationship with your God.

"What you should dwell on, what you should contemplate, what you should force yourself to think about, is this: Who is your God, how great He is, and how good He has been to you. Then, how could you mistreat Him? How could you have forgotten Him in the course of a year?

"Serving God is the purpose for which you were created. How could you have neglected His teachings, how could you have overlooked them, how could you have been careless about them?

"Think about how much you need Him, how much He does for you, how good He's been to you in the past year, how great He is in general, how true He is, and how holy He is.

"When you stop to reflect on this for even a moment – not a full day, but for one moment – you realize it is this God to whom you have been careless and lax in your devotion. It immediately hurts. You feel an intense stab of regret. How could you?

"How could you forget the purpose for which you were created? How could you be that way to such a God, to your God? And that is true repentance. Then you have truly taken an account of yourself, truly searched your soul, in the context of your relationship with God. Then you have begun to make things better."

–Manis Friedman
Doesn't Anyone Blush Anymore?

※※※※※※※※※※※※※※

Sins of Speech

The sins enumerated are listed in alphabetical sequence. Since each letter of the Hebrew alphabet is employed twice, forty-four culpable acts are cited in all.

Of these forty-four, ten refer to speech: a man's tongue is a major offender in causing him to sin. Not all the trespasses mentioned are, to be sure, of equal seriousness, yet all could be avoided by exercising greater care and self-control.

I offer herewith my own plea for caution in utilizing the lethal weapons at our verbal command:

The hasty judgment we passed upon another which sober deliberation revealed to be based on a single impression, an unproved rumor, or an unreasonable prejudice.

The quip we failed to repress which brought laughter to most but offense and hurt to one in our hearing.

The promise lightly given, which in our heart we never seriously meant to fill.

The calumny of another we heard uttered and knew to be untrue, and yet allowed to go unrebuked and unchallenged.

The gathered irritation and resentment born of unpleasantness elsewhere, which we brought home to darken and embitter the words we spoke to those nearest us.

The story we repeated presumably only for its humorous content, but which derided a whole class or race of people.

The time we spoke idly when we might have listened profitably.

The untruths we masqueraded under a plenitude of words.

The opinions we advanced with a certainty out of all proportion to the authority of the few facts we possessed.

The innumerable words we spoke which were born of envy, dipped in venom, or prompted by unjustified resentment.

The occasions when we failed to say the word of encouragement and friendliness though it was sorely needed.

The evasive statement, the ambiguous declaration, the misleading pronouncement in place of a forthright, clear, and honest expression of our views.

Who among us cannot extend the list?

-Rabbi Morris Adler
May I Have a Word with You?

※※※※※※※※※※※※※※

Sin and Repentance

Sin

Sin is anything that separates us from joy and enthusiasm, from loving our neighbor as ourself, from feeling our connection to everything else in the universe. This applies to murder, rape, theft, and all types of violence, which can occur only when we think we are separate from the person or thing we are violating, when we have no compassion or sympathy with another human being. It also applies to nonactions–sins of omission–such as staying in a marriage or a job where we are victimized, belittled, or otherwise stifled. In these cases, we have no sympathy for ourselves.

Repentance

Repentance is awareness, recognition of a blind spot, acknowledging the shadow so that we will be free to make more life-affirming choices in the future. This process can be very painful, for loss of our idealized self-image, our mask, is often frightening and depressing. But without repentance there is no forgiveness. We cannot forgive ourselves, nor can we receive the forgiveness of other people or of God until we are aware of and willing to admit our mistakes.

-Joan Borysenko
Guilt is the Teacher, Love is the Lesson

✻✻✻✻✻✻✻✻✻✻✻✻✻✻✻✻

Ashamnu: ABC's of Error

✻✻

Of these things we have been guilty: we have Acted out of malice; we have Back-bitten; we have been Contemptuous of others; we have Doubled-crossed; we have given Evil advice; we have Falsified the truth; we have Gloated over our achievements; we have Hated wrongdoers; we have been Insolent; we have Jeered convictions not our own; we have Knifed friends in the back; we have Lost our self-control; we have Manipulated; we have Nullified the humanity of others; we have Oppressed our brothers and sisters; we have told Petty lies; we have Quietly acquiesced in wrong; we have Refused to back down from positions we could see were incorrect; we have Sneered at serious matters; we have Trifled with other humans; we have Usurped others' positions; we have practiced Violence; we have supported War by our lack of long-term commitments; we have committed X-number of sins of which we have not been aware; we have said Yes when we should have cried out no; we have lacked the Zeal to struggle for our convictions through unrewarding months and years.

– Author unknown

✻✻

If you make a mistake, be big enough to admit it, smart enough to profit from it, and strong enough to correct it.

– Author unknown

✻✻✻✻✻✻✻✻✻✻✻✻✻✻✻✻

Ashamnu: An Alphabet of Wrongdoing

Dear Lord, we sin against you when we

Abuse our health
Betray the truth others place in us
Close our eyes to the poor and hungry
Dismiss serious matters with a joke
Enjoy the downfall of others
Forgive in ourselves what we condemn in others

Give in to illegitimate pressure
Hate others without cause
Ignore important issues in our community and country
Jeopardize our environment with our carelessness
Kid others without regard for their feelings
Listen to voices at odds with what we know is right
Make no time for those who need us
Notice only the faults of others
Openly criticize others without knowing the facts
Prevent others from showing their own strengths
Quietly accept hearsay as fact
Refuse to be generous
Stifle our conscience
Talk of others' failings instead of their successes
Use violence to achieve our goals
Vilify those with whom we disagree
Wait too long to restore relationships
eXcuse ourselves for hurting others by saying, "It's their fault."
Yield to that which is most convenient when a healthier option is available,
Zip past ideas worthy of deeper consideration.

—Rabbi Richard Sherwin

❊❊❊❊❊❊❊❊❊❊❊❊❊

Confessional

Ten times during the synagogue service of the Day of Atonement the *Viddui* or Confession of Sins is recited. According to Jewish tradition, repentance requires not only restitution or reparation, insofar as these are possible, but confession as well. "When a man or woman shall commit any sin that men commit, to commit a trespass against the Lord . . . then they shall confess their sin which they have done; and . . . make restitution . . . unto him in respect of whom he hath been guilty" (Numbers 5:6–7). The confession is not to be made before any human being, nor is any person regarded as having power to grant absolution; it is made before God who alone "forgives and pardons our sins."

The confession of the Yom Kippur liturgy begins with the plea, "Let our prayer reach You." This passage, in which the worshipper rejects the arrogance and obstinacy which might lead him to disclaim all wrongdoing, was already known in the Talmudic era (*Yoma* 87b). The litany of sins which follows it, "We have trespassed . . . ," is, however, first found in the ninth-century *Siddur* of Rav

Amram. In the Hebrew this litany is an acrostic, making use of each of the twenty-two letters of the Hebrew alphabet: *ashamnu, bagadnu,* and so on.

In post-Talmudic times there also developed as part of the *Viddui* another litany of sins, the *Al Het,* which in the *Mahzor* immediately follows prayers given here. This, too, is an acrostic. The oldest source containing it *(She'iltoth Rav Ahai),* which dates from the beginning of the seventh century, mentions only six lines. These were gradually expanded, until the Azhkenazic liturgy now has an *Al Het* that is a complete double alphabetical acrostic containing forty-four lines.

The alphabetical sequence in which these confessions, the *Ashamnu* and the *Al Het,* as well as many of the compositions of the *payetanim* in the High Holy Day Prayer Book are framed, may strike the modern mind as a highly artificial literary device and one, moreover, inconsistent with the deep seriousness of their theme. The artificiality is certainly present, and there is little doubt that many of the composers were concerned with displaying their verbal inventiveness and literary skill. The explanation that the acrostic device was largely adopted before printed prayer books came into existence, or when they were still quite expensive and scarce, as an aid to the worshipper's memory has considerable merit. Most important, however, to the devout Jew of the past was the content, not the form, of these prayers.

But it is on the score of content that many modern Jews are uncomfortable with these litanies. A confession, they feel, should be personal, reflecting the individual's own experiences, his own shortcomings and failures; here, however, are impersonal and general formulas, speaking of sin of which the individual may or may not be guilty. But this mood reflects a misunderstanding of the nature and purpose of the *Ashamnu* and the *Al Het.* There is opportunity for personal, individual confession on Yom Kippur; these formulas, however, are the collective confession of the community. They are couched in the first person plural: "We have trespassed . . . ," "For the sin which we have committed. . . ." The individual here associates himself with the community and acknowledges the collective guilt in which he shares. Moreover, even if the formulas are general and collective, only the rare person will not see in at least some of them the truth about his own life and his own deeds.

It is worth noting that both the *Ashamnu* and the *Al Het* deal only with moral violations, offenses against other persons and against one's self, not with infractions of the Jewish ceremonial or ritual law. Not that the latter are considered insignificant; both the ethical and the ceremonial law are regarded as divinely revealed by the tradition, and any violation of either is believed to be a sin against God. But there has been a general recognition that the moral commandments that are "between man and man" are weightier than the ritual commandments that are "between man and God." The Talmud (*Yoma* 86b) takes it for granted that only infractions of the former need to be detailed in the *Viddui* of Yom Kippur.

—Rabbi Bernard Martin
Prayer in Judaism

※※※※※※※※※※※※※※※

Moral Leprosy

A cocktail party has been defined as a place where they cut sandwiches and friends into little pieces. While the definition may be modern, the practice it describes is very old. In *Alice in Wonderland,* the Mock Turtle outlines the school curriculum of arithmetic: "Ambition, Distraction, Uglification, and Derision." Even before Lewis Carroll, the French philosopher Pascal declared that, "If all men knew what each said of the other, there would not be four friends in the world." And long, long before Pascal, the prophet Zechariah complained, "I was wounded in the house of my friends."

Why do we do it? Why do we engage in slander and malicious gossip? Well, there are many reasons. One English poet who is remembered more for his breakfast parties than for his poetry once explained: "I have a weak voice and unless I say something nasty no one will pay any attention to me." Saying something nasty is a great way of becoming the center of attraction.

Another reason for "uglification" is to be found in a distorted view that life operates on a kind of pulley system. When we pull someone else down, we think that we go up. Actually, when we belittle others, we are really trying to cut them down to our own size.

Whatever the motivations and however widespread the practice, Judaism denounced the sin of "the evil tongue" in the harshest terms. The Hebrew word for "leper" is *mitzora. . . .*

Our sages punned on the word *mitzora* and read it as *motzi ra* – he who spreads evil. They then went on to describe the slanderer as a kind of moral leper. His sin, one rabbi said, is equivalent to a violation of all the five books of the Torah. Another sage declared, "He who engages in the evil tongue is like one who denies God." Resh Lakish said, "In the future day of judgment, all animals will be assembled and they will ask the serpent why he poisons his prey. They will say, 'The lion destroys, so that he may eat. The wolf tears his prey for food. What do you gain, through your poison?' And the serpent will reply, 'Ask the slanderer, for he too destroys without benefit to himself.' "

Of the 44 sins we enumerate in the confessional on Yom Kippur, 10 are sins of the tongue. Does our tradition exaggerate the power of words? Who does not know their potency? How many families have they divided, how many reputations have they fractured, how many friendships have they broken, how many lives have they cost! For every word in *Mein Kampf,* 125 lives were to be lost; for every page, 4,700 lives; for every chapter, more than 1,200,000 lives! The price of moral leprosy is monstrously exorbitant.

But it would be a caricature of man and an insult to our Creator to dwell exclusively upon the destructive power of speech. Speech is also one of our most benevolent and distinctively human endowments. "A word fitly spoken," says the Bible, "is like apples of gold in settings of silver." Words soften grief, bolster our confidence, lift our sagging spirits, restore our wounded pride. A word of praise can send our souls winging, a word of encouragement can level mountainous obstacles. Words are transmitters of the accumulated wisdom of mankind. Kind words are the music of the world and the pass-key to every heart.

Three times each day, at the end of the Silent Devotion, we pray to be immunized against moral leprosy, "O Lord, guard my tongue from evil and my lips from speaking falsehood." In *Likrat Shabbat,* we added the petition of the anonymous poet:

> If any little word of mine
> May make a life the brighter,
> If any little song of mine
> May make the heart the lighter,
> God help me speak the little word
> And take my bit of singing,
> And drop it in some lovely vale,
> To set the echoes ringing.

–Rabbi Sidney Greenberg

❉❉❉❉❉❉❉❉❉❉❉❉❉

Sins of Speech

There is no such thing as idle gossip. It is always industrious. The same person who thinks of reporting the faults of others to us will also think nothing of reporting our faults to others. The gossiper is one who has mastered the art of saying nothing in a way that leaves nothing unsaid.

There is a story of a Jew who came to his rabbi to relieve him of his troubled conscience. He had circulated slander about his fellow man, only to discover that it was false. The rabbi said, "If you want to make peace with your conscience, you must fill a bag with feathers. Then go to every door in the village, and drop in front of each of them one of the feathers." After the Jew did as he was told he returned to the rabbi and announced that he had done penance. "Not yet," said the rabbi. "Now, take your bag, and gather up every feather that you have dropped." Again, he did as he was ordered. This time he returned and complained that the wind had blown them all away. "Yes, my good man," said the rabbi, "so it is with gossip. Words are easily dropped, but no matter how hard you try, you can never get them back again."

The milk of human kindness is never more diluted than when gossips gather together at the pump.

–Rabbi Saul I. Teplitz
(from a forthcoming book)

❋❋❋❋❋❋❋❋❋❋❋❋❋

Feel Like Gossiping? Read This Essay First

DEAR ANN LANDERS:

I am a hard-working, respectable 23-year-old woman from a middle class family. At the moment I am heartsick because of a vicious lie that has been spread about me.

I underwent minor surgery recently for a tipped uterus. It required one night in the hospital. Someone has circulated the story that I had an abortion. We are strict Catholics, and this lie is ruining my health and hurting my family.

Will you please run once again that wonderful essay about gossip? It needs to be seen by a lot of people. Thank you in advance.

–Worcester, Mass.

DEAR W.:

Here it is, one of the best essays I have ever published. It is one that should be repeated periodically.

Nobody's Friend

My name is gossip. I have no respect for justice.
I maim without killing. I break hearts and ruin lives.
I am cunning and malicious and gather strength with age.
The more I am quoted the more I am believed.
I flourish at every level of society.
My victims are helpless. They cannot protect themselves against me
because I have no name and no face.
To track me down is impossible. The harder you try, the more elusive I become.
I am nobody's friend.
Once I tarnish a reputation, it is never the same.
I topple governments and wreck marriages.

I ruin careers and cause sleepless nights, heartache and indigestion.
I make innocent people cry in their pillows.
Even my name hisses. I am called Gossip. Office gossip. Shop gossip. Party
gossip. Telephone gossip. I make headlines and headaches.
Before you repeat a story, ask yourself, is it true? Is it fair? Is it necessary?
   If not–SHUT UP.

–Ann Landers

❊❊❊❊❊❊❊❊❊❊❊

Missing the Mark

The Hebrew word "chet" does not have the same overtones as the English word
"sin." "Sin" has a much more theological connotation than "chet," which is
really a term from archery, meaning "missing the mark." When we achieve less
than we should, we are doing a "chet."

   Someone once said that every mistake or failure is the wrong amount of a
good quality. For example, hatred is an excess of self-protective anger. Selfishness
is an excess of a natural desire for one's necessary good concern. When we
under-shoot or over-shoot with regard to a positive quality, we miss the mark, or
commit a "chet."

   Rabbi Jules Harlow, editor of the Conservative Siddur, *Sim Shalom,* reports that
the following typographical error appeared in page proofs of the new Siddur:
"Praised is the Lord by day and praised by night; praised when we lie down and
praised when we *wise* up."

   Perhaps what the *Al Chet* prayer is telling us is really very simply–to wise up,
and become our best selves.

–Rabbi Dov Peretz Elkins

❊❊❊❊❊❊❊❊❊❊❊

Raising Our Consciousness

Someone once said that having a conscience does not prevent us from sinning, it
merely prevents us from enjoying it.

   Our recitation of the *Al Chet* prayers may not prevent us from repeating these
acts of failure and mistakes, but it may help us become more aware of the patterns

into which we fall by bad habits and unconscious errors. By raising our consciousness and awareness regarding the common mistakes of humanity, we thereby begin to slowly change our patterns of behavior and action.

–Rabbi Dov Peretz Elkins

✳✳✳✳✳✳✳✳✳✳✳✳✳✳

Sins in the World of Business

"For the sin we committed . . . in business dealings" *(be-masa u-matan).*

As we recite the litany of sins, or rather I prefer the word *failures,* I would like to ask you instead of racing through the long list, to select one or two and think carefully about them, meditate on them. Select one or two which may apply to your own life.

Perhaps it is *zilzul horim u-morim*–disrespect for parents and teachers. Or, perhaps it is the one about *masa u-matan*–ethical lapses in our business dealings. John Spalding once said that the test of the worth of a person's religion is to do business with him/her.

The story is told of an observant Jew who was schizophrenic in religion. He observed the mitzvot carefully, but was also a pick-pocket. One day, it seems, he visited the rabbi's office to return a watch he found, in fulfillment of the mitzvah of "*hashavat avedah*"–the obligation to return a lost article. After he left, the rabbi realized that he had lost his wallet, and assumed that the man who returned the watch had picked his pocket. He inquired, and the man had to tell the truth–it was indeed he.

The rabbi asked him how he could reconcile these two acts–returning the watch, and picking his pocket. "Well," said the man, "the Torah says you must return a lost article. That's a mitzvah. But business is business!"

Let's remember to be whole, integrated, moral people, who observe both the ritual and ethical principles of Judaism in a consistent fashion.

–Rabbi Dov Peretz Elkins

✳✳✳✳✳✳✳✳✳✳✳✳✳✳

We Set Our Own High Standards

[In Dostoevsky's *The Brothers Karamazov,* the] Grand Inquisitor accused Jesus of overestimating human capacity for spiritual strength and of setting standards so high that they could be met by no more than a small group of the elect. "I swear, man is weaker and baser by nature than Thou hast believed him! . . . Thou didst ask too much of him. . . . Respecting him less, Thou wouldst have asked less of him. That would have been more like love, for his burden would have been lighter."

The Grand Inquisitor, who sees humans as "weak, vicious, worthless, and rebellious," explains to Jesus, "We have corrected Thy work." His formula is starkly simple: proceed on the assumption that humans are children; keep them under heavy discipline; make them happy by sparing them the burdens of freedom.

Those who embrace religious or political systems based on individual moral responsibility cannot accept the Grand Inquisitor's formulation of the problem, much less his conclusion. Clearly there are elements in human nature antagonistic to high standards, but there is also an element in human nature that *sets those high standards* and seeks to meet them. The Grand Inquisitor's strategy prejudges the outcome, expects the worst, and creates social arrangements that seek to put a lid on human possibilities.

Ironically, it is not solely by moral criteria that the Grand Inquisitor's argument appears defective. If treating people like children really made them happy, no extraordinary force would be needed. But every contemporary example suggests that the ruler who sets out to treat his subjects like children needs quite a few machine guns. Evidently some of the children are reluctant to accept the arrangement.

—John W. Gardner
Morale

Confessional

I have always been impressed by the fact that the transgressions we list in these Yom Kippur prayers do not include the major sins. We do not beat our breasts and declare: "Forgive our sins of killing, of stealing, of adultery." We speak only of disrespect, of stubbornness, of evil meditations. Why? Is our prayerbook too squeamish, too gentle, too circumspect? I don't think so.

The transgressions of which most of us are guilty are not the cardinal ones, the once-in-a-lifetime, twice-in-a-lifetime sins. What corrodes our spirit, what nibbles away at our souls, are our tiny, almost imperceptible faults. It is these little sins that are most destructive, for we live and work and play in a society which sanctions—indeed encourages—*petty* larcenies, *petty* cheating, *minor* breaches of good taste.

An ancient talmudic law declares that when you pass your neighbor's house, you may not pick a single picket off his fence on the theory that he will not miss it. For if all his neighbors did the same, there would soon be no fence.

How often do we, in casual conversation, scratch a trifle off our reputation in passing a snide remark, a seemingly innocuous comment, and how strangely inconsistent we are. Any gossip which *we* indulge is, we are convinced, minor, casual, merely a passing of the time of day, but when we become the *objects* of these same comments, those who speak of us are vicious, malicious creatures who use their tongues to destroy a fellow human being.

—Author unknown

❋❋❋❋❋❋❋❋❋❋❋❋❋❋

Al Chet . . . Kazav

A Rabbi turns to his congregation just before the Al Chet, and tells them he wants to give a sermon on the subject of lying and liars. He asks them, "How many of you have read the chapter in the Book of Proverbs on Lying and Liars?" All the hands go up. "Good," he says, "you are just the group I want to speak to, then. Because there is no such chapter in the Book of Proverbs."

—Author unknown

❋❋❋❋❋❋❋❋❋❋❋❋❋❋

Al Chet

For the sin we have committed before You by taking Your created environment for granted.

For the sin we have committed before You by wasting Your priceless gifts: our natural resources.

For the sin we have committed before You by polluting our waters and fouling our air.

For the sin we have committed before You by caring more for things than for people.

For the sin we have committed before You by being open-handed when we spend for our own entertainment and tight-fisted when we give to charity.

For the sin we have committed before You by being more concerned with appearance than with substance.

For the sin we have committed before You by allowing our governments to spend more on office buildings and military hardware than on the needs of people.

For the sin we have committed before You by being more willing to give a poor man a dollar than to give him a job.

For the sin we have committed before You by being more concerned with special interest group rights than with human rights.

For the sin we have committed before You by not making our homes textbooks from which our children can further their Jewish education.

For the sin we have committed before You by being more willing to give our children presents as a substitute for our presence.

For the sin we have committed before You by encouraging our children to confine their horizons to the width of a television screen.

Oh God of forgiveness, help us to understand our imperfections and teach us how to really repent.

For the sin we have committed before You by polluting our bodies with tobacco and drugs.

For the sin we have committed before You by pursuing pleasure for its own sake.

For the sin we have committed before You by seeking happiness as a solution for our problems in a glass and in a capsule.

For the sin we have committed before You by looking for beauty in make-up and fancy clothing.

For the sin we have committed before You by valuing the sparkle in jewels above the sparkle in another human being's eyes.

For the sin we have committed before You by craving recognition for our acts of philanthropy.

For the sin we have committed before You by forgetting that we need nourishment for the mind, the heart, and the soul, in addition to the body.

–Adapted by Rabbi Morris Shapiro

※※※※※※※※※※※※※※※

Al Chet

For the sin which we have committed before You by the worship of success and status.

For the sin which we have committed before You by believing that people are less precious than property.

For the sin which we have committed before You by believing that in missiles there is real safety.

For the sin which we have committed before You by believing that we can afford to journey to the moon, but cannot afford to abolish poverty here on Earth.

For the sin which we have committed before You by spending more on cosmetics than on charity.

For the sin which we have committed before You by spending more on cigarettes than on cancer research.

For the sin which we have committed before You by dumping surpluses while human beings starve.

For the sin which we have committed before You by having dehumanized, profaned, and separated men.

Pardon our iniquities, oh God, and give us the courage to amend all of them.

For the sin which we have committed before You by filling Heaven with smog.

For the sin which we have committed before You by coating the beaches with slime.

For the sin which we have committed before You by subduing the earth and making it over in a technological image rather than in Your image.

Oh Lord, forgive us and help us not to always think the worst of Your children.

                                                        – Adapted by Rabbi Morris Shapiro

                              ※※※※※※※※※※※※※

Some Modern Sins

Is Photocopying against Jewish Law?

We often think that the "sins" listed in the Al Chet litany belong to the hoary past, and have little relevance to our world. Reading them carefully, however, we can see that many, if not all, of them still apply. However, they do not include many others which have become possible in our world of modern technology.

We quote the Teshuva of Rabbi Seymour Siegel z"l, late Professor of Talmud at the Jewish Theological Seminary, and former Chairman of the Rabbinical Assembly Committee on Jewish Law and Standards. The Teshuva was written on January 7, 1974, and passed by the Committee.

It is a violation of Jewish law and ethics to photocopy or otherwise reproduce and sell books or excerpts thereof, which are protected by the copyright laws of the USA.

It is wrong to reproduce large numbers of copies of copyrighted materials for use in classes or worship services without the permission of the publisher.

The practice of copying other people's works and publications without authorization would also seem to involve the following prohibitions:

Hasagat gevul: Interfering with the livelihood of others and impinging upon their rights. Unauthorized use of material belonging to others clearly involves this prohibition.

Geneyvat da'at: It is deceiving to publish something which is presented to the public as one's own writing or property, or as legitimately reproduced, when this is not the case. In cases where the public is given the impression that the "compiler" or reproducer is the original author or producer, *geneyvat da'at* is clearly involved.

Mitzva ha'ba ba'averah: It is particularly grievous that such unethical practices are used in conjunction with the *mitzvot* or *Talmud Torah* (Jewish education) and *Tefila betsibur* (public worship). The rabbis were justifiably censorious of those who used illegal and unethical means to fulfill a *mitzvah*.

Geneyva: Unauthorized copying of books and excerpts deprives authors and publishers of the just income which they have a right to expect from their labor and investment.

—Rabbi Seymour Siegel

❋❋❋❋❋❋❋❋❋❋❋❋❋

Ordinary Jews

Judaism is very conscious of man's sinfulness. The great Day of Atonement, Yom Kippur, is sufficient evidence of this. It is noteworthy, however, that the liturgy of Yom Kippur subtly suggests the mere commonplace nature of most of our sins. They are, in the main, the ordinary sins of men and women. We are offered no encouragement to indulge in an orgy of masochistic self-recrimination. Of the three main Hebrew words for sin, *het,* which means literally a missing of the mark, *avon,* sin resulting from a perverse twist of character, and *pesha,* wilful rebellion against God's laws, it is the most innocuous that is used in the lengthy *Al Het* formula of confession. As Rabbi Dr. Hertz remarks in his Commentary to the Prayerbook, the more vicious crimes such as brutal assault, bestial cruelty and murder are omitted from the list of sins to be confessed. We humbly abase ourselves before the divine Throne not as dissolute sinners, but as unworthy, ignorant bunglers. Indeed, almost at the beginning of the Yom Kippur service there occurs the threefold repetition of "for in respect of all the people it was done *unwittingly.*"

—Rabbi Louis Jacobs
Faith

Categories of Sin

In Biblical Hebrew there are three main terms for sin–*pesha, avon,* and *het.* . . .

Pesha means rebellion. It refers to the attitude of mind through which a man sets himself up as the sole judge of his actions, recognizing neither God nor His law. *Pesha* signifies the refusal of a man to consider himself accountable to God for his actions. For this type of man there are no external standards of right and wrong. Right is the name he gives to those actions which please him and further his aims, wrong, to those which displease him and frustrate his aims.

Avon comes from a root meaning "to be twisted," "to be crooked." It refers to the man whose course in life is deflected from the pursuit of the good. . . . It refers also to the twist in a man's character which seems to impel him to do wrong, to a queer perversity of temperament which propels him in the direction of wrongdoing. . . .

Het is the weakest of the three terms. It comes from a root meaning "to miss." The word is used, for example, of an archer whose arrows fail to hit the target. *Het* denotes failure to follow the good path, to lack of character or staying power which prevents a man from arriving at the goal he has set himself. . . . Blame is attached even to unwitting sin if it could have been avoided with the exercise of greater care. The careless driver, the slack teacher, the over-indulgent or the neglectful parent, the thoughtless son, all are guilty of *Het.*

–Rabbi Louis Jacobs
A Guide to Yom Kippur

Community

I was sitting on a beach one summer day, watching two children playing in the sand. They were hard at work, building a sand castle, with gates and towers and moats. Just when they had nearly finished their project, a wave came along and knocked it down. I expected the children to burst into tears, devastated by what had happened to all their hard work. But they surprised me. Instead, they ran up the shore, laughing and holding hands, and sat down to build another castle.

I realize that they had taught me an important lesson. All the things in our lives, all the complicated structures we spend so much time and energy building, are built on sand. Only our relationships to people endure. Sooner or later the wave will come down and knock down what we have worked so hard to build up. When this happens, only the person who has somebody's hand to hold will be able to laugh.

> —Rabbi Harold S. Kushner
> *When All You've Ever Wanted Isn't Enough*

❈❈❈❈❈❈❈❈❈❈❈❈❈❈

Sin Is Self-Defeat

If man sins because of his evil inclinations, he is misusing his *yetzer hara* and at the same time denying expression to his *yezer tov.* By thus misdirecting and betraying his vital inclinations, man confounds himself. According to the rabbis, a sin stupefies the human heart and defiles the soul. Every sin undermines a man's moral strength and diminishes his chances to meet the next temptation more hopefully. The Rabbis taught that a man's soul is the witness against him, whatever a man does, he does first of all to himself. A sin implies an act of self-defeat.

> —Rabbi Eliezer Berkovits

❈❈❈❈❈❈❈❈❈❈❈❈❈❈

Sin Becomes a Habit

❈❈

Sin dulls the heart.

> —Talmud, *Yoma*

❈❈

A sin leaves its mark; repeated, it deepens; when committed a third time, the mark becomes a stain.

> —*Zohar*

✳✳✳

If one places in front of the window many thin and threadbare sheets, they have the same effect in screening the light of the sun as one heavy blanket. Similarly it is not only the serious sins which act as a screen between the Divine Light and the soul, but also the lesser offenses, such as hiding oneself from the needs of the poor, indulging in slanderous talk, flying into a rage, pride, and many such offenses. Worst of all is the failure to engage in the study of the Torah.

–Shneor Zalman of Liady

※※※※※※※※※※※※※

Sinning through Religion

Religion has become a substitute for the couch of the psychoanalyst. It is expected to give us peace of mind, to bring us happiness, to guarantee us good health, and to assure us of never-ending prosperity. This religion is not God-oriented but man-centered; man is not required to serve God, but God is meant to serve man. It is the typical religion of a comfortable middle class. We have everything now: jobs, professions, homes, cars, insurance policies; and we also have a God. It is useful to have a God; one can never tell when one may need Him. Our religion is a prop for our prosperity and comforts. No one is concerned with the word of God; no one listens and no one obeys. The function of our awakened piety is to confirm us in our habits and our customary way of thought. We believe in God, but we also limit His authority. We prescribe for Him how to act toward us. Truth for Him is what *we* hold to be true; right what *we* consider right. He can ask of us no more than what we ask of ourselves. Most important of all, He is to be considerate; in no way may He inconvenience us or interfere with our comforts and pleasures.

–Rabbi Eliezer Berkovits

※※※※※※※※※※※※※

Confessions Are All in the Plural

The Need for Community

1. Hillel: *"Al Tifrosh min ha-tzibbur"* (Pirke Avot).

2. Next time you buy a train ticket, observe. It says, "No good if detached." None of us is.

3. Last year at High Holiday time, a pre-schooler who was a regular attender on Shabbat mornings, came to Yom Kippur services and was heard to say, "What are all these people doing in my synagogue?"

4. A woman came to me recently and said, "Rabbi you won't see me in temple these High Holidays because I've developed a fear of crowds, agoraphobia." I answered, "Then I suggest that you come the second day of Rosh Hashanah."

WE ALL NEED TO BE PART OF THE CONGREGATION!

–Rabbi Dov Peretz Elkins

3

ATONEMENT

On This Day of Atonement

On this Day of Atonement . . .
  We will not seek to escape
  responsibility for our own selves.
  We will not fault parents,
  siblings or childhood traumas
  for the weakness we display.
  Nor will we blame society, the
  economy, or our institutions for
  their failure to make us perfect.
  Judaism teaches us that we are free,
  not free to do anything we want,
  for we have obligations to others,
  nor free to be anyone we wish,
  for we are influenced by others.
  But free to choose,
  a dozen times a day
  how we shall react to life's challenges,
  and in this small way
  to mold ourselves to become
  better than we are.

On this Day of Atonement . . .
>   We need to accept
>   responsibility for our own selves.
>   We cannot be perfect,
>   continuously happy and successful,
>   always attractive, popular and healthy.
>   We seek only to be better;
>   to be a little kinder,
>   braver, and more patient,
>   To do a few more mitzvot,
>   To share a few more Simchas,
>   to be at one with ourselves,
>   our values and our dreams,
>   as well as being at one with
>   our people, our traditions and our God,
>   On this Day of Atonement . . .

> –Rabbi Allen S. Maller

✹✹✹✹✹✹✹✹✹✹✹✹✹

Thirteen Divine Attributes

The recurring final line of each stanza [of *kee hiney kachomer*] – *labrith habbeyt ve'al teyphen layyetzer* ("consider the covenant and disregard the evil inclination") – links the composition to the context of the Thirteen Divine Attributes of mercy. "The Covenant" actually stands as a synonym for those attributes, in an allusion to the talmudic statement that "a covenant *(brith)* was signed with the Thirteen Attributes that (whenever they are invoked in prayer by Israel) they will never be disregarded." The attributes are a kind of mystical key to unlock the treasury of mercy.

> –Rev. Dr. Jeffrey M. Cohen
> *Understanding the High Holyday Services*

✹✹✹✹✹✹✹✹✹✹✹✹✹

Mistakes

The story is told of the hunter who went out into the forest to shoot birds. He hit one bird, but it was only slightly wounded and fell to the ground. As the hunter lifted the bird to put it into the cage, the bird said, "Hunter, if you put me in a cage, I am going to tell people what a terrible shooter you are. If you let me go, I will give you three pieces of advice that will make you a wiser and more successful person." The hunter agreed to let the bird go.

"First of all," said the bird, "don't believe everything you hear, check and test it first. Secondly, don't try to do something that is beyond your limitations, because not only can you fail, but you destroy your reputation. Finally, once you make a mistake that can't be corrected, forget about it rather than rehashing the situation and wasting your energies. Tomorrow is another day."

With that, the hunter let the bird go and she flew to the branch of a nearby tree. From the branch she called out, "You are a fool! Inside of me is a precious jewel which could have made you a very rich man."

The hunter ran to the tree, tried to climb it but the bird flew higher. The hunter climbed higher, broke the branch off and fell to the ground, breaking his leg.

Again the bird called out, "You really are a fool! I just gave you three pieces of advice and in just a moment you disregarded them all. I told you not to believe everything you heard but you immediately believed that I have a jewel in me. I told you not to go beyond your limitations and you tried to climb higher than a bird can fly. I told you to forget the mistakes you could not correct and you regretted letting me go. You are really very foolish."

The message of this story is quite clear. To a large extent we who are starting the New Year must learn to know our strengths and limitations. We must learn what we can change and hopefully change for the better. What is beyond our power to change in this world must not be permitted to paralyze us and keep us from moving on into a better tomorrow. There is a need for positive guilt concerning those areas over which we have control and have failed; there is no room for an intolerable guilt trip for those aspects of our lives which are gone and best forgotten. Our calendar celebrated the dawning of a New Year with opportunity and challenge. Let's make the best of what we are being offered.

–Rabbi Stanley Platek

※※※※※※※※※※※※※※

Return to Jewishness

Remember: the Jew influences his environment only if he does not assimilate. Others will benefit from his experience to the degree that it is and remains unique. Only by assuming his Jewishness can he attain universality. The Jew who repudiates himself, claiming to do so for the sake of humanity, will inevitably repudiate humanity too. A lie cannot be a stepping stone to truth; it can only be an obstacle. . . . By working for his own people a Jew does not renounce his loyalty to mankind. On the contrary, he makes his most valuable contribution. . . . By struggling on behalf of Russian, Arab, or Polish Jews, I fight for human rights everywhere. By calling for peace in the Middle East, I take a stand against every aggression, every war. By protesting the fanatical exhortations to "holy wars" against my people, I protest against the stifling of freedom in Prague. By striving to keep alive the memory of the holocaust, I denounce the massacres in Biafra and the nuclear menace. Only by drawing on his unique experience can the Jew help others. A Jew fulfills his role as man only from inside his Jewishness.

—Adapted from Elie Wiesel

※※※※※※※※※※※※※※

On the Day of Atonement

"Heaven favors the daring." —*Sanhedrin* 105

Wrapped in white shawls with blue fringes,
    They move their heads and hands, and pray.
This is the Judgment Day,
    On which Existence hinges . . .

"On New Year's Day it is written,
    On Atonement Day it is sealed,
In Life's battle who shall be smitten,
    And who shall conquer the field.

"Who the Mount of Life shall climb,
    And who—descend;
Who shall fall before his time,
    Or reach the end.

"Who shall grow,
    And who decay;
Who must go,
    And who may stay. . . .

"A beneath the shepherd's rod
   Sheep are counted on their way,
So dost Thou, Almighty God,
   Count us one by one this day.

"Man's start and end is soil,
   A shard of broken pot;
The crumb he eats is toil,
, And he—a dream forgot . . ."

Wrapped in white shawls they pray,
   This is the Judgment Day!

To and fro as they move,
They look like trees in a grove,
   Wavered by the autumn breeze.
Gone are the summer days warm,
Winter comes riding on storm
   And what are men—but trees?

Yet silent among them I stand.
Their prayers I well understand,
   But cannot pray with them.
God, if I, too, am a tree—
Ah me!
   I am of different root and stem . . .

The tempest Jehovah may send,
   Can break me—not bend!
I will ask from heaven no gift,
Like an oak my head I will lift,
My sky-piercing eyes I will raise,
Nor flatter, nor beg, nor praise—
But claim!

Why hast Thou hidden in flame,
And drawn the sword from Thy sheath
On me, unweaponed, beneath?
Come down from Thy throne of fire,
With me to plod, like me to tire,
And then—judge!

Whoever Thou be, no matter,
I cannot pray, nor flatter,
I say to Thee as man to man,
And if confess I must,
I do not like Thy sordid plan
Of making Life a muddy span
Between eternities of dust . . .

Wrapped in white shawls they pray,
This is the Judgment Day . . .
But I alone,
Heart turned to stone,
Look on, look on,
    And cannot pray . . .

–Philip M. Raskin

❈❈❈❈❈❈❈❈❈❈❈❈

Can a Leopard Change Its Spots?

The prevailing conventional wisdom is that "you can't teach an old dog new tricks." People are formed by the third or fourth year, the Freudians tell us, and after that there is very little we can do to change. Both popular wisdom and science join together in giving us a defeatist attitude toward the potential of humans for growth and maturation.

Even one so prominent as Dr. Christian Bernard, world-renowned heart surgeon, once said, "I still believe it's all written in the Book. I believe in destiny, and there's very little you can do to change it."

Judaism has a philosophy, expressed in the *Une-taneh Tokef* prayer, that is diametrically opposed. It dares us to be big enough to break through our old patterns, and grow into a new image.

Corazon Aquino, President of the Philippines, had a viewpoint much closer to Jewish philosophy, when she said, "Why would I allow myself to think that things will be done the way they were always done? If I thought that way, Ferdinand Marcos would still be President!"

As we recite this prayer of God's Judgment, let us remember that Judaism gives us three important ways to build confidence in our capacity to mature: Teshuva, Tefila, Zedaka–improving our behavior, deepening our communion with God, and increasing our work for a better world and a better society.

–Rabbi Dov Peretz Elkins and Rabbi Stephen Chaim Listfield

The Key Is Sincerity

You don't need a ticket to pray on Yom Kippur. The Baal Shem Tov asked one of his disciples to prepare a special Nusah (melody) that the Baal Shem had taught him for the prayer of Une-taneh Tokef on Yom Kippur. When the time came to chant the prayer, the disciple forgot the Nusah. Heartbroken that he had disappointed his saintly teacher, he chanted the prayer in a broken voice with tears in his eyes. The Baal Shem Tov comforted him with the following parable: "A king was secluded in his palace in a private chamber. Only those of his intimates who had a special key could enter to see him. Once in an emergency a courtier broke down the door and gained entry to the king. On Yom Kippur, at the prayer of Une-taneh Tokef, Jews face an emergency. The King of Kings is deciding 'Who shall live and who shall die.' At such a time we don't wait for a special key, a special Nusah, but we break in right away with a prayer that comes from a sincere and contrite heart."

–Author unknown

Moral Accountability

The Rabbi of Sadgora once said to his disciples, "We can learn something from everything: we may learn not only from things God has created, but also from the creations of humans."

One of his students asked, "What can one learn from a train?"

"That because of one second a person can miss everything," he answered. "Another response might be (considering the one engine and the many cars behind it): 'That one hot one can shlep many cold ones.' "

"But what can we learn from the telegraph?"

"That every word is counted and charged."

"And what about from the telephone?"

"That what we say here," the rabbi responded, "is heard there."

–Author unknown

Responsibility for Each Individual

There is a predilection in our day to explain away evil deeds by invoking scientific terminologies. When we are selfish we psychologize and claim all actions have selfish motivations, hence we are not to be criticized. When we do violence to the moral code we quote Kinsey and say everybody does it. When we neglect our religious obligations we anthropologize and assert these were merely folkways of primitive man. Business dishonesty is rationalized by pleading the inexorability of the law of supply and demand. We follow the line of least resistance, but unctuously claim expediency as our primary criterion.

Against such hypocrisy Isaiah cried out (5:21), "Woe to those who are wise in their own eyes, and shrewd in their own sight!" I am reminded of this apocryphal retort Professor Morris Raphael Cohen addressed to a student defending a certain action of his, "You are right from your point of view but your point of view is all wrong." We create false values and then defend our actions on the basis of these spurious concepts. Seeking status under such a false guise must inevitably end in moral bankruptcy. Isaiah's stern reprimand (5:24) should become a grim warning to our contemporary age:

> Therefore as the tongue of fire devoureth the stubble,
> And as the chaff is consumed in the flame
> So their root shall be as rottenness
> And their blossom shall go up as dust;
> Because they have rejected the law of the Lord of hosts,
> And condemned the word of the Holy One of Israel.

Modern society can avert this doom if we repent and cleanse ourselves of the sins that beset civilization. The threat to mankind is not only from the atomic bomb. The lowering of moral standards is also a lethal danger involving every one of us. I underscored the following passage in a book I lately read, *What are We Living For?*

> Recently a group of engineers and scientists in London initiated an enquiry into the question: Can psychology help to prevent war? Representatives of various schools of psychological thought, and also several organizations founded for some purpose such as the promotion of international good will took part in the enquiry. I was allowed to see an analysis of the replies and found, as I had expected, that almost all were concerned with influencing other people but scarcely one even considered the central problem of changing the inner being of the individual himself.

That, of course, is our error too. We forget that it is we, each of us, who are being called and challenged. This is the meaning of the declaration in our ritual today, "All who enter the world dost Thou cause to pass before Thee as a flock of sheep." The emphasis is on the conduct and responsibility of every individual; upon every one of us devolves personal duties that cannot be shirked.

–Rabbi Isaac Klein
The Rabbis Speak (ed. Teplitz)

※※※※※※※※※※※※※※

Judgment Day

While walking, Elijah met a man who mocked at him and made fun of his words. Elijah said to the man, "What will you answer your Maker on Judgment Day?" The man responded, "I did not get wisdom and knowledge so that I could read and study." Elijah said to him, "My son, what is your work?" "I am a fisherman," said the man. "Who taught you to take flax and weave nets and cast them into the sea and draw forth fish?" Elijah asked. The man answered, "That knowledge came to me naturally, by instinct, from God." Elijah responded, "The wisdom to make nets, throw them into the sea and draw out fish was given to you from Heaven. But, for the words of Torah, it is said, 'The thing is very close to you.' You, too, have the wisdom and understanding to be able to read and study." Immediately the man raised his voice and began to cry. Elijah said to him, "Do not be overwrought, for all of God's creatures can return in repentance."

–Author unknown

※※※※※※※※※※※※※※

Atonement
A Higher Form of Religion

※※

The highest moment in a man's career is the hour when he beats upon his breast and tells all the sins of his life.

–Oscar Wilde
De Profundis

✳✳

To many of us, Judaism is a "Grade B" religion:
*B*irth
*B*rit
*B*ar-Mitzvah
*B*etrothal
*B*imah

On the Day of Atonement, we start with *A* (Atonement) – we are asked to upgrade our religion.

–Author unknown

✳✳✳✳✳✳✳✳✳✳✳✳✳✳✳

What Are We Doing?

. . . the land is Mine. You are My tenants. (Lev. 25:23)

You spread the heavens like a tent cloth.	holes in the ozone layer
You make the winds Your messengers.	Chernobyl
You make the springs gush forth in torrents.	chemical contamination of ground water
You make the grass grow for the cattle and herbage for man's labor, that he may get food out of the earth.	toxic pesticides
The trees of the Lord drink their fill.	decimation of rain forests
There is the sea, vast and wide, with its creatures beyond number, living things small and great.	oil spills
The earth is full of your creations.	destruction of whole species

(Psalm 104)

Think upon this, and do not corrupt and desolate My world. For if you corrupt or desolate it, there is no one to set it right after you. (Midrash, Qohelet Rabah)

Rabbi Abraham Joshua Heschel said: "In a free society, some are guilty, all are responsible." In this new year, The Jewish Theological Seminary of America implores everyone – all of us tenants on God's earth – to take responsibility for the preservation of our common home.

–High Holiday Message, Jewish Theological Seminary

✳✳✳✳✳✳✳✳✳✳✳✳✳✳

Atonement

Our Sins Are Covered Up

The translation of *kapper*, "to make atonement," does not render the original meaning of the word. But there is another translation which makes this clear: to cover. The sin is covered. That is atonement. An action cannot be undone, just as yesterday cannot be recalled. But something else is possible. The action can be atoned. Whether this be in the fire of judgment or in the compassion of forgiveness, in both cases it concerns the mystery of God, "who in His goodness reneweth the creation every day continually." The sin is covered, it no longer cries to Heaven, it does not pollute the land. Now life is possible. The sons begin in a renewed creation, unencumbered by the sins of the fathers. That is the miracle of the compassionate God.

–Ignaz Maybaum

✳✳✳✳✳✳✳✳✳✳✳✳✳✳

How Do We Change?

✳✳

A habit cannot be tossed out the window. It must be coaxed down the stairs a step at a time.

–Mark Twain

✳✳

I explained to the Confirmation Class that we beat the heart during Al Chet because, according to the Talmud, the heart is the source and seat of sin. One young lady replied, "Since we know more today about anatomy, maybe we should beat our heads in!"

–Rabbi Dov Peretz Elkins

✳✳

Confessional: "Chet" in Hebrew means "missing the mark." In other words, we don't become what we *can* become.

Nathaniel Hawthorne left notes with random ideas for future stories. One entry said, "Suggestion for a story, in which the principal character never appears." This is true of many of our lives – the principal character never appears. The person we might grow into, the person we might become, never shows up.

–Rabbi Sidney Greenberg

✳✳✳✳✳✳✳✳✳✳✳✳✳

Who Is Exempt from Improvement?

Sometimes we defeat the purpose of the High Holy Days by insisting that it is the "other person" who must change, not me. It's always someone else who is responsible for the world's problems. It's always my spouse who started the fight, not me. It's the President who messed up the country. I have no part in it.

Often I hear people who approach me after the service and say, "Rabbi, you really gave it to THEM!"

In a cartoon published recently, we see a parishioner talking to his priest in the confession box. The caption reads, "Well, that's enough about me, Father. What have YOU been up to lately?"

–Rabbi Dov Peretz Elkins and Rabbi Stephen Chaim Listfield

✳✳✳✳✳✳✳✳✳✳✳✳✳

Body and Soul

If we examine the list of confessions in *'Al cheyt* we find repeated references to parts of the body: *'immutz ha-leyv* (hardening of the heart), *bittuy sephathayim* (utterance of the lips), *dibbur peh* (words of the mouth), *chozeq yad* (violence of the hand), *lashon ha-ra'* (evil tongue), *'eynayim ramoth* (haughty eyes), *'azzuth metzach* (an obdurate brow), *qalluth ro'sh* (light-headed levity), *qashyuth 'oreph* (being stiff-necked), and *riytzath raglayim lehara'* (allowing one's legs to run to do evil).

As we stand on *Yom Kippur,* denying ourselves every bodily pleasure to enable our souls to soar upwards, unfettered, in order to plead our cause, this confessional's emphasis upon crimes committed by the body assumes a special significance.

It offers, in effect, a plea of extenuating circumstances by placing the blame upon the several parts of our bodily frame, and their propensity towards sin. The real "self," it is inferred, is our indestructible soul, whose purity we acknowledge each morning in the *'Elohai neshamah:* "My God, the soul which you have placed within me is pure. You have created it; You have formed it and breathed it into me. You preserve it within me; You will take it from me and restore it to me in the hereafter."

Thus, we assert that our nucleus is pure, for it is exclusively the physical frame which the soul inhabits that is its source of contamination. And in our confessional we leave God in no doubt as to the many organs of the body at whose door we lay the guilt. We ask, however, that the merit of the soul should secure forgiveness at the same time for its corporeal partner.

–Rev. Dr. Jeffrey M. Cohen
Understanding the High Holyday Services

※※※※※※※※※※※※※※

Healthy and Unhealthy Guilt

We must differentiate the Freudian type of superego from intrinsic conscience and intrinsic guilt. The former is in principle a taking into the self of the disapprovals and approvals of persons other than the person himself, fathers, mothers, teachers, etc. Guilt then is a recognition of disapproval by others.

Intrinsic guilt is the consequence of betrayal of one's own inner nature or self, a turning off the path to self-actualization, and is essentially justified self-disapproval. It is therefore not as culturally relative as is Freudian guilt. It is "true" or "deserved" or "right and just" or "correct" because it is a discrepancy from something profoundly real within the person rather than from accidental, arbitrary, or purely relative localisms. Seen in this way it is good, even *necessary,* for a person's development to have intrinsic guilt when he deserves to. It is not just a symptom to be avoided at any cost but is rather an inner guide for growth toward actualization of the real self, and of its potentialities.

–Abraham H. Maslow
Toward a Psychology of Being

❊❊❊❊❊❊❊❊❊❊❊❊❊❊

Our Highest Potential

Sin is "the failure to live up to the highest moral potentialities in one's self in any given situation."

−Rabbi Abba Hillel Silver

❊❊❊❊❊❊❊❊❊❊❊❊❊❊

A Few Holds

Hold on to your hand when you are about
    to do an unkind act.
Hold on to your tongue when you are just
    ready to speak harshly.
Hold on to your heart when evil persons
    invite you to join their ranks.
Hold on to your temper when you are
    excited or angry, or others are
    angry with you.
Hold on to the truth, for it will serve
    you well, and do you good throughout
    eternity.
Hold on to your virtue−it is above all
    price to you in all times and places.
Hold on to your character, for it is
    and ever will be your best wealth.

−Author unknown

❊❊❊❊❊❊❊❊❊❊❊❊❊❊

The Uses of Failure

❊❊

The foremost Jewish historian of the 19th century was Heinrich Graetz. His 5-volume work, "A History of the Jews," remains a classic, and must be referred to in any research in Jewish history until this very day.

Graetz graduated from the University of Jena in 1845. At that time the important community of Gliewitz was searching for a suitable man to fill the rabbinical vacancy in its synagogue. An invitation was extended to him to preach a trial sermon. Overcome by stage fright, Graetz lost the thread of his thoughts and he had to descend from the pulpit after muttering a few incoherent sentences. The young man was completely frustrated. His failure in the pulpit put an end to all the possibilities he had entertained.

But his failure proved to be a blessing in disguise. Graetz devoted his great powers to the study of Jewish history, and he eventually became the renowned Jewish historian of the age.

In his autobiography, Lee Iacocca writes, "There are times in everybody's life when something constructive is born out of adversity. There are times when things seem so bad that you've got to grab your fate by the shoulders and shake it. Setbacks are a natural part of life, and you've got to be careful how you respond to them. When times get tough, there's no choice except to take a deep breath, carry on, and do the best that you can."

–Rabbi Saul I. Teplitz
(from a forthcoming book)

※☼※

The truth of the matter is that the quality of regret belongs only to the mature and the secure.

Ships that sail the ocean gradually acquire a mass of barnacles, and this retards their speed. In order not to impair the usefulness of the ship or permit its deterioration, these barnacles are scraped off at intervals. The cultivation of a sincere feeling of remorse and regret will help greatly to clear away the barnacles of the ship of life–the mischosen words we have spoken and the unfortunate deeds we have done.

–Rabbi Saul I. Teplitz
Life is for Living

※※※※※※※※※※※※※※

Sin, Guilt, Morality, Religion, and Psychology

※☼※

We have found good reason to believe that psychopathology, instead of stemming from unexpressed sex and hostility, comes rather from an outraged conscience and violated sense of human decency and responsibility. This radically revised perception of the basis and nature of mental illness suggests an affinity with both classical and contemporary conceptions of the holy spirit and points the way to a new synthesis of religion and contemporary psychological and social science. . . .

The problem presented by psychopathology . . . is one that is best conceptualized, not as an illness, but rather as a kind of ignorance and moral failure. And the strategy of choice in preventing and correcting these conditions is manifestly educational and ethical.

–O. Hobart Mowrer
The Crisis in Psychiatry and Religion

※※

"Conventional psychiatry," says (Dr. William) Glasser, "scrupulously avoids the problem of morality, that is, whether the patient's behavior is right or wrong. Deviant behavior is considered the product of the mental illness, and the patient should not be held morally responsible because he is considered helpless to do anything about it." The basic premise of Reality Therapy is almost the exact opposite. The patient's problem is the result of his inability to comprehend and apply moral principles in his daily life.

–Frank G. Golbe
The Third Force

※※※※※※※※※※※※※※

Freeing Ourselves from Guilt

One of the reasons for reciting the Al Chet litany – besides the heightening of our moral conscience with the goal of becoming a better human being – is to assuage our sense of guilt for not being perfect.

Both religion and psychiatry have long developed methods to help people deal with the heavy burdens of guilt which all of us carry around. We are imperfect souls in an imperfect world.

In a cartoon in the *New Yorker,* a woman lying on her analyst's couch tells the doctor that after all these years of analysis she still feels very guilty. What should she do? His answer: "You still feel guilty after all I've done for you to help you let go of the guilt? You ought to be ashamed of yourself!"

Let us hope that the recitation of the Al Chet will help us not only to do both

of these things – remind us of our shortcomings and help us to purify our lives –
but also to help us let go of some of our unnecessary guilt for the times we did not
reach our highest goals and most noble aims.

– Rabbi Dov Peretz Elkins

※※※※※※※※※※※※※※

The Coach Advises Self-Responsibility

I'm just a plowhand from Arkansas, but I have learned how to hold a team
together. How to lift some men up, how to calm down others, until finally
they've got one heartbeat together, a team. There's just three things I'd ever say:

> If anything goes bad, I did it.
> If anything goes semi-good, then we did it.
> If anything goes real good, then you did it.
> That's all it takes to get people to win football games for you.

– Bear Bryant

※※※※※※※※※※※※※※

We Are Responsible

Prof. Joseph Epstein, of Northwestern University and editor of the highly
respected journal, *American Scholar,* wrote about the choices that you and I have in
making important life decisions:

> We do not choose to be born. We do not choose our parents. We do not choose our
> historical epoch, the country of our birth or the immediate circumstances of our
> upbringing. We do not, most of us, choose to die, nor do we choose the time or
> conditions of our death. But within all this realm of choicelessness, we do choose
> how we shall live: courageously or in cowardice, honorably or dishonorably, with
> purpose or in drift. We decide what is important and what is trivial in life. We
> decide that what makes us significant is either what we do or what we refuse to do.
> But no matter how indifferent the universe may be to our choices and decisions,
> these choices and decisions are ours to make. We decide. We choose. And as we
> decide and choose, so are our lives formed. In the end, forming our own destiny is
> what ambition is about.

The Unetaneh Tokef prayer reminds us that among our many choices to do good in the world are three crucial and indispensable ones: Teshuva, Tefilah and Zedakah – changing our ways, communing with our Creator, and helping to heal our broken world by helping other human beings.

– Rabbi Dov Peretz Elkins

❈❈❈❈❈❈❈❈❈❈❈❈❈

Teshuvah – Will United Germany Change?

The West Germans have truly changed. We value freedom and democracy – and so do the East Germans who have quite recently taught us a lesson in democratic fortitude. As we grow together again, we are both determined not to revert to our old ways. We harbor no hegemonic designs. The militarism of yesteryear has given way to robust antimilitarism. Reunification will not tear us from our postwar moorings.

Not only the Germans have forsworn their past – so have the other Europeans. The ground rules of European politics have been profoundly altered. The age of nationalism, of state rivalry, of destructive arms races between neighbors is over. European union is the mighty vision to which the Germans want to harness themselves. We will carry our weight – but not throw it around. We know that we'll have power, economic power above all – but we have no delusions of omnipotence. We say *"Deutschland"* again, but we say so quite diffidently – and we don't add *"über alles."*

– Theo Sommer
Newsweek

❈❈❈❈❈❈❈❈❈❈❈❈❈

Change the Future by Changing Ourselves

Today we see ourselves as we truly are. In a few moments we shall hear the Un'taneh Tokef prayer – an awesome prayer on an awe-filled day.

How do we review the record of our deeds from this past year?
How do we evaluate the quality of our existence?
We cannot blame our conduct on forces beyond our control.

With our own hand we seal the record of our deeds. We are fully responsible for the quality of our life, for making the most of it – or the least of it.

In the synagogue, a great Shofar sounds to call us to account.
In the congregation, Un'taneh Tokef is chanted to set the
record straight. In our hearts, a still small voice is heard. God
speaks through the conscience of people.

On Rosh Hashanah it is written. On Yom Kippur it is sealed:

Who shall be pierced by envy,
And who shall be torn by resentment;

Who shall be tormented by the fire of ambition,
And whose hopes shall be quenched by the waters of failure;

Who shall hunger for approval,
And who shall be stuffed with selfishness;

Who shall be content with his lot,
And who shall wander in search of satisfaction;

Who shall be poor in his own eyes,
And who shall be rich in Mitzvot;

Who shall be serene,
And who shall be distraught;

Who shall stand out as a Jew,
And who shall fade away and assimilate;

Who shall study Torah,
And who shall grind for grades;

Who shall be openminded,
And who shall be tight-fisted;

Who shall be interdependent with others,
And who shall be independent and alone;

Who shall be truly alive,
And who shall merely exist.

But Yom Kippur has not ended,
The door is not yet closed.
We can yet change the decree.
For we are a people that does not
Resign itself to fate.

    We can annul the decrees.
    We can re-open the future.
    We can reclaim our lives.
    We can change the future by changing ourselves.

We are flesh and blood.
Our origin is in dust and our end is to be dust.
But we have been created in the divine image.

    Implanted within us is the ability to pray
    The urge to do right, the power to repent.
    This is the theme pervading the awesome melody of the Un'taneh Tokef.

                                   —Rabbi Allen S. Maller

✕✕✕✕✕✕✕✕✕✕✕✕✕✕

A Litany of Atonement

FOR REMAINING SILENT WHEN A SINGLE VOICE WOULD HAVE
MADE A DIFFERENCE
FOR EACH TIME THAT OUR FEARS HAVE MADE US RIGID AND
INACCESSIBLE
    We forgive ourselves and each other;
    We begin again in love.

FOR EACH TIME THAT WE HAVE STRUCK OUT IN ANGER
WITHOUT JUST CAUSE
FOR EACH TIME THAT OUR LACK OF CONFIDENCE HAS DIMIN-
ISHED OUR POTENTIAL
    We forgive ourselves and each other;
    We begin again in love.

FOR EACH TIME THAT OUR GREED HAS BLINDED US TO THE NEEDS
OF OTHERS
FOR THE SELFISHNESS WHICH SETS US APART AND ALONE
    We forgive ourselves and each other;
    We begin again in love.

FOR FALLING SHORT OF THE ADMONITIONS OF THE SPIRIT
FOR LOSING SIGHT OF OUR UNITY
    We forgive ourselves and each other;
    We begin again in love.

FOR THESE AND SO MANY ACTS BOTH EVIDENT AND SUBTLE,
WHICH HAVE FUELED THE ILLUSION OF SEPARATENESS
    We forgive ourselves and each other;
    We begin again in love.

                                  –Rev. Robert Eller-Isaacs

※※※※※※※※※※※※※

What Are Your Excuses?

A recent advertisement for a hospital talked about a National Heart Attack Risk Study. The study dealt with various risk factors, such as cholesterol, blood pressure, diabetes, smoking, weight, etc. The top part of the ad, the section that is supposed to capture the reader's attention, quoted some of the standard causes people give – ways that we rationalize away why we are not taking better care of ourselves. Some of these included:

    –It's just a few extra pounds.
    –I can quit anytime.
    –Work's a little crazy right now.
    –I don't have time to exercise.

These excuses are typical of the ones you and I use, not only why we don't take care of our bodies, but also why we don't do many other things to take care of our total intellectual, spiritual, emotional, as well as our physical health. Excuses such as:

    –I'm too old to change my habits.
    –Even if I called more often, they're too busy to talk to me.
    –I'll do it when the kids grow up.
    –Some day I'm going to get into the habit of regular reading and study.
    –I'll volunteer more when my business gets better structured.

At this moment, I'd like you to think about one or two goals you have for your self, for your spiritual health especially, for your family, for your relationship with God, with the deeper and more important things in life. And then think of your favorite excuses – like the ones I mentioned. What are they? Take a minute to think about them, and how you can change for the New Year.

–Rabbi Dov Peretz Elkins

※※※※※※※※※※※※※※

Bein' Good, Bein' Bad

※※

Two Sunday school children were returning home in serious discussion of their lesson. "Do you really believe there's a Devil?" one asked. The other replied, "Naw, he's like Santa Claus. It's your Dad!" Well, human beings can be as genial and generous as St. Nick or as devilish and destructive as "old Nick," unsainted.

As Shakespeare put it, "Men are sometimes masters of their fate." Which is to say that we are to some degree at least free and can choose to use our freedom for good purposes or abuse it by destructive acts. Indeed, some theologians contend that human nature is more inclined toward evil than good. Mark Twain expressed the view, through Huckleberry Finn's remark, "Bein' good is so hard, while bein' bad ain't no trouble at all."

–Anthony Fries Perrino
Holyquest: The Search for Wholeness

※※

The moving finger writes – and having writ
moves on: nor all your piety or wit
shall lure it back to cancel half a line
nor all your tears wash out a word of it.

–Anonymous

※※※※※※※※※※※※※※

Pledge for the Future

Avinu Sheh Bashamayim
Let not my prayers be in vain.
This day I resolve:
To live by the teachings of Torah
In all that I do.

I pledge to bind myself to my fellow Jews,
Wherever they may be.
I pledge to remember Jerusalem and Israel.
To work to keep them safe and secure.
I pledge to accept Your commandment
To give equal dignity to all Your children.

I will love and care for my family.
Giving them, not only material things, but
My time and instruction.
Let me be an example to my children
Of the right way, the Jewish way.

I will conduct my business affairs
In truth and righteousness.
I will seek to improve my character,
To overcome my faults.

Help me, O God, to keep these resolutions.
When I forget, forgive me.
When I falter, remind me.
When I weaken, correct me.
In my efforts, be with me.

—Rabbi Bernard Raskas

※※※※※※※※※※※※※※

The Hell There Is!

Hell
is not a place
of endless torment:
forevered, physical pain
that satisfies the wrath
of vengeful deity.

It is awareness
of hurt inflicted
beyond undoing:
remorse born
of recognized wrong.

It is
the sense of isolation,
the awful alienation
which sears a sensitive soul
with sorrow.

But sadder still
and finally,
there is
the hopeless hell:
a sensitivity to
no remorse,
no loneliness,
nothing.

–Anthony Fries Perrino
Holyquest: The Search for Wholeness

❋❋

The hell to be endured hereafter, of which theology tells, is no worse than the
hell we make for ourselves in this world by habitually fashioning our characters
in the wrong way. If we realize the extent to which we are mere walking bundles
of habits we would give more heed to their formation. We are spinning our own
fates, good or evil, and never to be undone. Every smallest stroke of virtue or of
vice leaves its ever so little scar.

–William James

❈❈❈❈❈❈❈❈❈❈❈❈❈

Faith and Courage Determine Our Destiny

Dear friends, there is a way of turning our guilt into creative purposes. Instead of
permitting the effects of guilt to torture and depress us, we can open the door to

forgiveness and change. For the purpose of Al Chet is not to drive us into deeper feelings of shame and remorse. It should enable us to redirect our guilt feelings into areas of wholesome change.

Many people have succeeded in doing this, and I would mention only a few that come to mind:

Frances Bacon did it. Following a political career as Lord Chancellor of England, he was forced out of office because of his graft and corruption. His life could have ended in disgrace. Instead, he underwent a process of creative atonement, and this enabled him to write one of the greatest books in philosophy.

Florence Nightingale did it. After experiencing a deep guilt at the indifference of her social class to the soldiers who were dying in the Crimea, she underwent a process of creative atonement, and became an angel of the nursing profession.

Charles Dickens did it. The guilt he felt about the horrid life of the people of London was channeled into a creative talent. His novels, which described the poverty of the down-trodden class of England, helped change its political system.

Mahatma Gandhi did it. When he was a student of law in London, he was a dandy and a fop. Later in life, the sight of the vermin-covered untouchables filled him with remorse, and he channeled his guilt into the philosophy of non-violence which helped bring freedom to the new India.

Sir Jacob Epstein did it. When he was a young man, he killed a bird, and when he realized what he had done with his own hands, he developed a profound sense of guilt. But this did not lead to an incapacitating neurosis or an allergic rash. Instead, a creative atonement motivated him to use his hands which molded, shaped and fashioned the great sculptures of our time.

We cannot tell what may happen to us in the strange medley of life. Fate often changes our best laid plans, but we can decide what happens in us – how we take it, what we do with it. Fate may bring two people together, but it is their *faith* in themselves and in one another that keeps them together. The test of living is not what fate does to us. The test of living is what *faith* can do for us. How to take the raw stuff of life and make it a thing of worth and beauty, that is the true test.

Nothing can stop a determined man. Cripple him and you have a Sir Walter Scott; put him in prison and you have a John Bunyan; bury him in the snow at Valley Forge and you have a George Washington; have him born in abject poverty and load him with bitter racial prejudice and you have a Disraeli; afflict him with asthma as a boy and you have a Theodore Roosevelt; stab him with rheumatic pains until he cannot sleep without opiate and you have a Charles Steinmetz; paralyze his legs and you have a Franklin Roosevelt. In short, it's one's faith and courage that determines one's destiny.

–Rabbi Joel Zion

※※※※※※※※※※※※※※

Confessing: Our False Priorities

We often ask why we repeat this long litany of confessions again and again and again in the course of the ten days of repentance – the *Aseret Yemai Teshuva.*

There are many answers – many reasons for reminding ourselves one day of the year of the sum total of all our shortcomings.

Let me discuss just one of these many reasons: because we so often mix up our priorities, and we need to be reminded that first things must come first, and last things last. We often spend our time, our energy, our creativity, our resources, and our dollars on things which are temporary, vain, and sometimes even harmful. In a world in which there are so many serious problems facing us – the threat of nuclear devastation, the destruction of our environment, the need to provide food for the hungry, cures for the sick, and beds for the homeless, why do we waste so much of ourselves on transient, foolish, and petty satisfactions and luxuries?

Just by way of example: the tobacco industry spends $2 billion every year only on advertising around the world. The American Cancer Society and American Lung Association spend $7 million on anti-smoking education.

As we recite the Al Chet and the Ashamnu, let us remember our priorities – in the way we spend our funds, in the way we use our time, in the way we serve God, our synagogue, and the Jewish community, in the way we care for our health, and in the way we nourish our families and friends.

– Rabbi Dov Peretz Elkins and Rabbi Stephen Chaim Listfield

※※※※※※※※※※※※※※

Constructive Guilt

Not all guilt is harmful. Constructive guilt, in fact, is beneficial.

Three decades ago, the playwright Archibald MacLeish produced the memorable Broadway production, "J.B.," based on the story of Job. Job was a biblical character who suffered without knowing why. In the MacLeish play, three comforters – a Christian, a Marxist, and a psychiatrist – approach J.B., the modern Job, and use the no-guilt approach.

The Christian says, "It's not your fault. You are the victim of original sin."

The Marxist tells J.B.: "It's not your fault. You are the victim of economic determinism."

The psychiatrist also absolves J.B. by saying: "It's not your fault. You are the victim of unconscious drives you can't control."

J.B., however, does not accept this no-guilt approach. He sees the value of constructive guilt when he says: "No, I want to be responsible. I want it to be my fault. Because that's what it means to be a human being. It means to say: 'I have the power to choose the moral content of my life.' "

Constructive guilt is helpful because it teaches us a sense of responsibility. It reminds us that we are held accountable for what we do. Of course, constructive guilt can torture and torment us.

We have duties to other people. When we do not fulfill these, our guilt is appropriate. Constructive guilt impresses upon us the acceptance of the consequences of our actions, even when they are unpleasant and painful. Sometimes we need to be punished for our misdeeds.

Yet, constructive guilt is not intended to engender gloom and depression because of what we have done. Rather, it is to foster hope. No matter how serious our misdeeds, we have the power to change and do good.

Constructive guilt enables us ultimately to regenerate ourselves, to gain renewed self-esteem, and to become responsible and caring adults.

—Rabbi Samuel M. Stahl

⬙⬙⬙⬙⬙⬙⬙⬙⬙⬙⬙⬙⬙⬙

The Paradoxes of Sin

For the sin we committed before you . . .

- By not reading enough.
- By reading too much and not acting on our reading.

- By not serving our community.
- By serving our community and neglecting ourselves and our families.

- By having a narrow point of view and not listening to those who disagree.
- By listening to others always and not having convictions of our own.

- By chasing after material possessions.
- By thinking we are unworthy of owning nice things.

- By neglecting our dearest friends.
- By chasing friends and running away from ourselves.

- By saving the world and ignoring our own people.
- By saving Jews and ignoring the rest of mankind.

- By disobeying our parents.
- By obeying our parents and suspending our rational mind.

- By ignoring our children.
- By indulging our children.

- By letting our anger control us.
- By suppressing our rage and righteous indignation.

- By foolishness and childishness.
- By not laughing enough and not playing enough.

- By being selfish.
- By not loving ourselves and not caring enough for ourselves.

- By ignoring God.
- By relying on God instead of ourselves.

- By ignoring the past.
- By living only in the past.

- By saying "We don't make a difference."
- By pretending we can save the world.

–Rabbi Dov Peretz Elkins

✷✷✷✷✷✷✷✷✷✷✷✷✷✷✷

Whatever Became of Sin?

It took place in a Baptist Church on a sweltering hot day. The preacher was delivering a lengthy sermon and one of the parishioners fell asleep. The preacher went on and on; the man slept on and on. Suddenly the preacher noticed him, became enraged, and called out: "All those of you who are for salvation, stand up!" and the entire congregation rose except for that one sleeping soul. The furious preacher motioned to the assembly to be seated and then screamed at the top of his lungs: "All of you who are for sin, stand up!" The sleeping man woke with a start, jumped to his feet, and stood shocked, rubbing his eyes. He looked about at the seated congregation, thought for a moment, and then addressed the preacher, "Reverend, I confess that I don't know what we're voting on, but it looks like you and I are the only ones for it."

Well, I *am* in favor of sin . . . the word "sin" . . . and I hope that you are too. The problem is that too many of our contemporaries are not. Over the past decade the word "sin" has been all but exorcised from our vocabularies.

In his book, *Whatever Became of Sin?*, Dr. Karl Menninger writes: ". . . the popular leaning is away from notions about guilt and morality. Some politicians, groping for a word, have chanced upon a silly misnomer, permissiveness. Their thinking is muddy, but their meaning is clear. Disease and treatment have been the watchwords of the day and little is said about selfishness or guilt in the morality gap. And certainly no one talks about sin . . . no longer is there an emphasis on self-control, on individual moral responsibility, on a code of behavior stronger than technical legality or illegality." Now Menninger is not some old fuddy-duddy or naive priest. He has been a practicing psychiatrist for over 50 years, and I would be insulting your intelligence to present before you his credentials. Suffice to say, he has authored 12 books and is the founder of the world famous Menninger Clinic in Topeka, Kansas.

And Menninger is concerned, deeply concerned, over the disappearance of the word "sin" from our vocabularies. In his analysis, the good Doctor points out how some sins have simply disappeared, how others have come to be viewed as either crimes, symptoms of emotional disturbance, or collective irresponsibilities. Whatever the specific metamorphosis, they are no longer "sins." Menninger is deeply concerned over this phenomenon and disappointed by the way some of his colleagues practice psychiatry.

Take a typical example. A patient feels guilty over some wrong that he has committed. He explains his feelings of guilt to his doctor. "Terrible, awful," says the doctor. "One should not feel guilty. No matter what you did, don't feel guilty over it. Guilt is old-fashioned, it's unhealthy, it's religious! Society bears the ultimate blame for your misdeeds; it's your family that is responsible, not you." I exaggerate, of course, but does this not sound familiar?

According to Menninger, this phenomenon of displacement of blame is the first step in the transformation of a moral human being with guilt into an amoral creature who can feel no guilt. It is the removal of the "I" from "sin," and if there is no sin, then we all live under a "no-fault morality" where no one can be responsible for anything.

This is precisely one of the theories advanced to explain the popularity of the "exorcist," exorcism and various types of mysticism and even devil-worship. All this affords one an ingenious cop-out. "I'm not to blame . . . the devil made me do it! It really wasn't me, I was possessed!" In other words, we have here a remarkably convincing rationale for the displacement of guilt.

–Rabbi Elijah J. Schochet

All Jews Are Responsible for Each Other

The two prayers, *Ashamnu* and *Al Chet* constitute the Jewish confession. You will observe that each of these confessional prayers is followed by prayers in which we seek forgiveness.

Atonement is more than a wish for forgiveness; it is the desire to be *at-one* with God.

To be *at-one* with God implies a desire to "bend our will to God, to observe His precepts and to revere His law in truth."

Confessions in Judaism, you will notice, are always in the plural: "*We* have sinned, *we* have transgressed," etc. They are always meant to be said by the entire congregation, even by those individuals who feel that they themselves have not been guilty of the sins enumerated.

The reasons for the use of the plural and the recitations of the confessions by the entire congregation are manifold. When one Jew sins, it is as though all Jews have sinned. This is in accordance with the principle that all Jews are responsible for one another. The confessional prayers for the High Holidays are constructed to intensify our feelings of responsibility for one another.

When an individual Jew celebrates, the whole community rejoices; when he weeps, the community shares his grief with him; when he sins, the whole community shares his sin.

The group recitation of the confessional is intended to remind us that the failure of the individual is very often the result of the shortcomings of the society or community in which one lives.

According to Judaism, the individual and the group make their confessions directly to God. There are no priests in the synagogue. The whole house of Israel is looked upon as a kingdom of priests and each Jew can turn directly to God without the assistance of an intermediary. The function of the rabbi is to *teach,* not to act as the bridge between Jew and God.

–Author unknown

Healthy and Unhealthy Guilt

Forgiving Self and Others

Forgiveness is not a lack of discrimination whereby we let all the criminals out of prison; it is an attitude that permits us to relate to the pain that led to their errors and recognize their need for love. Whereas judgmentalism focuses on flaws, forgiveness focuses on wholeness. As we learn to act from the sphere of forgiveness in all our relationships, we become conduits for a greater energy, a lifeforce that we vibrantly "feel" as love, peace, compassion, power, wisdom, and an enthusiastic gratitude for life. . . .

I used to think that making a mistake was the worst thing on earth. Mistakes meant I wasn't good enough and people wouldn't like me. I might be ridiculed, rejected, or abandoned. Making a mistake meant that I would immediately forget all of the good things I'd ever done and focus on that one error until it seemed to become the totality of who I was.

Mistakes were an open invitation to self-criticism, anxiety, depression, paranoia, and even panic. The omnipresent fear of error created physical tension, stress, frequent illness, and a pervasive sense in me that the other shoe was about to drop. It created a kind of *unhealthy guilt* that bore no relation to the genuine and important remorse of *healthy guilt* that teaches us conscience by providing emotional feedback about the consequences of hurtful behavior.

Unhealthy guilt made me feel bad about almost everything I did because, after all, I could have done a better job. Having to be perfect made it hard for me to take risks and stifled my creativity. It made me competitive, tight-lipped, defensive, and awfully serious about myself. It made for constant comparisons between me and others, during which I always worried about being one up or one down. It made me hypersensitive to criticism, which I heard even where it wasn't intended. I was like a fortress constantly prepared for attack. . . .

While the physical and psychological level of mind/body healing are extremely powerful, they attain their full benefit only when combined with an entity that is generally left out of both medical and psychological treatment. That entity is *soul,* our personal reflection of the Spirit or Lifeforce that is the energy from which mind and body arise. Without considering soul and Spirit, our healing from guilt and the stress, anxiety, helplessness, depression, and physical symptoms it creates cannot be complete. As one of my patients expressed it, "I've had eight years of therapy and the best medical treatment, but there's a place inside me nothing has touched." That place is the soul, and our healing must go deep enough to reach it.

–Joan Borysenko
Guilt is the Teacher, Love is the Lesson

4

FORGIVENESS

Forgive Us!

It is told in Chassidic literature that a *Mithnaged,* who would not forgive Rabbi Levi Yitzchok Berdichever for becoming a Chassidic Rebbe, would constantly molest the latter with various difficult Talmudic inquiries. When this *Mithnaged* attempted to do the same to Rabbi Boruch of Mezbish, the latter posed to him the question: "Do you know the Talmud well?"

"Of course," replied the *Mithnaged.*

"Then you know," continued the Rebbe, "that the Talmud states that when a child is in the mother's womb, a light is kindled above its head and it learns the entire Torah. However, when it is about to be born an angel strikes it on the mouth and thereupon it forgets everything. Now, why should it learn everything only to forget it?"

The *Mithnaged* was silent.

So Rabbi Boruch continued, "At first, it is not clear why God created forgetfulness. But the reason is this: if there were no forgetting, man would incessantly think of his demise. As a result, he would not engage in any worthwhile pursuits, nor would he raise a family or build a home, and he would not engage in anything for his own welfare or the welfare of the human race. Therefore God planted forgetting within him. That is why an angel strikes the child on the mouth to make it forget. Occasionally the angel forgets to do it, so it becomes my task to do it. Now, what did you desire to ask me?"

The *Mithnaged* attempted to speak, but could not recall anything. He left Rabbi Boruch, returned to Berdichev, joined the House of Prayer of Rabbi Levi Yitzchok and became one of his ardent disciples.

If we heed the words of the poet and this Chassidic story we *will* forgive *and* forget.

–Rabbi Morris A. Gutstein
Frontiers of Faith

※※※※※※※※※※※※※※

Thoughts on Forgiveness

※※

Not Only God Must Forgive – So Must We!

A woman in Florida was raped, shot in the head, brutally mutilated, and left to die. Miraculously, she survived. The host of a TV talk show asked her, "Is the bitterness overwhelming?" She answered, "No! That man took one night of my life. I refuse to give him one additional second."

–Leo Buscaglia
Loving Each Other

※※

Unless we are able to forget the past, we'll never be free of its power to reawaken hate and pain.

–Leo Buscaglia

※※

"Judge not your friend until you are in his place." It is easier to forgive if you do not judge others. Leave judgment to Heaven.

–Talmud, *Pirke Avot*

❈

Whoever takes vengeance or bears a grudge acts like one who, having cut one hand while handling a knife, avenges himself by stabbing the other hand.

–Jerusalem Talmud

❈

Rabbi Nechunia: "How did you attain longevity? I never went to sleep with a grudge in my heart."

–Talmud, *Megillah* 28a

❈

General Oglethorpe once said to John Wesley, the 18th-century founder of the Methodist Church, "I never forgive and I never forget." To which Wesley answered, "Then, sir, I hope you never sin."

–Author unknown

❈

Vengeance is self-defeating. In a world of insanity, we must be sane.

–Elie Wiesel

❈

Who is truly mighty? He who makes an enemy into a friend.

–Talmud

❈

Forgive and forget. The first helps your soul. The second, your liver.

–Author unknown

❈

Ralph Waldo Emerson said of a friend, "His heart was as great as the world, but there was no room in it to hold the memory of a wrong."

–Author unknown

※※※※※※※※※※※※※※

The Meaning of Forgiveness

Forgiveness is a charged word. Everybody has a different opinion about what it means. To some it is a religious commandment that sounds okay in theory but is difficult to execute in practice. It calls forth images of Jesus dying on the cross, looking compassionately at his tormentors as he prays, "Forgive them, Father, for they know not what they do." Some people relate very positively to this image. To others it seems like abdicating responsibility, becoming a victim.

There's another understanding of forgiveness that is both theoretically sound and practically feasible. It is consistent with any belief system, secular or religious. *Forgiveness means accepting the core of every human being as the same as yourself and giving them the gift of not judging them.* You can be clear about whether or not a person's behavior is acceptable without judging the person. Psychologists caution parents never to criticize their child, only the child's behaviors. "You are stupid," is a very different statement from, "Your behavior is not acceptable to me." If a person knows that you respect and value him or her, your comments about behavior are welcome. If you are attacking the person's character, however, no comment, no matter how perceptive, will be heeded. Forgiveness starts with ourselves and extends to others. Accepting that the core of your own being is as precious and wonderful as that of any other person is the greatest gift you can ever give yourself.

–Joan Borysenko
Minding the Body, Mending the Mind

※※※※※※※※※※※※※※

A Three-Fold Formula

The prayer of "Une-taneh Tokef" is climaxed by the culminating verse, which the congregation proclaims as one: "Penitence, prayer, and righteous acts avert the severe decree."

In some of the older machzorim, there appear three other words, above "*teshuvah, tefillah, tzedakah,*" in a smaller print: "*tzom, kol, mamon*"–fasting, voice, money. These represent the means or methods whereby one can practice the three virtues of penitence, prayer, and righteousness. For the ordeal of fasting leads to repentance; the voice is the medium of soul-stirring prayer; and the contribution of money to a worthy cause represents an act of "*tzedakah.*"

If we analyze *"tzom, kol, mamon"* even further, we discover, as many commentators point out, that the *"gimmatria"* or numerical equivalent of each of the three words is the same. The sum total in each case is equal to 136. This remarkable fact is one way of teaching us that *"teshuvah, tefillah, tzedakah"* are all interrelated, that penitence, prayer, and righteous deeds are all aspects of the same ideal of living a good and Godly life. Also, it's interesting to note that 136 is twice 68, which happens to be the number value of *"chayim."* This means that we are thus blessed with a "double life," both in the physical and spiritual sense.

To go one step further, repentance implies returning to the ways of Torah; prayer means turning to God through *"Avodah"* or divine worship; and *"tzedakah"* means the carrying out of deeds of loving kindness by *"gemilut chasadim,"* benevolent acts. This is reminiscent of the familiar passage in the first chapter of *"Pirkei Avot"*: "The world is based upon three principles: Torah, worship, and kindliness" (Simon the Just).

—Shlomo Rapoport

✸✸✸✸✸✸✸✸✸✸✸✸✸✸

Judge Ourselves Gently

Remember:
> If you judge and criticize yourself, others will judge and criticize you.
> If you hurt yourself, others will hurt you.
> If you lie to yourself, others will lie to you.
> If you are irresponsible to yourself, others will be irresponsible in relation to you.
> If you blame yourself, others will blame you.
> If you do violence to yourself emotionally, others will do violence to you emotionally, or even physically.
> If you don't listen to your feelings, no one will listen to your feelings.
> If you love yourself, others will love you.
> If you respect yourself, others will respect you.
> If you trust yourself, others will trust you.
> If you are honest with yourself, others will be honest with you.
> If you are gentle and compassionate with yourself, others will treat you with compassion.
> If you appreciate yourself, others will appreciate you.
> If you honor yourself, others will honor you.
> If you enjoy yourself, others will enjoy you.

—Shakti Gawain
Living in the Light

❋❋❋❋❋❋❋❋❋❋❋❋❋❋

Two Monks

Two monks on a pilgrimage came to the ford of a river. There they saw a girl dressed in all her finery and obviously not knowing what to do, for the river was high and she did not want her clothes spoilt. Without more ado, one of the monks took her on his back, carried her across, and put her on dry ground.

Then the monks continued on their way. But the other monk started complaining, "Surely it is not right to touch a woman; it is against the commandments to have close contact with women. How can you go against the rules for monks?" and so on in a steady stream.

The monk who carried the girl walked along silently, but finally he remarked, "I set her down by the river, but you are still carrying her."

–Irmgard Schlogel
The Wisdom of Zen Masters

❋❋❋❋❋❋❋❋❋❋❋❋❋❋

Don't Judge Motives

I hereby offer a simple proposal that could profoundly enhance the quality of life in our society and our private lives.

I propose a one-year moratorium on assessing people's motives.

When not destructive, assessing motives is simply pointless. First, we rarely know our own, let alone others' motives. Second, we tend to exaggerate the purity of our own motives, and to assign nefarious motives to others. Third, even when we are certain that we do know motives, we should still be assessing *actions*–our own and others'–not motives.

In the personal realm, when we discover that we have hurt someone's feelings, our first reaction is, "I didn't mean it." And because we rarely do deliberately and consciously set out to hurt another person, we feel exonerated. And when we do nothing when we should have done something good, again, we exonerate ourselves – this time by saying, "I meant to."

This is very dangerous. By judging our motives rather than our actions, we can assuage all guilt over any action or inaction. *Everybody* thinks his motives are pure and good. And on a conscious level, they probably are.

That's why motives just aren't the issue. What do we do, not what do we intend, is what counts.

On the global level, assessing motives rather than actions has led to serious moral distortions. A particularly important example concerns assessments of capitalism and communism.

Communism has resulted in the loss of freedom by more nations and to the deaths of more individuals than has any other doctrine in human history. Yet because it is perceived as emanating from good *motives* – abolition of poverty, greater equality – many people refuse to accord it the antipathy that its *deeds* deserve.

Capitalism, on the other hand, has led to greater freedom and to less poverty than perhaps any other political-economic doctrine in history. Presumably, it ought to be widely admired. Yet it is often vilified and even its supporters rarely consider capitalism to be a particularly moral system. The reason? It is based on selfish motives.

Defense of communism and opposition to capitalism emanate from the same flaw – assessing motives, not results.

As a talk show host in constant debate with people, I have had to learn that people with opposing opinions are often equally well-motivated. I therefore try never to cast aspersions on their motives.

For example, while I strongly differ with people who oppose capital punishment, I take it as a given that they are well-motivated. Yes, I believe they are advocating an injustice by allowing murderers to live and that their position reveals greater mercy to the murderer than to the victim's friends and relatives. But I do not doubt the decency of their motives.

I only wish that this attitude characterized opponents of my views. For example, I was constantly amazed at how widespread the view was among supporters of Walter Mondale's presidential campaign that anyone who voted for Ronald Reagan was motivated by selfish – pocketbook – considerations. Virtually every Mondale supporter, whether private citizen or public commentator, expressed the belief that his motives were more idealistic than those of Reagan supporters.

And when it comes to supporting a large defense budget and building of nuclear weapons, all constraints on assessing motives simply break down. Those of us who are hawkish toward the Soviet Union have our motives constantly challenged. We are accused of loving war, hating Russians, wanting to fatten the military-industrial complex, having a "Rambo" mentality and suffering from missile envy. The possibility that we, too, are motivated by love of peace and justice is rarely granted as a possibility.

Yet we who support a strong defense believe that our motives – ensuring peace by remaining strong, protecting democracy, opposing Communist tyranny, helping little nations survive against Soviet imperialism – are quite idealistic.

So, please, no more assessments of motives in the macro realm, let's debate results, not motives. And in the micro, let's assess ourselves by our actions.

–Dennis Praeger
Ultimate Issues

❀❀❀❀❀❀❀❀❀❀❀❀❀

Don't Be Judgmental

One of several names by which Rosh Hashanah is known is Yom-Hadin, the Day of Judgment. In the picturesque imagery of the Machzor, we see ourselves on this day standing before the divine bar of justice. The Heavenly Judge holds court, and all His creatures pass in review. He considers not only our deeds, but also our motives.

Perhaps one area of our lives which should be of special concern to us at this season is this very matter of judging. We, the judged, are also the judges. Often, in our daily lives, we pass judgment; we would do well at High Holy Day time to consider how often we, the judges, are prone to misjudge.

We misjudge our fellow human beings. All too often we are superficial, impressed by externals, focusing upon what a person "has," rather than what a person "is."

We are like that beggar in the story. He approaches a kindly looking man and makes his pitch. When he finishes, the man replies, "My friend, I have no money, but I can give you some good advice."

Whereupon, the beggar interrupts and says: "If you ain't got no money, I reckon your advice ain't worth hearing."

How often do you and I use the beggar's method of judgment, confusing a person's valuables for his value, his wealth for his worth?

In addition, we often misjudge others because we are quick to impugn motives and misinterpret deeds. An excellent illustration can be found in the Haftorah chanted on the first day of Rosh Hashanah. Hannah's silent prayers for a child are thought by Eli, the High Priest, to be nothing but the raving of a drunken woman. Charitably, the Book of Samuel does not record how Eli felt when Hannah explained her behavior.

Not only are we prone to misjudge ourselves. There is an old Yiddish expression which goes, "No one will fool you as much as you will fool yourself."

We persistently delude ourselves. Our cruelest acts mask themselves to appear like noble deeds. We cover our own failures with the cloak of self-deception so that others, not we, assume the blame.

We do not succeed in establishing harmony with our spouses, not because we have not tried hard enough, but because, "She doesn't understand me, or he doesn't understand me."

If we are truly honest with ourselves, we could find impressive evidence of our tendency to misjudge ourselves.

And finally, at this season, when we pray for life, it is sobering to realize how often we misjudge the purpose and meaning of life itself.

We bypass the lasting things for the latest things.

We sacrifice health for wealth and then try in vain to undo a bad deal.

We try to keep up to the minute, and our interests become momentary.

We have accelerated our speed of travel and lost our sense of direction.

We have confused the Pursuit of Happiness with running after pleasure.

We have so many beautiful houses and an unprecedented number of broken homes.

We have added knowledge, but we have not increased wisdom.

We have overfed our bodies, and at the same time, starved our souls.

We have become preoccupied with making a living and have paid little attention to making a life.

During this season, there is no shortage of prayers. But perhaps one more would be in order. It would be the prayer wise King Solomon uttered. When the Lord came to him in a dream and offered him anything he wanted, Solomon asked, "Give your servant an understanding heart . . . for who is able to judge?"

—Author unknown

※※※※※※※※※※※※※※

Our Hearts Are Warm

A distinguished doctor was called to a patient who had passed out and couldn't be revived. The doctor examined him and found all his limbs cold. He felt the patient's head—no warmth of life; he felt the patient's hands which were cold; his feet were icy. The family saw that the doctor found no warmth and began to weep. The doctor said: "Don't despair yet, because I have not yet felt his heart." And so it was—when he felt the heart, he found it warm and pulsating. The doctor said to the family with joy, "Dear children! There is hope that your father will recuperate for there is still a thread of life in his heart. Get warm water to warm him and he'll revive. But don't delay with the warm water—it is vital!"

The great healer, Yom Kippur, arrives—for it can cure the spiritual illnesses of Jews. But he finds the patient in a fainting condition. He feels our head—it is cold (due to false thoughts); he feels our lips—they are cold because we used them for Leshon Harah; he feels our hands and they are cold because we used them for that which is prohibited; he feels our feet and they are cold because we used them to go where they should not go! BUT nevertheless, we should not despair! When he feels our heart, it is still warm because the Jewish heart is warm. There is hope. Get warm water—hot tears! We'll warm our hearts!

–Rabbi Simcha Kling

※※※※※※※※※※※※※※※

What Is the Most Precious Thing in the World?

An angel was sent down from heaven to bring back the most precious thing in the world. When the angel reached earth, he came upon a wounded soldier who had given his life for his people and his country. The angel brought back to heaven the soldier's last drop of blood. In heaven he was told, "This blood is precious, but it is not the most precious thing in the world."

So the angel descended to earth a second time. This time he brought back the soul of a person who had given his life to save another. They said to him in heaven: "This soul is precious, but this too is not the most precious thing in the world."

Again the angel returned to earth in search of the most precious thing in the world. He saw a robber enter the home of a very rich man. The robber planned to kill the rich man and take all his money. Just as the robber was about to do this, he noticed the rich man's wife in another room of the house. She was saying the bedtime prayer with her small son. Suddenly the robber remembered how his mother used to say the same prayer with him. A tear fell from the robber's eyes, and he ran from the house.

It was this tear that the angel brought back to heaven and everyone there said to him: "This tear is the most precious thing in the world, because there is no one greater than one who repents."

–Anonymous

Returning to the State of Purity

Quite distinct from Christianity which teaches that every human being is born in "original sin," Judaism teaches the sublime doctrine that every human being comes into the world in a state of purity. In our traditional prayers, we assert this doctrine as follows: "The soul which Thou, O God hast given unto me came pure from Thee."

But while creating us with a soul immersed in purity, God also implanted "free will" within each of us. We are not puppets of fate, doomed to dangle from strings over which we have no control. Rather, we are endowed with a capacity to make personal choices in life. We know the difference between right and wrong, and no one can force us to make a choice against our will. Our ancient Rabbis have clearly emphasized this principle of Judaism: "Everything is foreseen by God, yet freedom of choice is given." (*Abot* 3, 19).

Being human, we sometimes err and go astray. Therefore, Judaism includes the confessional on Yom Kippur. But we need no priest to intercede for us when we confess. United with our brethren in prayer, we raise our voices together directly to God; and we thus reestablish the soul-purity which makes us at one with Him.

–Rabbi Alexander Alan Steinbach

Ashamnu – A to Z

(After reciting the alphabetical list of sins we committed, let's listen now, for a moment, to a list of *positive* things we can do in the year ahead. They are also listed A to Z. By doing these things, we will be able to help avoid the list in Ashamnu.)

The ABC's of Happiness

ASPIRE to realize your potential
BELIEVE in yourself
CREATE a good life

DREAM about what you might become
EXERCISE frequently
FORGIVE honest mistakes
GLORIFY the creative spirit
HUMOR yourself and others
IMAGINE great things
JOYFULLY live each day
KINDLY help others
LOVE one another
MEDITATE daily
NURTURE the environment
ORGANIZE for harmonious action
PRAISE performance well done
QUESTION most things
REGULATE your own behavior
SMILE often
THINK rationally
UNDERSTAND yourself
VALUE life
WORK for the common good
X-RAY and carefully examine problems
YEARN to improve
ZESTFULLY pursue happiness.

–Robert Vallett
Prescriptions for Happiness

※※※※※※※※※※※※※※※

Making Our Lives Less Imperfect

No human being is perfect. Sin, however, need not doom us if it is recognized, admitted, and not repeated. Therefore, we acknowledge the transgressions committed by any one of us and by all of us. We do so because we have faith in the possibility of atonement.

We do so hoping that we will not err again. We do so in order to become closer to the divine, to recognize our having been created with the ability to distinguish between good and evil.

We confess our sins publicly and thereby declare our determination to make our lives less imperfect and more holy in the days and months to come.

–Anonymous

⁂⁂⁂⁂⁂⁂⁂⁂⁂⁂⁂⁂⁂

Nothing Escapes You

"You know the mysteries of the universe as well as the secrets of every mortal. You search the deepest recesses of the human soul, and probe all our thoughts and motives. Nothing is hidden from You, nothing escapes You."

— Author unknown

BEING GROUNDED: A MEDITATION

Go deep inside yourself
Find that treasure that
is known by your name.

Look at this treasure
Look at the resources
that are universal
You have them all.

You can see
think
hear
feel
taste
smell
choose
move
sort

To *sort*—the ability to
let go of that which once fit
but no longer does, and
see clearly what
fits now.

Now say to yourself,
"I am able,
I can do this.
I have the energy through my
groundedness, my relationship to the heavens,
and my interconnectedness with others.
I am able."

— Virginia Satir
Meditations and Inspirations

❋❋❋❋❋❋❋❋❋❋❋❋❋❋❋

The Highest Level of Sensitivity to Injustice

Professor Edmund Cahn accentuated the need for the cultivation of a "sense of injustice." We can not always discern and delineate the way to absolute justice but we do react almost instinctively to an injustice. A Yiddish saying declares: "A yid ken nisht leiden kein avlah." "The mark of a Jew is that he cannot tolerate an injustice." "Leiden" implies that he feels hurt by an injustice. There are three distinct types and occasions for reacting to injustice: The first is when a person is the victim of an injustice done to him, either as an individual or as a member of a group. Here the principle, "If I am not for myself, who will be for me" is self-evident and compelling. Increasingly, in our day, the victims of discriminations and the underprivileged assert their rights with increasing vehemence and too often they practice towards others the very discriminations from which they seek liberation.

Quick action against an injustice done to us is natural and needs no extraordinary stimulation. But there is a second, higher level of the "sense of injustice" which alas, is becoming more and more rare. It is our response to an injustice done to another person or group. Here the moral mandate applies, "Do not stand by the blood of your fellowman" (Lev. 19:16), or as our *haftarah* puts it "deal your bread out to the hungry, bring the poor that are cast out into your house . . . and hide not yourself from your own flesh" (Isaiah 57:6–7). We are prone to say "I like to mind my own business, I do not wish to be involved and I will not stick my neck out." The protesting college youth of the 1960s expressed their indignation at the smug indifference of people by wearing buttons carrying the legend "Give a Damn!" Of the enormous sin of callous indifference and iniquitous inaction was the silence of the leaders of the civilized world to the agonized appeal for help addressed to them from the death camps by the victims of Hitler. Neither Churchill, nor Franklin D. Roosevelt nor Pope Pius XII to whom these appeals were sent, took definitive action to save six million Jews from the Nazi gas chambers. Everyone of us who was in a position of influence in those desperately tragic years, has reason to be remorseful for not doing enough. Prof. A. J. Heschel rendered a severe but just verdict when he said "many are guilty, but all are responsible."

There is an even higher level of sensitivity to injustice. This higher level is reached when we react with indignation at an injustice which we ourselves perpetrate toward our fellowman. The average person too often has an eagle's eye toward the faults of others but is blind as a bat towards his own shortcomings. Bahya Ibn Pakuda gave us sound advice when he admonished us, "When in the mood of praising, praise God and when in the mood of blaming, blame yourself." Yom Kippur should not only be a liturgical ritual and an exercise in physical self-mortification. It should be a day for removing the evil that is in our hands, for a contrite confession of those attitudes and acts which have brought misery and humiliation to other human beings. This is the true purpose of the *Al Het* confessions. They should be more than a familiar refrain but should move us to think of those deeds about which we must say "I cannot forgive myself for what I have done." Only then can we expect God's forgiveness. The words *salahti ki-devarekha* should mean to us that the extent of God's forgiveness is determined by the depth and intent of our own words of contrition. Only through remorse and repentance can reconciliation be achieved, only then can the evil within us be eradicated.

–Rabbi Max Arzt
The Rabbis Speak (ed. Teplitz)

✸✸✸✸✸✸✸✸✸✸✸✸✸✸

Revenge

Yehi ratzon . . . she-tislach lanu al kol chatotenu.
Lord our God, forgive all our sins.

I have reflected on the theme of revenge, which comes to people's minds on occasion. In rare instances, it is acted upon. A distinguished jurist, Richard A. Posner of the Seventh District Court of Appeals, wrote an insightful book, *Law and Literature,* in which he skillfully diagnoses the subject of revenge. Revenge is a primitive form of law. Posner analyzes an act of revenge that makes the avenger both the investigator, prosecutor, judge, sheriff, and executioner. He states that acts of revenge tend to be too frequent and too savage. The avenger misjudges the balance of right and wrong. Acts of revenge beget feuds, and a feud can be far more destructive than the original aggression.

Law, rather than revenge, gives a victim or his adherents a day in court. Revenge breaks out whenever legal remedies are blocked or when public enforcement is lax. In the play "Hamlet," which Posner analyzes at length, the Danish prince's act of revenge leads to no less than *seven* deaths. This play makes clear that revenge places responsibilities on people who are "temperamentally not suited to bear them." Posner points out that a great line in the play has Hamlet saying, "The time is out of joint. O cursed spite that I was born to set it right." The emphasis upon "I" is significant. Each avenger does what is right in his eyes.

Against this background, it would be well to consider the tradition of our people as reflected in our literature. Some texts command vengeance, others condemn it.

Most instances of mass brutality against Jews were reflected in cries for revenge. From the Holocaust era, we have surviving messages that ask for a continuing fight to the death with the Nazis and their ilk. From Kovno, we hear: "Brothers, avenge us. Vengeance, vengeance, with no mercy." On the other hand, Elie Wiesel once wrote that vengeance is self-defeating. A fine teacher once said: "In a world of insanity, we must preach sanity."

In our liturgy, there are references to catastrophes suffered at the hands of the cruel. This was the case with the Crusades (1096) and the Chelmnicki massacres (1649–50). In "the Father of Mercies" prayer (Av Harachamim), we ask: "God, remember them (the martyrs) for good . . . render retribution for His servants' blood." Rabbi Samson Raphael Hirsch commented on this prayer: "Our people throughout the ages have committed to God, and God alone, the task of avenging the blood of their murdered. Our people were kept free from bitter and burning lust for vengeance against their oppressors. They left retribution up to God." In the spirit of the psalmist, we plead: "God of retribution appear. Rise up, Judge of the earth, give the arrogant their deserts."

God, law, must be our sources of judgment. As for an individual's action, the Bible speaks clearly: "You shall not take vengeance nor bear any grudge against any of your people, but you shall love the Lord your God as yourself." Joseph's conduct towards his brothers is among the noblest instances of forgiveness. A modern commentary cites a classic statement: "He who has a forgiving spirit is himself forgiven; whosoever does not persecute them that persecute him." The ideal persons are those who are insulted but do not retaliate with insult.

While there are invocations of wrath against the enemy, Jewish tradition, in the main, reaffirms the redemption and renewal of the whole earth and the moral regeneration of our people and all mankind. Those who died as martyrs will be vindicated in the Messianic Age when there will be a vital spiritual life that shall lead all to God (Bokser, Mahzor, p. 436). Bokser quotes a 16-year-old young man, Moshe Finker, who perished in a Nazi death camp. He left a diary in which he reflected his reactions to the gathering storm that was to engulf him. He pleaded for nekamah, retribution. "When I speak about nekamah, I ask you to concern yourselves with the positive aspects of nekamah. Our nekamah, to compensate for the tragedies of today and the tragedies of the long night of exile we have endured for 2,000 years will be the restoration of our people to the Holy Land."

The young man had a heart that beat for his people and for humanity. He did not demand brute force, but rather redemptive life. His answer to the cruelty was to save the people and build the land. Our tradition teaches us: "Who is mighty? He who makes an enemy into a friend."

                                                        –Rabbi Seymour J. Cohen

✺✺✺✺✺✺✺✺✺✺✺✺✺✺✺

Ashamnu: The Plural Form

It is significant that our formulae of confession are all couched in the plural, as if to suggest that it is society which fosters the climate and conditions wherein sin is engendered in the heart of the individual. An unfeeling society will nurture despair on the part of the disadvantaged. From despair flow crime and sin. An irresponsible society will, similarly, breed delinquency, violence and sin. The plural formulation indicates that, though the individual commits the act, society at large must bear the responsibility.

It will be noted that, through the confession, there is not one reference to sins of neglect or omission in the performance of specific ritual practices. The catalogue of sins is restricted to the domain of ethics and morals, as if to emphasize that no Jew who strives after piety may ignore his responsibilities to his fellow man.

–Rev. Dr. Jeffrey M. Cohen
Understanding the High Holyday Services

✺✺✺✺✺✺✺✺✺✺✺✺✺✺✺

Why Are Our Prayers in the Plural?

Why was the Confession composed in the plural, so that we say, "We have sinned," rather than, "I have sinned"? Because all Israel is one body and everyone of Israel is a limb of that body; that is why we are all responsible for one another when we sin. So, if one's fellow should sin, it is as though one has sinned oneself; therefore, despite the fact that one has not committed that iniquity, one must confess to it. For when one's fellow has sinned, it as though one has sinned oneself.

–Rabbi Isaac Luria

✺✺✺✺✺✺✺✺✺✺✺✺✺✺✺

Knowing That We Are All Sinners Helps Us Avoid Arrogance and False Pride

What blinds us to the fact that we are the principal actor in this drama of Yom Kippur, that our prayers are not set speeches by some master playwright but the speeches of our own heart which should be coursing within and disturbing us during the meditation of this day? What is it that blinds us to the meaning of Yom Kippur in our own lives? Pride. False pride.

The coronation of the emperors of the Austro-Hungarian empire took place in Vienna in the Cathedral of St. Stephen. This magnificent religious building was a fitting place for a royal ascension. But before the emperor designate was allowed to enter the cathedral for his coronation there was one ritual which he had to undertake. As he approached the gates he found them locked. The Emperor was obliged to summon a church attendant and to cry out, "I, Emperor Franz Joseph of all Austria-Hungary, demand admittance." The canon replied, "We do not know the emperor of all Austria-Hungary. Who is it who desires admittance?" The Emperor cried out, "I, Franz Joseph, demand admittance." And again the answer came, "We do not know Franz Joseph. Who is it who demands admittance?" A third time the emperor cried out, but this time his words were of a different tone: "I, a sinner, request admittance."

"Permission is granted: enter, sinner. Thou art known to us."

The purpose of this ritual is self-evident. Here was a man who had the power of life and death over millions of subjects. The future of his people would rest entirely upon his shoulders, and only a man who was conscious of his limitations, of his frailties, of his folly, who was willing to listen and to reason – only such a man was fit to rule.

– Rabbi Daniel Jeremy Silver

Conscience: Clear or None at All

The well-known master of brief and humorous rhyme, Ogden Nash, has this to say about how we should deal with a guilty conscience:

> There is only one way to get through life
>   on this terrestrial ball.
> And that is to have a clear conscience,
>   or none at all.

Since we Jews are a people with a deep and strong sense of right and wrong, and our conscience is highly evolved over many millennia, we don't have the choice of having "none at all." So if we take the advice of Ogden Nash, then our conscience must be clear. The Confessional prayers will help us toward achieving that goal.

—Rabbi Dov Peretz Elkins

❊❊❊❊❊❊❊❊❊❊❊❊❊

The Uses of Forgiveness

In the words of William A. Ward, "Forgiveness is a funny thing. It warms the heart and cools the sting." In the Yom Kippur Confessional we are reminded that we not only ask God to forgive us, but we too must, in God-like fashion, forgive those who ask our forgiveness. The benefits, as William Ward explains, are clear. Forgiveness brings satisfaction and more closeness to both the offender and the offended.

—Rabbi Dov Peretz Elkins

❊❊❊❊❊❊❊❊❊❊❊❊❊

Confession: The Jewish Way

I saw on television recently that there is a new 900 telephone number 540-TELL. You call this number, speak to someone, and confess your sins. For some, it may help them feel better to talk to a faceless stranger and bare one's soul. For Jews, we find that doing it together in synagogue with our fellow Jews, through the Al Chet and other passages in the Mahzor, it is much more spiritually uplifting and emotionally satisfying.

—Rabbi Stephen Chaim Listfield

❊❊❊❊❊❊❊❊❊❊❊❊❊

When Forgetting Is Not Complete

We ask God's forgiveness in our prayers, and at the same time we are asked to forgive ourselves and our neighbors, especially when they ask to be forgiven. Sometimes, however, that forgiveness is not complete. We say we forgive our loved ones, but we nurture a grudge inside, and really do not let go fully of our psychological injury.

Let me illustrate: A man becomes intoxicated at a party and makes a terrible fool of himself in front of his wife and all their dear friends and neighbors. He begs forgiveness from his wife, who accepts his apology with these words: "I'll forgive and forget." Nevertheless, she continues to remind him of his past misdeed. When he complains to her and says, "I thought you agreed to forgive and forget?" she replies, "Yes, I did, but I didn't agree to let you forget that I agreed to forgive and forget."

The qualification in forgiveness is that it must be full and complete, so that we start with a *tabula rasa* in our relationships, with no past stains on the record book of our lives.

–Rabbi Stephen Chaim Listfield

✺✺✺✺✺✺✺✺✺✺✺✺✺✺✺

We Sin against You

We sin against You when we sin against ourselves; for our failures of truth, O Lord, we ask forgiveness:
    For pretending to emotions we do not feel;
    for using the sins of others to excuse our own;
    for denying our responsibility for our own misfortunes;
    for refusing to admit our share in the troubles of others;
    for condemning in our children the faults we tolerate in ourselves;
    for condemning in our parents the faults we tolerate in ourselves;
    for passing judgment without knowledge of the facts;
    for remembering the price of things but forgetting their value;
    for teaching our children everything but the meaning of life;
    for loving our egos better than truth.

V'al kulam elo-ah s'lihot.
    S'lah lanu.
    M'hal lanu.
    Kaper lanu.

We sin against You when we sin against ourselves; for our failures of truth,
O Lord, we ask forgiveness:
    For using people as steppingstones to advancement;
    for confusing love and lust;
    for withholding love to control those we claim to love;
    for hiding from others behind an armor of mistrust;
    for treating with arrogance people weaker than ourselves;
    for condescending towards those whom we regard as inferiors;
    for shunting to a side those whose age is an embarrassment to us;
    for giving ourselves the fleeting pleasure of inflicting lasting hurts;
    for cynicism which eats away our faith in the possibility of love.

V'al kulam. . . .

We sin against You when we sin against ourselves; for our failures of justice,
O Lord, we ask forgiveness for us and all humanity:
    For the sin of false and deceptive advertising,
    for the sin of keeping the poor in the chains of poverty;
    for the sin of withholding justice from the world;
    for the sin of racial hatred and prejudice;
    for the sin of denying its existence;
    for the sin of using violence to maintain our power;
    for the sin of using violence to bring about change;
    for the sin of separating ends from means;
    for the sin of threatening the survival of life on this planet;
    for the sin of filling the common air with poisons;
    for the sin of making our waters unfit to drink and unsafe for fish;
    for the sin of pouring noxious chemicals upon trees and soil;
    for the sin of war;
    for the sin of aggressive war;
    for the sin of appeasing aggressors;
    for the sin of building weapons of mass destruction;
    for the sin of obeying criminal orders;
    for the sin of lacking civic courage;
    for the sin of silence and indifference;
    for running to evil but limping to do good.
    For all these sins, O forgiving God, teach us to forgive ourselves and
    help us overcome them.

V'al kulam. . . .

– Author unknown

※※※※※※※※※※※※※※※

Prayer Flights

Once someone accepted me –
me, with my somewhat long nose
and skinny features.
Someone accepted
the way I speak,
the way I act in public, and
the way I really am.

Because I was accepted,
I can see more clearly who I am
and accept myself without reservation.
I no longer want to be another.

I am myself – simply and surely.
Love has finally defined for me
the man I really am, and always was.
And I am not troubled or ashamed
by this definition.

Please, God, never let me despair
because I am who I am.

–Mark J. Link, S.J.
In the Stillness is the Dancing

※※※※※※※※※※※※※※※

Change

Man alone, of all the creatures of the earth, can change his own pattern. Man
alone is the architect of his destiny. The greatest discovery in our generation is
that human beings, by changing the inner attitudes of their minds, can change the
outer aspects of their lives.

–William James

God and Man

Al Chet is a prayer of confession, *viddui,* that lists at length a long series of sins men and women are prone to commit during the course of the year. The list is broken up by the refrain *v'al kulam*–"for all of these sins, God of forgiveness, forgive us, pardon us, grant us atonement." Clearly it takes a certain *hutzpah* to enumerate those terribly heinous transgressions and beg God's pardon. But that is precisely what we do in *Al Chet,* year after year on Yom Kippur.

Paradoxically, although we ask for, pray for, and even *expect* God's forgiveness, we find it difficult to ask forgiveness of fellow men whom we've wronged. And we find it even harder to forgive those who have wronged us. Yet the Halakhah insists: there is no atonement on Yom Kippur until you first ask forgiveness and forgive. God cannot forgive sins committed between man and man; only human beings can achieve that. We must learn to say, "I'm sorry" and beg pardon of others. And we must also learn to forgive, to pardon, to accept sentiments of remorse. He who does not accept apologies is called "cruel" by the sages. Halakhah demands that we must ask forgiveness three times. If the offended person does not then accept the apologies, the offender has done his duty.

On Yom Kippur we ask the "God of forgiveness" to accept our apologies. We must ask our fellowman the same. And even as we pray and trust that God will pardon, so must we pardon each other–husbands and wives, parents and children, neighbors and friends, clans and nations.

–Rabbi Gilbert S. Rosenthal

Should We Forgive the Nazis?

Professor Abraham Joshua Heschel asked the question, when would the Jews forgive the Nazis? Rabbi Heschel told the following story: "There once was a Rabbi travelling on a train through Russia. He was shabbily dressed and small in stature and was sitting in a railroad car studying the Mishnah. Two Poles began to make fun of him and deride him. They cursed him and the Rabbi did not reply to them, continuing to study the Mishnah. They then took his suitcase and threw it on the floor. The rabbi maintained his composure–did not rebuke them–gathered all of his belongings and put them back in the suitcase. They continued to revile the Rabbi.

"When they reached the town where the Rabbi was going, a large crowd was waiting for some important dignitary. The two Poles discovered to their amazement that the little old Jew whom they were taunting, was an esteemed and revered Rabbi. They later asked him to forgive them for their taunts and jeers. The Rabbi said, 'You are asking the Rabbi to forgive you, not the little old Jew who was in the railroad car. You have to ask him to forgive you. He is the one you injured by your insults and your jeers.' "

That was Dr. Heschel's answer. Namely, only the victims can forgive. We do not have a proxy vote to forgive in their stead.

–Author unknown

Confession

The Nazis could never say, "I sinned."
Confession requires sensitivity, humility.
The bigot is brutal and arrogant.

–Author unknown

Free to Take Chances

During an interview for a magazine in November, 1976, President Jimmy Carter talked about his faith:

> Belief in the forgiveness of God gives me the freedom to take chances and make mistakes. . . . I feel contention with God at times–why is there suffering and doubt and death and hunger?–but even the struggle is contributing to a deeper sense of assurance. The alternative is a belief in permanent death.

–Author unknown

✖✖✖✖✖✖✖✖✖✖✖✖✖✖✖

The Ten Precepts of Interpersonal Relationships

The nature of all relationships is paradoxical.

Our first and most important relationship is with our Self.

We are all mirrors. What we want from another is our Self. What we can give to another is their Self.

The purpose of relationship is to position our Self in the world.

Relationships are vehicles for sharing experiences and for expressing emotions.

Relationships need space, harmony, and rhythm in order to grow.

Relationships cannot grow without individual expansion and growth.

The quality of a relationship is far more important than the form it takes.

We can't really have a relationship unless we are willing to *not* have a relationship.

Relationships never end; only their form changes.

–Deon Kaner
Briarpath Review

✖✖✖✖✖✖✖✖✖✖✖✖✖✖✖

As God Forgives Us, We Forgive Others

Family strife is most painful. Last night we thrashed through private matters of joint concern to a tight-lipped impasse. This afternoon while walking in the woods, a way opened towards a common place where each of us could stand his ground in mutual acceptance. I felt a warmth from my brother and a small tenderness towards him. Our battle of opposing convictions yielded a tiny flow of grace. A moment of intimacy was born from honest combat. Lord, quiet our sibling fears and soften our suspicions. Let the soil of our heritage, now ploughed up, be fertile ground for fresh hopes shared. Let hard bargaining yield more than justice and reach beyond mercy toward the magnanimity of those who have walked the narrow edge of separation, and been saved, this time, from stumbling over the precipice. Let your tenderness yearn over us.

–Rev. Robert A. Raines
The Ridgeleaf

※※※※※※※※※※※※※※

Our Spirit Soars
Laws of the Spirit

1. Happiness comes from spiritual wealth, not material wealth. Happiness is always a by-product, never a product. Happiness comes from giving, not getting. If we pursue happiness for ourselves, it will always elude us. If we try hard to bring happiness to others, we cannot stop it from coming to us also. The more we try to give it away, the more it comes back to us multiplied. If we try to grasp happiness, it always escapes us; if we try to hand it out to others, it sticks to our hands like glue.

2. The more love we give away, the more we have left. The law of love differs from the law of arithmetic. Love hoarded dwindles, but love given grows. If we give all our love, we will have more left than he who saves some. Giving love, not receiving, is important; but when we give with no thought of receiving, we automatically and inescapably receive abundantly. Heaven is a by-product of love. When we say "I love you," we mean that "a little of God's love flows from me to you." But, thereby, we do not love less, but more. For in flowing the quantity is magnified. God's love is infinite and is directed equally to each person, but it seems to gain intensity when directed to sinners. This is the wonder and mystery of it, that when we love God we get an enormous increase in the quantity flowing through us to others.

3. It is better to give than to receive. Giving is a sign of psychological and spiritual maturity. There are few diseases so childish and so deadly as the "gimmies," a disease that separates us from friends and from God and that shrinks the soul. The secret of success is giving, not getting. To get joy we must give it and to keep joy we must scatter it. The greatest charity is to help a person change from being a receiver to being a giver.

4. Loneliness is the punishment for those who want to get, not give. Helping others is the cure for loneliness. If we feel lonely, we are probably self-centered. If we feel unloved, we are probably unloving. If we love only ourselves, we may be the only person to love us. Whatever we give out, we get back.

5. Thanksgiving opens the door to spiritual growth. If there is any day in our life which is not thanksgiving day, then we are not fully alive. Counting our blessings attracts blessings. Counting our blessings each morning starts a day full of blessings. Thanksgiving brings God's bounty. From gratitude comes riches— from complaints, poverty. Thankfulness opens the door to happiness. Thanksgiving causes giving. Thanksgiving puts our mind in tune with the Infinite. Continual gratitude dissolves our worries.

6. To be forgiven, we must first forgive. Forgiving brings forgiveness. Failure to forgive creates a hell for the unforgiver, not the unforgiven.

–John Marks Templeton
Riches for the Mind and Spirit

Forgiveness

Forgiveness is the exercise of compassion and is both a process and an attitude. In the process of forgiveness, we convert the suffering created by our own mistakes or as a result of being hurt by others into psychological and spiritual growth. Through the attitude of forgiveness, we attain happiness and serenity by letting go of the ego's incessant need to judge ourselves and others. . . . Forgiveness is not a self-righteous or Pollyanna-like turning of the other cheek by which we condone anathema behavior. But if we can understand the deep pain from which hurtful actions inflicted upon us arose, then we have suffered with the other person; we have been compassionate. In that act of compassion, we move out of the role of victim and see beyond their actions to the person who is acting. Forgiveness does not require us to become friends with, for example, an abusive parent, to care for them in their old age, or to do anything in particular. Forgiveness is a state of mind that may give rise to specific actions but is not defined by those actions. . . .

Forgiveness requires us to give up our ideas of better and worse and to finally see ourselves as equals and colearners. This is a hard lesson when we've been hurt and our debtor seems unrepentant, but regardless of what they learn or don't learn in the process or how fast or slow they are at it, forgiveness is up to us. *Forgiveness is not conditional on someone else's behavior.* If we insist that it is, we cannot move out of the victim position. Holding on to being the victim is the surest way of staying stuck and blocking our healing.

–Joan Borysenko
Guilt is the Teacher, Love is the Lesson

The psychological case for forgiveness is overwhelmingly persuasive. Not to forgive is to be imprisoned by the past, by old grievances that do not permit life to proceed with new business. Not to forgive is to yield oneself to another's control. If one does not forgive, then one is controlled by the other's initiatives, and is locked into a sequence of action, a response of outrage and revenge. The present is overwhelmed and devoured by the past. Those who do not forgive are those who are least capable of changing the circumstances of their lives. In this sense, forgiveness is a shrewd and practical strategy for a person or a nation to pursue, for forgiveness frees the forgiver.

–*Time* essay

✖✖✖✖✖✖✖✖✖✖✖✖✖✖

The Meaning of Forgivensss

The rabbis offer the following fascinating story based upon the Torah commandment "You shall not hate an Edomite, for an Edomite is your fellow human
being." (Deuteronomy 23:8)

Rabbi Elazar ben Shammua was once walking by the seashore when he
noticed a boat sinking at sea. A moment later he watched as a man holding
onto a plank of wood floated onto shore. Other Jews were walking by.
Because the man was naked, he covered himself and pleaded: "I am a son
of Esau, your brother. I have lost everything. Please give me a garment to cover
myself." The Jews refused and said: "Your people have treated our people with
cruelty. Therefore, may all your people be stripped bare as you are today." The
man then turned to Rabbi Elazar and said, "You are an honorable man; please
help me." Rabbi Elazar took off a garment and gave it to him. Then he brought
him to his home, fed him, and gave him money with which to begin his life
again.

When the emperor died, the rescued man succeeded him. He ordered that all
Jews in his state be killed. The Jews turned to Rabbi Elazar and asked him to
plead for them. When the man, who was now the ruler, saw Rabbi Elazar
standing before him, he said: "Does not your Torah teach 'You shall not hate an
Edomite, for he is your brother?' I told your people that I was the son of Esau, and
they treated me with hatred, not with kindness."

Rabbi Elazar replied: "Though they are guilty of breaking the law of the
Torah, forgive them."

The king, recalling what Elazar had done for him answered: "Because of what
you did for me I will forgive them."   (*Ecclesiastes Rabbah* 11:1)

Rabbi Elazar ben Judah taught that "the most beautiful thing a person can do
is to forgive." (*Rokeach* 13c) Bearing grudges only prolongs hostility. Forgiveness
and understanding are the only genuine ways to reconciliation, cooperation, and
peace. Perpetuating prejudices through slogans and names only increases human
suffering. Perhaps that is why the Torah warns us: "You shall not hate an
Edomite, for he is your brother. You shall not hate an Egyptian for you were a
stranger in his land." (Deuteronomy 23:8)

–Harvey Fields
A Torah Commentary for Our Times, Vol. I: Genesis

※※※※※※※※※※※※※※

Forgiveness

Yom Kippur teaches us that *forgiveness is real,* that it is not a figment of our imagination, or an illusion fostered by our desires. In our rich and expressive Hebrew tongue there are many terms for forgiveness, and we repeat them time and again in the *'Al Het: Ve'al kullam, 'eloah selihot, selah lanu, mehal lanu, kapper lanu,* "For all these sins, O God of forgiveness, forgive us, pardon us, grant us remission." While the three verbs used in this moving prayer are synonyms, they each suggest a different conception of the nature of forgiveness.

The minimum view is expressed by the Hebrew term *selah.* The root has an Akkadian cognate, *salahu,* which means "to besprinkle, to water." There are those who conceive of forgiveness as a kind of deodorizer. The sin remains intact, but we add a little perfume, so that the odor is not quite so pronounced, or clean it up a little by besprinkling it with water, so that it is easier to bear.

At the other end of the spectrum is the term *mehal,* which is derived from the Hebrew root *mahah,* "to wipe out." According to this maximum view, forgiveness means blotting the sin out completely, erasing it as though it had never taken place. Unfortunately, however, once the face of innocence is corrupted, it can never be restored in its pristine purity. Deception, theft, cruelty, unfaithfulness, let alone a major crime like murder, cannot be blotted out, because they cannot be undone.

Basically, forgiveness is more than besprinkling the sin, but it is less than blotting it out. It is noteworthy that neither of these two terms gives its name to our Sabbath of Sabbaths. Yom Kippur derived its name from a root *Kafara,* which in Arabic means "to cover over." Forgiveness does not mean pretending that the offense was never committed, but neither does it mean constantly recalling the wrong and reviving the resentments and hurts of the past. "Kippur" means "covering over," and beginning afresh.

To be sure, forgiveness is desperately hard to practice. The reason for the difficulty is highlighted by the French proverb, *"Tout comprendre, c'est tout pardonner,"* "To understand everything is to forgive everything." But human beings, unlike God, never understand all, either about themselves or about their fellow men, and therefore they find it difficult to practice the divine art of forgiveness. An injury, we find, is hard to forgive, but even worse is an insult, a blow to our pride, to our self-esteem, to the trust we find misplaced, and so we say, "revenge is sweet," and we call it justice. "An eye for an eye," we say, quoting Scripture and misinterpreting it.

But the sweetness of revenge is transitory; it quickly turns to gall and wormwood, to bitterness in our hearts. Hard as forgiveness is to practice, it is harder still to live without it. The Count of Monte Cristo had been grievously wronged in his youth, and he decided to devote his life to avenging himself upon his enemies. When it was all over, he discovered that he had sacrificed his life and destroyed himself in the process.

The divine art of forgiveness will become easier to practice if we remember that not only is this virtue possible, but it is real; that it is not only real, but absolutely necessary. Life cannot go on without it, not only for the sinner, but also for the victim, as well as for the society of which both are a part.

–Rabbi Robert Gordis
Leave a Little to God

5

HEAR, O ISRAEL

Let Us Commit

Let us commit our hearts and might
to accept in love the sovereignty of Heaven,
to do that which is expected of us,
to live the covenant day and night.

"HEAR"

Let not egotism, personal or national, seal our ears
to the cry for compassion
or the voice of divine command.

"O ISRAEL"

We are linked by a bond we are not free to break.
We are of the covenant people whose ancestors
heard God's voice, whose prophets beheld the Almighty in visions.
We have been compared to the lamb, torn by vicious wolves,
and to the lion, unafraid to walk alone among the peoples.

"THE LORD OUR GOD"

In a pagan world which treated nature as divine
and adored gods with the vices of humans,
our people stood apart, witnesses to a daring faith:
The God of holiness, who loves us,
demands justice and mercy;
God will, one day, be the God of all humanity.

"THE LORD IS ONE"

The universe,
its diversity, complexity, and seeming contradictions,
all derive from one source, the One Creator.
We, unlike by history, race, and temperament,
are yet of one family, the children of One Father.
He is the King, and his Kingship is not in a far-off age;
it is in us, and upon us, if we will now accept its yoke.

–Rabbi Nahum M. Waldman
Likrat Shabbat (ed. Greenberg and Levine)
Copyright © 1987, Media Judaica

❈❈❈❈❈❈❈❈❈❈❈❈❈❈❈

The Lord Is Unique

"Hear O Israel, the Lord our God," inevitably implies a variegated perception of God; for no two human beings, due to their unique individualities, could conceptualize God in the same way. Nevertheless, "the Lord is One," the Lord is unique for we all perceive God as a unique transcendental entity.

"You shall love the Lord, your God, with all your heart." All your heart, the Rabbis in the Talmud say, implies that man should serve his Creator with both dispositions, his disposition to do good, and also with his disposition to do evil. For instance, man should use his disposition to hate, to hate evil. Man should use his disposition to create, to create good.

"With all your soul"—man should be willing to defend the principles of his heritage with his very life, for the only life worth living is a life committed to an ideal worth dying for.

"And these words shall be engraved on your heart and you shall teach them to your children" – it is only when our Jewish values are genuinely engraved on our hearts that we shall be able to transmit them to our children.

"And thou shalt bind them for a sign upon thine hands and as frontlets between thine eyes" – one should commit himself totally, his physical strength and mental endowment to the service of God.

"And thou shalt write them upon the doorposts of thy house" – a house should not become a mere place of relaxation, but a miniature sanctuary.

"In order that your days and the days of your children shall be prolonged on God's Earth" – for when man lives a life of commitment, a life of sanctity, then he eternalizes every hour, every minute of his existence. As the Rabbis in the Talmud put it, "One hour of good deeds on this earth is more significant than the eternal bliss, the eternal joy, of the world to come." Indeed, man's mission here on earth is to transform the earthly days into heavenly ones.

"And thou shalt see it and remember all of God's commandments and do them" – man has no choice; either he sees and lusts and does evil, or he sees and is awed and does good.

"Wherefore you shall remember and do all of my mitzvot and be holy unto your God" – God demands of us more than ethical behavior. We are enjoined to become holy to our God as the Prophet Micah puts it: "You have been told, O man, what is good and what the Lord requires of you to do justly, to love mercy (ethical behavior), and to walk humbly with your God (holiness)."

– Rabbi Morris Shapiro

✷✷✷✷✷✷✷✷✷✷✷✷✷✷✷

A Challenge

Doctor Viktor E. Frankl, Viennese psychiatrist and survivor of Auschwitz, relates an incident which he refers to as the deepest experience he had at Auschwitz. He had hidden the manuscript of his first book in his coat which was taken away from him when he arrived at the camp in exchange for an old ragged one belonging to an earlier victim. Instead of the many pages of his manuscript, he found in the pocket of the newly acquired coat a single page torn out of a Hebrew prayer book, containing the words of the Sh'ma.

He interpreted this incident as a challenge to live his thoughts instead of merely putting them on paper.

– Rabbi Morris Shapiro

❋❋❋❋❋❋❋❋❋❋❋❋❋❋❋

Sh'ma: The Battle-Cry of the Jewish People

❋❋

Throughout the entire realm of literature, secular or sacred, there is probably no utterance to be found that can be compared in its intrinsic intellectual and spiritual force, or in the influence it exerted upon the whole thinking and feeling of civilized mankind, with the six words which have become the battle-cry of the Jewish people for more than twenty-five centuries.

– Rabbi Kaufman Kohler

❋❋

The scientific faith is essentially akin to the ancient religious faith in holding that the infinity in which we live and move is in reality one, not many. The scientific faith that all things are variants on a single system, that one law rules the Cosmos from end to end, from the biggest to the littlest, is a faith that grows stronger with each succeeding discovery.... Today this faith is so high that we have little doubt but there is a continuity from man to amoeba to molecule. There is no separation of man from his origin nor from his fellow man. We are indeed all brothers.

– Ralph W. Burhoe

❋❋❋❋❋❋❋❋❋❋❋❋❋❋❋

World Unity

Mystics of all ages have described the intense experience of unity with the universe during their deepest mystical encounters. It is a trans-national and trans-denominational phenomenon reported by mystical personalities of all faith traditions.

When we recite "Sh'ma Yisrael" – that one line which is the central core of the Jewish faith – it is customary to close our eyes, and even to cover our eyes with our hands or our tallit, to shut out the normal sensations of the environment, and concentrate intensely on the unity of God and of God's universe.

In a recent book entitled *Global Mind Change–The Promise of the Last Years of the Twentieth Century,* Dr. Willis Harman, a noted social scientist and formerly a professor of electrical engineering, describes this sense of global unity. "In higher states of consciousness," he writes, "there is an awareness of being one with the universe and all its creatures, [a feeling of being] related to the Creator. Because these insights are so different from the ordinary experience our language usually expresses, they are not easily conceptualized and verbally communicated. Myth and symbol, paradox, poetic metaphor become more effective means of communicating these insights and experiences."

For the past several thousand years, Jews have found their own unique way of expressing this extraordinary feeling of unity with the Creator and the Universe by reciting, with great feeling and concentration, the "Sh'ma Yisrael."

–Rabbi Dov Peretz Elkins

With All Thy Soul

"And thou shalt love the Lord thy God with all thy . . . soul." (Deut 6:5)

Berachot 61b:

When the Romans brought Rabbi Akiba to execution, they began to comb his body with iron combs. As it was time for reading the Sh'ma, he began its recitation, and despite the tortures to which he was being subjected, he continued to take upon himself the yoke of the Kingship of God (i.e. to recite the Sh'ma). His disciples said to him, "Master! Thus far?" (Meaning: why, amid such agonies, do you concentrate on saying the Sh'ma?) Rabbi Akiba answered them: "Throughout my life I was troubled with this verse: 'And thou shalt love the Lord thy God with all thy soul.' This means: even if He takes your life. I have been thinking: 'When will I have the opportunity to fulfill this? Now that the opportunity is mine, shall I not fulfill it?' " He prolonged the word *Ehad* (one) and the word was on his lips as he expired. A heavenly voice then proclaimed, "Happy are you, Rabbi Akiba, that you died with *Ehad* on your lips."

–Author unknown

A Treasured People

Jewish existence is a tapestry woven of silk on a loom of steel, woven with tears and blood, mystery and martyrdom, threnody, exultation, anguish, ecstasy, peril and paradox.

–Rachel Rabinowicz
New York Times

"When You Lie Down and When You Rise Up"

The Eternal Jew

A wandering Jew once met a man
With blood-spattered clothes and an axe
in his hand.
The Jew whispered "God!" as he started aback;
The man, too, was startled, his visage
grew black.
"Why are you wandering here, Jew?" he
cried.
The Jew said his word: "God will always
abide."
The man cried in fury: "What whisper
you there?"
The Jew made reply: "God is judge, I
declare."
He swung up his axe, smote the Jew on
the head.
The falling Jew cried: "God avenges the
dead!"
Now when that same man to the seashore
did go,
The Jew he beheld as he walked to and
fro.
Astonished, he cried: "What, are you still
alive?"
The Jew made him answer: "In the Lord
I do thrive."

He seized on the Jew, flung him into the
    sea.
The Jew sank, and never a word uttered
    he.
Now when that same man went forth on
    the chase,
He found the Jew meeting him, face
    unto face.
He raged and he shouted: "Alive yet are
    you!"
"With the aid of the Lord!" responded
    the Jew.
He took aim, a bullet right through him
    he shot.
The Jew fell; and falling, he called on his
    God.
That night the man dreamt. And what
    did he dream?
Before him the Jew stood. Alive he did
    seem.
He stared at him piercingly, and murmured
    once more:
"God sees what befalls, He is judge as of
    yore."
He leapt up to clutch him, he brandished
    his fist.
The Jew rose in the air, and he vanished in
    mist.
In the morning he heard him knock at
    his door.
In the evening he saw him still striding
    before.
He returned in his dreams. He returns to
    this day.
He troubles him dreaming and waking,
    they say.
What power is hid in him? What secret
    at call?
He has "God" on his lips in his rise and
    his fall.

—Jacob Cohen
Translated from the Hebrew by I. M. Lask

✳✳✳✳✳✳✳✳✳✳✳✳✳✳

Everything in Moderation?

Two friends who had not seen each other for some time were engaged in an animated discussion when one of them asked, "Would you want me to read your horoscope?"

"I didn't know you believe in astrology," her friend replied.

"Oh," said the first friend, "I believe in everything a little bit."

Many of us are that way – we believe in many things a little bit. We hedge our spiritual bets. We are reluctant to make total commitments. We don't mind too much being classified as "religious" but we would not want to be considered "fanatics." Everything in moderation.

Sidney Lanier, the nineteenth-century American poet and critic, captured the mood of our time when he wrote:

We live in an age of half faith and half doubt,
Standing at the Temple doors head in, heart out.

To those of us who share the spiritual ambivalence of our time, there is a well-known biblical verse that ought to shake us up: "You must love the Lord your God with all your heart and with all your soul and with all your might" (Deuteronomy 6:5). The Scriptures ask us to love God totally, completely, with our whole being. Moderation is not enough.

Indeed, as we stop to think about it, we realize that the statement "Everything in moderation" is only moderately true.

In studying the credentials of a prospective employee, a bank executive would not be overly impressed by a letter of recommendation describing the applicant as being "moderately honest." A defendant on trial for his life would not choose a lawyer who was moderately competent. A parent with a desperately ill child would not choose a doctor who is moderately skillful. And there is not too much hope for a marriage in which the partners are moderately faithful. When a man is drowning twenty feet offshore, a fifteen-foot-long rope will not do. In certain areas, moderation is simply not enough.

The love of God is one of those areas. Every morning and every evening, the Jew recites the words found in the mezuzah, the small traditional ornamental container that Jews affix to their doorframes: "You must love the Lord your God with *all* your heart and with *all* your soul and with *all* your might."

–Rabbi Sidney Greenberg
Say Yes To Life
Copyright © 1983, Crown Publishers

※※※※※※※※※※※※※※

Meaning, Purpose, and Belonging in Life

I am a single cell in a body of three billion cells. The body is mankind.

I glory in the individuality of self, but my individuality does not separate me from my universal self – the oneness of mankind.

The portion of that substance that is mine was not devised; it was renewed. So long as the human bloodstream lives I have life. Of this does my immortality consist.

I do not believe that humankind is an excrescence or a machine, or that the myriads of solar systems and galaxies in the universe lack order or sanction.

I may not embrace or command this universal order, but I can be at one with it, for I am of it.

I see no separation between the universal order and the moral order.

I believe that the expansion of knowledge makes for an expansion of faith, and the widening of the horizons of mind for a widening of belief. My reason nourishes my faith and my faith my reason.

I am diminished not by the growth of knowledge but by the denial of it.

I am not oppressed by, nor do I shrink before, the apparent boundaries in life or the lack of boundaries in the cosmos.

I cannot affirm God if I fail to affirm humanity. If I deny the oneness of humanity, I deny the oneness of God. Therefore I affirm both. Without a belief in human unity I am hungry and incomplete.

Human unity is the fulfillment of diversity. It is the harmony of opposites. It is a many-stranded texture, with color and depth.

THE NATURE OF A HUMANE SOCIETY

The sense of human unity makes possible a reverence for life.

Reverence for life is more than solicitude or sensitivity for life. It is a sense of the whole, a capacity for inspired response, a respect for the intricate universe of individual life. It is the supreme awareness of awareness itself.

I am a single cell. My needs are individual but they are not unique.

I am interlocked with other human beings in the consequences of our thoughts, feelings, actions.

Together we share the quest for a society of the whole equal to our needs, a society in which we neither have to kill nor be killed, a society congenial to the full exercise of the creative intelligence, a society in which we need not live under our moral capacity, and in which justice has a life of its own.

Single and together, we can live without dread and without helplessness.

We are single cells in a body of three billion cells. The body is humankind.

–Norman Cousins
The Nature of a Humane Society

Let Us Take Each Other's Hands

Let us take each other's hands
and walk toward the light of God.
Let us stay in the presence of God
and in the nowness of Joy.

Let us be free from separation
of all kinds.
Let us resist the temptation
to judge each other's behavior.

Let us stop our suffering.
Let us, together, once and for all,
let go of all our past hurts,
and unmet desires.
Let us put our total trust in God and
then see only the God-Self in each other
and feel God's never-ending Love
filling us to the brim and over.

Let us let go of all our self-doubts
that we have projected to each other.
Let us join our wills as one
and be directed only by God's Plan.

Let us join in Love
Let us join in Joy
Let us join in Peace.
Let us LOVE, LOVE, LOVE . . .

—Gerold Jampolsky, M.D.
Out of Darkness Into Light

Listen to Yourself
Using the "Sh'ma" as a Personal Meditation

The Shema can be said as a prayer or a declaration of faith, and it is said as such by Jews all over the world, but if the words are said very slowly, and if a person prepares himself mentally, the Shema can be an extremely powerful meditation. Indeed, the Torah itself prescribes that the Shema be said twice daily, and it seems highly probable that this was originally prescribed as a short daily meditation for all Israel.

The technique consists in saying the words very slowly, in a manner very similar to that of using the Amidah for a meditation. In the Amidah, the prescribed rate was approximately one word every seven seconds. The Shema can be said even more slowly. You can dwell on each word for as long as fifteen or twenty seconds, or with experience, even longer. During the silences between words, let the meaning of each word penetrate your innermost being.

It is easier to use the Shema as a meditation than the Amidah, since the main portion of the Shema consists of only six words, which are easy to memorize. Before you can use these words as a meditation, you must know them well and by heart. You should be seated while saying the Shema and keep your eyes closed. Strive to be perfectly still, with no body motion whatsoever.

– Rabbi Aryeh Kaplan
Jewish Meditation

※※※※※※※※※※※※※※

Sh'ma: Harmony and Unity of the Cosmic System

I hypothesize that there is a formative directional tendency in the universe, which can be traced and observed in stellar space, in crystals, in microorganisms, in more complex organic life, and in human beings. This is an evolutionary tendency toward greater order, greater complexity, greater interrelatedness. In humankind, this tendency exhibits itself as the individual moves from a single-cell origin to complex organic functioning, to knowing and sensing below the level of consciousness, to a conscious awareness of the organism and the external world, to a transcendent awareness of the harmony and unity of the cosmic system, including humankind.

It seems to me just possible that this hypothesis could be a base upon which we could begin to build a theory for humanistic psychology. It definitely forms a base for the person-centered approach.

– Carl R. Rogers
A Way of Being

✹✹✹✹✹✹✹✹✹✹✹✹✹✹✹

A Near-Death Experience

Thanksgiving and Sukkot are not the only contexts in which to give thanks. There is a wonderful blessing "Gomel" (gratitude for kindness) which is recited upon delivery from danger or illness. Two weeks ago, on a flight to New York, the pilot informed us that he was not certain whether the nose gear was locked into place. He was thus unsure whether there would be a crash landing—which is always dangerous. We were diverted to the Newark airport which has a longer runway and is not adjacent to a body of water. (Should the plane go out of control, it could conceivably go into the bay.)

I recited the Shema. I recalled the words of Rabbi Zalman Schachter that there is a special intensity when the Shema is recited in what could be for the last time. I felt that the Shema connected me to Jews who had preceded me and would follow me. This prayer, thousands of years old, was recited in the days of Moses and, hopefully, will be by my descendants. I also sensed a connection with God. I recalled the Rabbinic insight that "everything is in the hands of Heaven except the fear of Heaven." This reminds us that, although we cannot control everything which happens to us, we can determine our response. The willingness of people to help one another, the bonding that took place among the passengers and the crew, was an extraordinary experience.

Finally, I was reminded once again that life is uncertain. We never know what tomorrow will bring. When the plane landed safely, I vowed that whenever I begin a trip or a voyage, I will recite the Traveler's Prayer. It is a beautiful expression of our hopes for a safe trip and a happy landing.

–Rabbi Arnold M. Goodman

✹✹✹✹✹✹✹✹✹✹✹✹✹✹✹

Sh'ma: A Modern Midrash

You shall love the Lord your God with all your mind, with all your strength, with all your being.
The entire self is a vessel of potential born in the image of the Divine.

Set these words, which I command you this day, upon your heart.
The laws of the Torah are the way to a better Jewish life if we fully digest them.

Teach them diligently to your children;
Each and every person is responsible for the Jewish education of all children so they can grow Jewishly.

speak of them in your home and on your way, when you lie down and when you rise up.
Study and teach about this Jewish way of life so it becomes as important to you as your life's work.

Bind them for a sign upon your hand;
May the Mitzvot of Jewish life become inseparable from your everyday actions.

let them be a symbol before your eyes;
Give them enough thought so they become part of your way of life.

inscribe them on the doorposts of your house and upon your gates.
Be willing to confirm publicly, "I am a Jew."

Be mindful of all my Mitzvot, and do them; so you shall consecrate yourself to your God.
Whatever your Jewish idea of God, accept the heritage and tradition of Jewish life as part of the whole.

I, the Lord, am your God who led you out of Egypt to be your God; I the Lord am your God.
There is no substitute! We are made in the image of the Divine and have that potential to achieve holiness by following in God's path.

–Shirley Barish
Bikurim

❊❊❊❊❊❊❊❊❊❊❊❊❊

Sh'ma Yisrael – Some Hidden Meanings

In his commentary on the liturgy, the 14th century Spanish scholar Abudarham gives two unusual explanations of the word "Sh'ma." He interprets them as acronyms for the following:

The three letters of "Sh'ma" *(Shin Mem Ayin)* stand for the words *"S'u aynaychem marom"*–"Lift your eyes heavenward" (Isaiah 40:26). Another interpretation is that the three letters stand for the names of the three daily prayers which Jews recite: *Shacharit, Mincha, Aravit.*

Through these interpretations, Abudarham tells us that the Sh'ma is best recited with our eyes (our souls) lifted toward our Creator; that is, with kavanah, feeling, and meaning. In addition, the feeling we derive from the recitation of the Sh'ma should permeate all of our prayers each day of our lives.

–Rabbi Dov Peretz Elkins

❈❈❈❈❈❈❈❈❈❈❈❈❈❈

Sh'ma Yisrael

Not long ago, I was in the San Diego airport waiting for a flight. All of a sudden, a policeman came up to a woman and a four- or five-year-old girl waiting for the same plane.

He said to them, "I know this will seem strange, but a four-and-a-half-year-old girl has disappeared. The description given by her parents very much fits this girl–blonde, blue eyes, curly hair, wearing a red dress and black shoes. I don't want to alarm you, but I am going to have to ask you some questions to prove that this little girl is really yours, that she isn't the girl who is missing."

What a situation! This woman had to prove that her daughter was really her daughter.

The policeman asked the woman's name, address, hometown, and husband's name. Then he said to the little girl, "What's you name?"

"Mary," she said.

"What's your last name?" Silence.

"Well, where do you live?"

"At home."

"Do you know the name of your city?"

"Nope."

"What's your daddy's name?" he asked.

"Daddy."

"What does he do?"

"He goes to work."

Since he wasn't getting anywhere with the little girl, the policeman turned to the woman. "Do you have any pictures of your little girl in your wallet? Any pictures of your husband that your girl might recognize?"

"No," she said, "I don't carry any pictures."

"Well, what about your plane tickets? Let me see your tickets."

"We're on stand-by," she said. "We don't have our tickets yet."

So, what would you do? How would you prove that your child is actually your child? How would your prove that the little boy or girl with you isn't really someone else's child whom you've kidnapped?

Frightening, isn't it?

Eventually, the policeman must have been satisfied, because he apologized for the intrusion and left. If only he had been able to hear the dialogue immediately following his departure, there would have been no problem in the first place.

"Mommy, Mommy," cried the little girl, "what did that man want from us?"

But the incident got me to thinking. How would I have identified my young sons (oh, those many years ago) if I had been in the same situation? What could we have done to prove that we were actually father and son?

If I had had the presence of mind to think clearly in that scary moment, the answer for us would have been fairly easy. I would have said, "Scott, tell the policeman what we say before we eat."

And Scott would have said, "Baruch Attah Adonai, Elohenu Melech HaO-lam, HaMotzi Lechem Min HaAretz."

And then, I would have said, "Seth, tell the policeman what we say before we go to bed at night."

And Seth would have said, "Sh'ma Yisrael, Adonai Elohenu, Adonai Ehad."

And the policeman would have known that these were my sons.

–Rabbi Wayne Dosick

✵✵✵✵✵✵✵✵✵✵✵✵✵✵

The Thoughts That Should Be in the Mind When the Sh'ma Is Read

The plain meaning of the words *Hear O Israel* has been explained by Abudarham who writes: "This is a form of testimony as if each Jew says to his neighbor: Hear that I believe that the Lord our God is unique in His world. This is why the letter *ayin* of the word *Shema* and the letter *dalet* of the word *ehad* (one) are found written in the Torah scroll larger than the other letters so as to form the word *ed* (witness) to hint at this testimony."

The New Zohar (p. 60a) has this to say: "This verse (Hear O Israel) had meaning when Jacob's sons said it to him (since his name was Israel) or when Moses said it to the people of Israel. But now when everyone says *Hear O Israel,* to which Israel do they address themselves? We have been taught that Jacob our father did not really die and God has sealed him in His precious Throne that he should be a permanent witness for his sons who affirm the unity of God's name, as is fitting, twice a day. So that when they do affirm the unity of God's name they say: '*Hear O Israel!* Be thou our witness that we affirm the unity of God's name as is fitting.' At that time Jacob avails himself of four wings spread out in all four directions and he ascends to the Holy One on high and blesses Him with seven benedictions. Happy is the father who bore his seed upon the earth and happy the children who crown their father in this manner. At that moment all the heavenly hosts proclaim: 'Blessed is His glorious Kingdom for ever and ever.' And Jacob is crowned with thirteen rivers of pure balsam and he stands continually over his children like a wall around a city to prevent strong judgments from having any dominion over them."

Still a further meaning is found in the holy Zohar. This is that the word "Israel" refers to God who is called "Israel." For God is called by many names and among these is Isra-el which means "God is right." So that the meaning of the words *Hear O Israel* is as if man is speaking directly to God: "Hear Thou who art called Israel that I believe with perfect and truth faith that Thou art the Lord and our God and that Thou art the one Lord." What the Zohar really means here is so very profound who can grasp it? But my purpose is not to reveal mysteries but to explain the meaning of *Hear O Israel* as the Zohar understands it in its plain sense. You now have three possible explanations of the words *Hear O Israel*. Choose whichever you like provided your heart is in it.

And thou shalt love the Lord thy God with all thy heart. When a man recites these words he is obligated to bring into his heart a strong and mighty love for God. This love is a positive commandment for the holy people and the duty is derived from this verse. If a man is easy-going about this, apart from having failed to fulfill his obligation of loving God, he also speaks a lie, God forbid. The strategy for attaining to this love is for man to awaken with great energy all his limbs and his mind together with all his other senses and to prepare himself to bring this tremendous love into his heart. Then in proportion to his effort at demonstrating his capacity to act, his heart will be all the more on fire in great love.

I shall give you an illustration. We notice that when a mother kisses her baby to whom she is attached in her innermost heart she kisses with all her might because of the tremendous love her heart bears the child and all her being goes into the kiss. So it is with regard to man's love for God, may His name be exalted. This is how the holy Zohar puts it: "And thou shalt love" – a man should worship God in love for there is no greater form of worship than the love of God.

R. Abba said: These words of the *Shema* contain all the principles of the Torah because all the Ten Commandments can be found in these words and our colleagues have found them there. Come and see that God loves nothing so much as the man who loves Him as he should. What does this imply? As it is written – *with all thy heart.* This is the gist of the passage. So how can a man fail to set his heart on fire, to bring into it the most powerful sense of the love of God with all his might, as above. This note is enough.

And with all thy soul. Our Rabbis comment: "Even if He takes away your life." Consequently, he should not speak untruths, God forbid. He should depict to himself that he is suffering martyrdom for God's sake.

And with all thy might. The Rabbis comment: "With all they wealth." Therefore he should not speak untruths but should depict to himself that he is told: "Either bow down to this idol or we will take away all that you possess," but he retorts: "Take all my wealth but I shall not bow down to your idol or worship it." And he should depict to himself that they take away all he has, even a whole chest of gold coins, and leave him penniless, and all because of his love for God may He be exalted.

And these words which I command thee this day shall be upon they heart. When he finishes the verse he should say to himself: "I accept it upon myself that this love will always be in my heart."

And thou shalt teach them diligently to thy children. He should take this obligation upon himself by saying to himself: "I accept upon myself the duty of teaching my children Thy holy Torah."

[Commentary:]

The book from which this passage is taken is a guide to prayer. Alexander Süsskind advises his readers on the kind of thoughts they should have in mind when reciting the various prayers. This passage is part of his commandments on the *Shema*. No doubt the *Kabbalists* did not take literally the idea of Jacob flying upwards on wings. The reference to Jacob on God's Throne is to the ancient belief that the face of Jacob (Israel) was engraved on the Throne. This, too, was in all probability understood in a figurative sense. The second explanation is very beautiful. Jews, the descendants of the Patriarch Jacob, reassure him that they have kept the faith and not departed from his ways.

> —Alexander Süsskind
> *Yesod Ve-Shoresh Ha-Avodah*
>
> Rabbi Louis Jacobs (translation, commentary)
> *Jewish Ethics, Philosophy & Mysticism*

❊❊❊❊❊❊❊❊❊❊❊❊

Choice: An Experiential Meditation

❊❊

"Ve-haya im shamo-a."
"If you will earnestly obey the commandments I command you this day . . ."

> —Leviticus 11:13

❊❊

Clasp your hands . . .
Feel the energy flow.
Let yourself feel that connection,
the energy that moves around.
Put yourself where you've always been,
in the universal life-force.
Very gently bring your hands to rest
in your lap.
Breathing comfortably, tell yourself:
"I am a life form based in divinity.
I am able to see,
to hear,
to feel,
to smell,
to touch,
to move,
to speak,

to choose."

−Virginia Satir
Meditations and Inspirations

6

HEAR, O GOD,
OUR VOICE

Healing through Meeting

The help of the therapist is not, in the first instance, a matter of finding the right word, still less techniques of communication. It is a matter of the dialogue of touchstones coming into being between one who cannot reach out and one who can. "When one person is singing and cannot lift his voice," said a Hassidic rabbi, "and another comes and sings with him, another who can lift his voice, then the first will be able to lift his voice." "That," said the rabbi, "is the secret of the bond between spirit and spirit."

If patients fear exposing themselves for fear that the therapist or their family or friends will invalidate what they have to contribute as worthless, then they will not be able to enter into the venture of the dialogue of touchstones. The goal of healing through meeting, of confirmation, and of the dialogue of touchstones is, therefore, the same – to establish a dialogue on the basis of trust.

–Maurice Friedman
The Healing Dialogue in Psychotherapy

❊❊❊❊❊❊❊❊❊❊❊❊❊❊

Hear! Listen!

We all need to be reminded to be better listeners. Listening (in Hebrew, Sh'ma) is the primary skill in communication.

I note with great interest an article in a recent issue of the *N.Y. Times* which talks about an important lesson about listening learned by Governor Dukakis. Let me quote a few paragraphs:

> In Michael Dukakis' first semester in 1979 as an unemployed politician and Harvard faculty member, he got bad grades from his students.

> Their evaluations said Mr. Dukakis did not listen to anyone but himself, comments that recalled the criticism he had heard in his first term as Massachusetts Governor and a quality that may have contributed to his stunning defeat in the 1978 Democratic gubernatorial primary.

> By many accounts, Mr. Dukakis took the criticism to heart in the years that followed, before he left the John F. Kennedy School of Government, re-entered politics and was re-elected Governor in 1982.

> "The most important thing he learned here was to listen, and even more, to hear what people were saying," said Graham T. Allison, Jr., the dean of the Kennedy School who had a key role in hiring Mr. Dukakis. (Allen R. Gold, *N.Y. Times*)

Mr. Dukakis learned a lesson that all of us must continually learn, one which is at the heart of our relationships with others. It is the theme of Sh'ma Kolenu— as we turn to God, who is the ultimate model of a good listener.

–Author unknown

❊❊❊❊❊❊❊❊❊❊❊❊❊❊

The Past Got in My Eyes

"Do not forsake us. . . . Bring us closer to Your Torah."

Just recently a "Peanuts" cartoon caught my eye. In case you missed it, I would like to share it with you for it is "food for thought" for the High Holy Days.

In the cartoon, Lucy walks toward Charlie Brown, who is standing on the pitching mound, tosses him the baseball and says, "Sorry, I missed that easy fly ball. I thought I had it, but suddenly I remembered all the others I've missed, and the Past got in my eyes!"

As I see it, the whole purpose of the High Holy Days is to acknowledge the past, deal with it and ask for forgiveness for our failure to live up to God's expectations; and then leave it behind and begin our lives over again with a clean slate.

This cartoon reminds us that if we choose to allow it, the past can continue to influence our present and, in turn, the future.

To what avail, we might ask? Are we to let our past misdeeds be the sole determinant of what happens to us? Or perhaps, if we enter the New Year with a new image, one in which the past does not get in our eyes, this time we may catch on to the importance of taking a renewed look at dealing with life.

–Rabbi Daniel A. Roberts

※⊗※⊗※⊗※⊗※⊗※⊗※⊗

Skills for Leadership

In Barbara Tuchman's book, *The March of Folly,* the author discusses four historical events which she thinks are turning points in history. In each of these four great events, there were similar aspects of folly which were the dynamics that ultimately brought about the disaster.

The four disastrous events are: the Trojan War, the reign of six Renaissance Popes from 1470 to 1530, the loss of the American colonies by the British, and the war in Vietnam.

Barbara Tuchman identifies three aspects of folly that were at work in each of those periods of history to which those in power paid no attention. The three aspects of folly are:

1. the growing disaffection of constituents.

2. the glorification of self.

3. the illusion of invulnerability.

In the final chapter of *The March of Folly,* Barbara Tuchman quotes Machiavelli, who said that the prince "ought always to be a great asker and a patient hearer of truth, and he should be angry if anyone has scruples about telling him the truth." Tuchman adds: "What government needs is great askers."

As Barbara Tuchman shows, listening is one of the most important skills for leadership anyone can have.

–George Eppley
Cleveland *Plain Dealer*

❂❂❂❂❂❂❂❂❂❂❂❂❂

Listening with the Heart

In a recent cartoon, our pathetic but lovable friend Ziggy passes a rather shabby-looking character who is sitting on the sidewalk propped up against a building. Beside him there is a sign that announced: "Good Listener – 25 cents for 5 minutes."

The sidewalk solicitor had greatly underpriced his services, for we happen to be suffering from a terrible shortage of good listeners. Like the biblical woman of valor, a good listener's worth "is far above rubies."

Almost any day the classified sections of our newspapers announce courses and seminars that promise to make us better speakers. But where are the courses to make us better listeners? Among the prizes awarded at commencement exercises there is usually one for the graduate who has shown excellence in public speaking. But did you ever hear of a prize awarded to a student for excellence in private listening?

When a prominent TV personality decided to quit a popular network program, he gave his explanation for his surprising action: "I've become increasingly aware of late that for the past ten years I've been on the air doing a great deal of talking. I want to start looking, thinking, and listening to people."

Anatomically speaking, you and I are so constructed that we should devote more time to listening than to speaking. The Divine Architect endowed us with two ears but only one mouth. Yet for most of us the mouth is a sorely overworked organ and the ears are in a state of semiretirement.

A good listener is worth considerably more than twenty-five cents for five minutes. Psychiatrists' offices are crowded with people willing to pay substantial fees to satisfy their hunger to be heard. Many a family breakup is directly traceable to a failure in communication. There's a great deal of talking and even shouting, but very little listening.

One family therapist who has achieved much success in his work explains his method: "I really don't do much of anything to get families together. I simply give each member a chance to talk while the others listen – without interrupting. Often it's the first time they've listened to each other in years."

His words have the sharp sting of recognition. The next time we are sorely tempted to give our children a "talking to," let us first pause to ask ourselves when we last gave them a "listening to." And this goes for husbands and wives too.

When God appeared to King Solomon in a vision in the night and offered him any gift he wished, the wise monarch asked for neither power nor wealth, nor glory. He asked instead for "a listening heart." It is a gift worth cultivating. For, ultimately, true listening is not done with the ears. It is done with the heart.

–Rabbi Sidney Greenberg
Say Yes to Life
Copyright © 1982, Crown Publishers

※※※※※※※※※※※※※※※

Cast Me Not Out in Old Age

I Am Me

I am not the stroke in Bed 2,
Or the hip replacement in room 4,
Or the Foley that needs changing in 7.
    I AM ME.

I used to have responsibilities like you.
There were people dependent on me.
I had a wife,
I raised 7 children,
I have made decisions.

My body was young and strong.
I ran, I flew, I made love,
I ran with the wind, –
Skimmed the lake in a sailboat,
I have lain alone on smooth grass.

I have kissed hurts away from skinned knees,
And felt a baby's face nuzzling into my neck.
I remember the fragrance of baby powder.
I have been brave.
I have won honors.

I have failed in some things,
But please see ME.
You will be old someday just like ME.
Then you will understand how I want you to know ME–
But then it will be too late.

–Author unknown

✵✵✵✵✵✵✵✵✵✵✵✵✵

A Crabby Old Woman Wrote This

What do you see, nurses, what do you see?
Are you thinking when you are looking at me,
A crabby old woman, not very wise,
Uncertain of habit, with far-away eyes.
Who dribbles her food and makes no reply
When you say in a loud voice "I do wish you'd try."
Who seems not to notice the things that you do.
And forever is losing a stocking or shoe.
Who unresisting or not, lets you do as you will,
Is that what you are thinking is that what you see?
Then open your eyes, nurse, you're not looking at me.
I'll tell you who I am as I sit here so still;
As I do your bidding, as I eat at your will.
I'm a small child of ten with a father and mother,
Brothers and sisters, who love one another,
A young girl of sixteen with wings on her feet,
Dreaming that soon now a lover she'll meet;
A bride soon at twenty–my heart gives a leap.
Remembering the vows that I promised to keep;
At twenty-five now I have young of my own
Who need me to build a secure, happy home;
A woman of thirty, my young now grow fast;
Bound to each other with ties that should last;
At forty, my young sons have grown and are gone,
But my man's beside me to see I don't mourn,
At fifty once more babies play round my knee,
Again we know children, my loved one and me.
Dark days are upon me, my husband is dead,
I look at the future, I shudder with dread,

For my young are all rearing young of their own,
And I think of the years and the love that I've known.
I'm an old woman now and nature is cruel.
'Tis her jest to make old age look like a fool.
The body it crumbles, grace and vigour depart,
There is now a stone where I once had a heart;
But inside this old carcass a young girl still dwells,
And now and again my battered heart swells.
I remember the joys, I remember the pain
And I'm loving and living life over again.
I think of the years all too few gone too fast,
And accept the stark fact that nothing can last.
So open your eyes, nurses, open and see
Not a crabby old woman look closer – see ME!

– Anonymous

※※※※※※※※※※※※※※※※

Prayer of an Aging Woman

Lord, you know better than I know myself that
I am growing older, and will some day be old.
Keep me from getting talkative, and particularly
from the fatal habit of thinking that I must say
something on every subject and on every
occasion.

Release me from craving to straighten out
everybody's affairs. Make me thoughtful, but
not moody; helpful, but not bossy. With my
vast store of wisdom it seems a pity not to use it
all, but you know, Lord, that I want a few
friends at the end. Keep my mind from the
recital of endless details – give me wings to
come to the point.

I ask for grace enough to listen to the tales of
others' pains. But seal my lips on my own aches
and pains – they are increasing, and my love of
rehearsing them is becoming sweeter as the
years go by. Help me to endure them with
patience.

I dare not ask for improved memory, but for a growing humility and a lessening cocksureness when my memory seems to clash with the memories of others. Teach me the glorious lesson that occasionally it is possible that I may be mistaken.

Keep me reasonably sweet. I do not want to be a saint–some of them are so hard to live with–but a sour old woman is one of the crowning works of the devil.

Give me the ability to see good things in unexpected places, and talents in unexpected people. And give me, O Lord, the grace to tell them so.

–Anonymous

Hear My Voice, I Am Dying

Yes, I am dying, but . . .
. . . I'm still the same person you have known all along. My name and address haven't changed, and you can still reach me at the same phone number.

Yes, I am dying, but . . .
. . . I still need to be needed. Now, more than ever. I need places to go, people to be with, and things to do. I'm not trying to escape the reality of my situation, but neither do I want to sit at home with nothing to do except dwell on my situation.

Yes, I am dying, but . . .
. . . You can still get close to me. You can sit by me, shake my hand, even give me a hug. My disease is not contagious. I've not been put in isolation by my doctors.

Yes, I am dying, but . . .
. . . You can still send notes and cards. After my surgery, the postman must have thought I was a celebrity! Today I faced an empty mailbox. Even a bill or an advertisement would be something to look at.

Past failure and present fear restrict the range of our feelings and the purview of our thinking.

While these days of meditation awaken us to the truth of what we are, they must also quicken within us the reality of what we can be.

—Adapted from Eugene O'Neill

�֎֎֎֎֎֎֎֎֎֎֎֎֎֎

Leaping to Spiritual Heights

There is an ancient myth that describes that when humans were being created, each of the angels brought a special gift. From one we received muscle so that we might be able to work and to defend ourselves. From another we gained fleetness of foot. From a third we gained keen vision. Another gave us skills of analysis and wisdom. And still another angel gave us the gift of tenderness and compassion. Thus, mankind grew in the image of God.

The story, however, also tells of the gift of the Devil. The Devil, in his desire to make our lives utterly miserable, conferred upon us the gift of memory. Every failure, every false step, every missed opportunity, every misdeed would remain with us to haunt us. Thus, we no longer could love ourselves or our neighbors. We never would be able to have self-confidence. The Devil's gift of memory was indeed demonic. To counter this, God gave us the gift of forgiveness. Personal failure exists, but we have the power to surmount the past and face the future with new possibilities.

Rabbi Asher ben Yechiel, who lived in the 14th century, said: "Each night before retiring, forgive anyone who may have offended you."

There was a legendary Russian dancer by the name of Nyjinsky, who became famous for his uncanny ability to leap in the air. When asked how he accomplished his remarkable feat, he smiled and responded, "I simply pause and leap." Rosh Hashanah is our chance to pause and leap to spiritual heights we never reached before. We can break away from the old patterns, and free ourselves from the chains of our past to new discovery for the benefit of ourselves and the Jewish people.

—Rabbi Saul I. Teplitz
(from a forthcoming book)

※※※※※※※※※※※※※※※

Listening with Our Spiritual Ear

Earlier this year, the International Fellowship of Reconciliation agreed to consider a proposal for a Listening and Reconciliation Project.

Three of us worked to develop the project: Adam Curle, senior Quaker mediator, teacher and author; Herb Walters, founder of the Rural Southern Voice for Peace (RSVP); and I. The focus is adaptable to any conflict.

This listening requires a particular mode. The questions are nonadversarial; the listening is nonjudgmental. The listener seeks the truth of the person questioned and makes an effort to see through any masks of hostility and fear to the sacredness of the individual. Listeners do not defend themselves but accept whatever others say as *their* perception and validate their right to it.

A Listening and Reconciliation Team is not meant to supersede other modes of nonviolence, but it may be a prelude to them. We hope it will be composed of people skilled in listening to grievances. It may well be brought into play before demonstrations of other nonviolent activities are set in motion.

People often engage in acts of terrorism and violence because they have grievances they feel have not been heard and will never be heard or addressed. The common denominator is fear; the common condition is separation. Such a process opens new avenues of communication and enables those heard to be more aware of what they think and to change their opinions. It does the same for listeners. Through listening, we believe we will better discern what might be done and thus reduce fear. Confident listening will teach us how to proceed.

We are not talking about listening with the human ear. To discern means "to perceive something hidden or obscure." We must listen with our "spiritual ear." This is very different from deciding in advance who is right and who is wrong, and then seeking to rectify it.

Here are three definitions of reconciliation that we used. Thich Nhat Hanh (well-known Vietnamese Buddhist priest) describes it as "understanding both sides." To Adam Curle, it means to "work for harmony wherever we are, to strive to bring together what is sundered by fear, ignorance, hatred, resentment, injustice – any conditions which divide us." To me, it's the bringing together of parties whose relationship has been broken.

To do this work, Adam Curle feels we must have a particular perception of human beings. He writes, "I begin with a concept of human nature based on the belief in a divine element within each of us . . . which is ever available, awaiting our call to help us restore harmony. . . . We must remember this good exists in those we oppose."

The call, as I see it, is for us to see that within all life is the mystery, God. It is within the Contra, the Nazi, the Afrikaner and the American. By nonjudgmental listening, we may awaken it, and thus learn the partial truth the other is carrying. For another aspect of being human is that we each carry some portion of the truth. To reconcile, we must listen for, discern and acknowledge this partial truth in everyone.

Here are some "partial" processes. Thich Nhat Hanh asks this of us. "In South Africa, the black people suffer enormously, but the white people also suffer. If we take one side, we cannot fulfill our task of reconciliation. Can you be in touch with both sides, understanding the suffering and fears of each, telling each side about the other? Can you understand deeply the suffering of both sides?"

Central to reconciliation is to maintain a relationship with both sides. Listening is the way of maintaining that contact: listening to the grievances of both sides, affirming the partial truth of each side by recognizing each party's suffering and describing it to the other.

Again, Adam Curle writes: "Listening, coupled with *befriending* is the unquestionable basis of all mediation efforts. . . . When I started, I was told to 'just listen quietly'; words like mediation and negotiation were never mentioned, and still are not in our actual dealing with our embattled friends."

Herb Walters encourages us to begin reconciliation with listening. He went with another trained listener to Honduras to interview the Contras in 1988, because they and the U.S. peace movement were not communicating. Neither of them was naive enough to think that everything they heard was true, but both were impressed with the sincerity and depth of conviction many Contras held. When he returned, Herb wrote: "The Contra Listening Project has raised new questions for me. One is: Why weren't we peace people calling for dialogue between the Contras and Sandinistas? My answers are that we didn't trust the Contra leadership, and that we saw the Contras only as the enemy, therefore not worthy of talking to. What we know was part of the truth, but we failed to seek the whole truth. At least I did."

Then Herb asked a key question: "Is there a place for an organization that could be trusted by both sides, that could find the human faces of 'the enemy' and carry that message across the battle lines? I am convinced now more than ever that my job as peacemaker is not to take sides. It is to seek the truth. It is to humanize rather than dehumanize the 'enemy.' It is to understand and seek out the best in all sides. . . ."

Finally, Adam recommends, "Do not make any rigid decisions about the design of this listening-reconciliation body. Keep flexible. Keep your eye on the world scene to see what is needed, then meet to see what is feasible. Do not have preconceived ideas of what you will do or the results you want; there are constantly new possibilities. Make your team available to the world. What is most important is to find the people, people of understanding and compassion who are tactful and who don't talk too much!"

I will leave you with a talisman that inspires me. Gandhi reminded us that there exists within each person an energy equal to the force of an atom bomb: a loving power, a caring power, a healing power for peace. I believe it is time to release that power in new ways, and this is one of the ways.

—Gene Knudsen Hoffman
Fellowship

7

SCRIPTURAL READINGS

Self-Affliction

The Torah reading on Yom Kippur ordains the commemoration of this day by self-affliction, cessation from work, and by various rites of atonement performed by the High Priest in the Temple.

The reality of sin is the starting point for the need of atonement. Life must be lived according to a standard, and any deviation from this standard creates a disturbance that must be removed. The disturbance is in the world, as well as in man himself, in the feeling of guilt, which tells him that he is under judgment and in need of penitence.

There are two kinds of offenses that a person may commit, an offense against God and an offense against man. The offense against man must be redressed by trying to make good the wrong done against him, but even the wrong done against man has a dimension of sin against God. Sincere penitence is expressed in the remorse felt over one's wrongdoing and the resolution to shun such wrongs in the future.

The rites performed by the High Priest as spokesman of the people focused attention on the universality of sin; it reached deeply into the inner person with the call for the renunciation of sin; it directed the hearts of the people to God in earnest prayers for forgiveness; and it offered the people the reassurance that they had been forgiven and that they could now face the future clear of the taint of sin which had clung to them over their past misdeeds.

−Rabbi Ben Zion Bokser
HAMACHZOR: The High Holiday Prayer Book
Copyright © 1959, Hebrew Publishing Company

❈❈❈❈❈❈❈❈❈❈❈❈❈

"You Shall Practice Self-Denial" (Fasting)
Leviticus 16:29

The Rev. Robert J. Egan, a Jesuit priest who teaches theology and the history of spirituality at Gonzaga University in Spokane, Wash., says inquiries about fasting come frequently from those seeking spiritual guidance. Other religious counselors confirm this.

"The use of fasting in protest movements," Father Egan said, "has given it an acceptability it might otherwise have lost." He also noted that the pervasiveness of dieting in American culture, although it may have a motive quite different, even opposite, from that of fasting, familiarizes people with the idea of denying themselves food for their own good.

Further, groups concerned with worldwide hunger have encouraged fasting in order to raise both public awareness and funds. For instance, families enrolled in Operation Ricebowl promoted by Catholic Relief Services, forego one meal a week during Lent and contribute the money saved to local and overseas antipoverty projects. Last year, Operation Ricebowl raised about $4 million.

Initially, fasting achieved a place in almost every major religion as a way to make oneself receptive to a divine message or vision, to prepare oneself for an important event or to expiate guilt and win compassion from a deity.

Many early Protestants rejected what they saw as the excessive fasting that had taken place in the Middle Ages, examples, in their view, of trying to gain salvation by human effort rather than faith in Christ, according to Richard Lovelace, who teaches the history of Christian spirituality at Gordon-Conwell Theological Seminary in South Hamilton, Mass. The Puritans, however, encouraged fasting, and national days of "fast and prayer" were more frequently declared than days of thanksgiving during the American Revolution and the first decades of the Republic.

Father Egan finds that fasting has not lost its traditional purposes. It is "a kind of voluntary suffering that can remind you of other people's suffering," he said. "Or it can be an act of expiation, something hard to do that helps deepen your resolve" to change behavior.

"A big part of spiritual advancement," Father Egan said, "is not only breaking bad habits but becoming conscious of habits in general, of the automatic in our lives." Fasting allows one to do that, he said, in that "it deroutinizes your day."

For a number of years, Margaret R. Miles, the Bussey Professor of Historical Theology at Harvard Divinity School, has been re-evaluating fasting and other Christian spiritual disciplines in terms of contemporary culture.

Questioned about fasting, Ms. Miles said, "In a world that could be destroyed by nuclear war, it is terribly important not to devise spiritual disciplines that seem to disparage the natural world or the human body." She agreed with the criticism by feminists that Christian teaching has often linked women and the human body and disparaged both. The "body-denying and world-denying asceticism" in the Christian tradition "should just be acknowledged and deplored," she said.

But Ms. Miles believes that fasting, especially short fasts with juice and water, can serve both body and spirit by helping people break with habits that stultify their awareness. Fasting "can give you some leverage to examine your life," she said. "Many people feel that it significantly clarifies the mind to break that constant link to the world" of food and meal times, and "a change in physical condition alters consciousness."

–Peter Steinfels
New York Times

❉❉❉❉❉❉❉❉❉❉❉❉❉❉

Fasting

The pious Rabbi Abraham Joshua Heschel of Apt (19th century) used to say, "If it were in my power, I would do away with all the afflictions, except for the afflictions of the bitter day, which is the Ninth of Av–for how could one eat on that day?–and the afflictions on the holy and awesome day, Yom Kippur; who needs to eat on that day?"

–Sifran Shel Zaddikim
Days of Awe

❉❉❉❉❉❉❉❉❉❉❉❉❉❉

The Sabbath of Sabbaths

The Rabbi of Rymanov was asked, "Wherein lies the superiority of Yom Kippur, that it is called 'A Sabbath of Sabbaths'? Is not the weekly Shabbat also referred to as 'A Sabbath of Sabbaths unto the Lord' (Exodus 35:2)?" Replied the Rabbi, "Read the Bible more carefully. Of the weekly Shabbat it says, 'A Sabbath of Sabbaths *unto the Lord,*' but of Yom Kippur it is written 'A Sabbath of Sabbaths *unto you*' (Leviticus 23:32)."

This keen interpretation highlights the importance of Yom Kippur as the high point of Jewish teaching. This day is the most sacred in our calendar because it focuses attention on the individual, on the need of personal improvement and for ultimate human betterment.

– Anonymous

※※※※※※※※※※※※※※

The Scapegoat

The word "scapegoat" is widely misused. In the Bible, the *sa'ir la'azazel,* the scapegoat, did not automatically remove everyone's guilt. It was not a *Kapporoh* (like the chicken and rooster used in Jewish custom on the eve of Yom Kippur) which took the rap for everyone else.

The Bible stresses that atonement came about when there was sincere confession, honest self-evaluation and frank confrontation with the guilt of each individual and society as a whole. "And Aaron shall lay both his hands upon the head of the live goat, and confess over him all the iniquities of the people of Israel, and all their transgressions, and all their sins, and he shall put them upon the head of the goat, and send him away into the wilderness by the hand of a man who is in readiness" (Lev. 16:21).

The need of the hour is a total moral self-evaluation in our society. We must see ourselves from a vantage point beyond national, racial, and individual egotism. We all are involved, in varing degrees, from the bottom to the top of society. A token expiation, the selection of a suitable victim, will solve nothing.

–Rabbi Nahum M. Waldman
Jewish Exponent

※※※※※※※※※※※※※※

Choosing Our Scapegoats

The Torah reading for Yom Kippur morning comes from Leviticus Chapter 16. The main theme of the reading is the scapegoat ceremony, in which a goat symbolically carries the sins of Israel into the desert. In fact, there are two goats, one which is sacrificed and one which is led to AZAZEL, the wasteland. It is taught (Mishneh Yoma 6:1) that "the two goats of Yom HaKippurim, their mitzvah is that they should be equal in their appearance, their height, their worth, and the way they were acquired." There is nothing to distinguish between the goat which is sacrificed to the Lord and the scapegoat. In human society, scapegoats are not innately different from others. But, as psychologist Robert Coles has written, "we crave scapegoats, targets to absorb our self-doubts, our feelings of hopelessness." The scapegoat of Yom Kippur symbolically removed the sins from Israel. Human scapegoats are an expression, not of their own shortcomings, but rather of those that choose them.

—Rabbi Jonathan Perlman

✖✖✖✖✖✖✖✖✖✖✖✖✖

An Enchanting Spell Is Cast over Us

The Day of Atonement is the holiest day in the Jewish calendar. On this awesome day we should exclude the thought of everything except man's relation to God and the relation of man to his fellowman. Yom Kippur revives the confidence of the Jew in the ultimate triumph of God's love and justice, and awakens within him a craving to elevate his spiritual life.

However sadly a Jew may have fared throughout the year, however deep may have been his remorse at the misfortunes and the tribulations that overwhelmed him, he finds solace in the Synagogue on Yom Kippur. He derives comfort in communing with the Divine Spirit. Somehow, Yom Kippur casts an enchanting spell over us. Not only does it influence the Jew in every part of the globe, but it also affects even those whose spirit has been beclouded by materialism.

Yom Kippur calls every Jew back to the fold. It enjoins man and woman to arm for the battle against evil and temptation. It reminds us that the battle is to be waged, not through priest or mediator, but through the personal efforts of the individual himself. Thus does Yom Kippur teach us this most momentous fact of human life: although man's destiny is in the hands of the Great Architect of the Universe, the reins of his conduct are in his own hands.

The Day of Atonement is with us. Let each of us give himself wholeheartedly to genuine atonement. With contrite spirit, let us resolve to place stronger reliance upon the kinship between us who are finite and the Almighty who is Infinite. We should realize that the most valuable treasure of life is the blissful accord of man's soul with its Creator, and the relation of his life to the Giver of all life.

—Rabbi Alexander Alan Steinbach

✶✶✶✶✶✶✶✶✶✶✶✶✶✶✶✶

Forever

Forever?
God, forever?

Then what will we achieve today?
What good is our fasting?
What good is our solemnity,
If we and our children must repeat it Forever?

Why do we have to repeat our prayers?
Why must we always seek fresh atonement?

Everything seems to be changing.
God, is anything forever?

Today we need not pray for health.
We have wonder drugs and skilled surgeons.

We need not stare in wonder at the moon.
We can go there.

We exorcise no devils anymore.
We have drugs to change our personalities.

We need not read old books
When new ideas sweep the earth.

Why, then, do we have to do today
What our grandparents did?

Or have we not changed?
Are we still primitive people
Doing again and again
Things we know are wrong?

Must we always fight against ourselves?
Is that battle never won?

"And you shall afflict yourselves.
It is a law forever."

If we cannot win the battle,
Help us, at least, not to lose it.

It is better to struggle forever
than to die once.

—Rabbi Michael Hecht
The Fire Waits

✱✪✱✪✱✪✱✪✱✪✱✪✱

No One Is Too Far Removed to Repent
"Peace, peace! To the far and the near"—Isaiah 57:19

Scripture and rabbinic literature never tire of assuring sinful man of the unfailing availability of redemption through repentance and of the transforming power of divine grace. Isaiah 57:19, read as: "Peace, peace, to the far and the near: to all who draw near to me I draw near and heal them," is used by a midrashic commentator to attribute to God the moving words: "My hands are stretched out toward the penitent; I reject no creature who gives me his heart in repentance." No life is so derelict, so sin-hardened, so lost in self, that it is beyond redemption: "Though your sins be as scarlet, they shall be white as snow" (Isaiah 1:18).

—Will Herberg
Judaism and Modern Man

✱✪✱✪✱✪✱✪✱✪✱✪✱

Sometimes

✱✪

"Shalom, shalom—
Shalom to those who are far off,
Shalom to those who are near,"
saith the Lord—
And I shall heal them.

—Isaiah 57:19
Haftarah, Yom Kippur

❊❊

Sometimes God is seen, and sometimes He is not. Sometimes He listens, and sometimes not. Sometimes He can be sought, and sometimes not. Sometimes He can be found, and sometimes not. Sometimes He is near, and sometimes far.

–Midrash *Tanchuma, Ha'azinu* 4

❊❊❊❊❊❊❊❊❊❊❊❊❊❊

A Prayer of Responsibility for Children
"To Undo the Bonds of Tyranny"–Isaiah

We pray for children who put chocolate fingers everywhere, who like to be tickled, who stomp in puddles and ruin their new pants, who sneak popsicles before supper, who erase holes in math workbooks, who can never find their shoes. . . .

And we pray for those who stare at photographers from behind barbed wire, who can't bound down the street in a new pair of sneakers, who never "counted potatoes," who are born in places in which we wouldn't be caught dead, who never go to the circus, who live in an X-rated world.

We pray for children who bring us sticky kisses and fistfuls of dandelions, who sleep with the dog and bury goldfish, who hug us in a hurry and forget their lunch money, who cover themselves with Band-aids and sing off key, who squeeze toothpaste all over the sink, who slurp their soup.

And we pray for those who never get dessert, who have no safe blanket to drag behind them, who watch their parents watch them die, who can't find any bread to steal, who don't have any rooms to clean up, whose pictures aren't on anybody's dresser, whose monsters are real. . . .

We pray for children who spend all their allowance before Tuesday, who throw tantrums in the grocery store and pick their food, who like ghost stories, who shove dirty clothes under the bed and never rinse out the tub, who love visits from the tooth fairy, who don't like to be kissed in front of the school bus, who squirm in church or temple and scream in the phone. . . .

And we also pray for those whose nightmares occur in the daytime, who will eat anything, who have never seen a dentist, who aren't spoiled by anybody, who go to bed hungry and cry themselves to sleep, who live and move and have no being.

We pray for children who want to be carried and for those who must, for those we never give up on and for those who will grab the hand of anyone kind enough to offer it.

Hear our cries, Adonai, and listen to our prayers. Amen.

–Ina Hughes

❊❊❊❊❊❊❊❊❊❊❊❊❊❊❊❊

Mending the World

Herman Hagedorn has written a poem describing a man's face-to-face encounter with God. It contains these words:

I hastened to reassure Him, "There's nothing the matter with me. It's the other fellow that's the trouble, a hundred and thirty-five million of him." "I know all about the hundred and thirty-five million," said the Lord, and I thought He seemed a little tired as He said it, "but I don't at the moment seem able to see anyone but you."

"Me, Lord?" I said, "How odd! I'm sure you must be mistaken. There's nothing about me that need give you even a moment's uneasiness."

Silence rose out of the ground, straight, hard and thick as a wall. Rose like a wall between us, between the Lord and me. And my nose flat up against it, and the Lord on the other side.

"I'm one of your troopers, Lord," I said, "I've been fighting your battles . . . for years and years . . ."

The wall was so cold it sweated and I began to sweat, too. "You know all about it, Lord. I've run my business by the Golden Rule . . . Been a vestryman in the Church, a trustee of hospitals . . . Fought in a dozen good causes. Not an awful lot happened, but then You know how things are in this world."

The wall got higher and thicker and colder and wetter. I had to shout to make sure that the Lord could hear me at all.

"You can't do this to me! I'm a pillar," I cried. "I'm a corner stone! I'm not a materialist, a scoffer. I'm one of those Christians that hold the social structure together."

The Lord said not a word, but space began to speak. Space spoke in icicles pointed like knives. Icicles dropping on me 'til I froze and burned and bled. "I'm a good man, Lord!" I called, "I don't get the idea!"

But we "get the idea," don't we! The one thing which most assuredly rises up like a wall to separate us from the Source and Sustenance of life is our own unwillingness to acknowledge our involvement in the sins of humankind, a self-righteousness that is insensitive, unrepentant and irredeemable.

To know that at this very moment there are babies crying themselves to sleep because they are starving and to refuse to experience the pain of listening to their cries is to plunge ourselves into the hopeless hell of hard-heartedness.

I suspect that none of you has reached that point or you probably wouldn't be reading this. If you can still feel restlessness which recognizes that your life is not all that it could be, that you're not doing all that you might be doing in response to the pain and suffering in this world, recognize what a wonderfully worthwhile thing that is: that very awareness which hurts like hell – is a sign of life and a source of hope.

Just as fire cleanses and purifies while it burns, the pain of conscience contains the power to heal and make us whole.

–Anthony Fries Perrino
Holyquest: The Search for Wholeness

8

YIZKOR – FOR
THE DEAD

Kaddish
Symphony No. 3

I
INVOCATION
(TEXT BY THE COMPOSER)

SPEAKER:

O, My Father: ancient, hallowed,
Lonely, disappointed Father:
Betrayed and rejected Ruler of the Universe:
Angry, wrinkled Old Majesty:
I want to pray.
I want to say *Kaddish.*
My own *Kaddish.* There may be
No one to say it after me.

I have so little time, as You well know.
Is my end a minute away? An hour?

Is there even time to consider the question?
It could be here, while we are singing,
That we may be stopped, once for all,
Cut off in the act of praising You.
But while I still have breath, however brief,
I will sing this final *Kaddish* for You,
For me, and for all these I love
Here in this sacred house.

I want to pray, and time is short.
Yit'gadal v'yit kadash shme' rabah . . .

> —Leonard Bernstein
> Copyright © 1963, 1965, 1983 by Amberson, Inc.

❊❊❊❊❊❊❊❊❊❊❊❊❊

Colonel Marcus on Death

I am standing upon the seashore. A ship at my side spreads her white sails to the morning breeze and starts for the blue ocean. She is an object of beauty and strength, and I stand and watch her until at length she is only a ribbon of white cloud just where the sea and sky come to mingle with each other.

Then someone at my side says, "There, she's gone!" Gone where? Gone from my sight—that is all. She is just as large in mast and hull and spar as she was when she left my side, and just as able to bear her load of living freight to the place of destination. Her diminished size is in me, not in her!

And just at the moment when someone at my side says, "There, she's gone!" there are other voices ready to take up the glad shout, "Here she comes!" And that is dying!

> —Colonel David (Mickey) Marcus

❊❊❊❊❊❊❊❊❊❊❊❊❊

Grieving

Today I speak of death.
If loss were all,
There would be no need to grieve:
We would merely end;
But the journey continues.
So put your arms around me
And allow the tears
To wash away my sorrow;
Hold my hand
And allow the silence;
I may speak in whispers
Or not at all,
But my message will be clear
In the absence of sound;
My words, when they come,
Will tell the pain
In my own special way:
You need not feel it—
I need to say it;
Do not comfort me with hushing
Or stay the noise
I would make;
If grief be a part of this time,
Let me feel it
For it is a part of me;
Let me say Death;
Let me talk of Loneliness;
Let me feel my Missing—
I need to know its meaning;
The pain must be felt
In its own significance;
I come from yesterday
And when any part of that dies,
A part of me ends
And I feel diminished;
Let me say goodbye
So I can let go
And learn to hold on
In a new way;
When I have said farewell
To what was,

I will be able to define
What is
And then can contemplate
What can be;
For as I mourn,
There grows in me
a new recognition
Of my connections
And when I look up at last,
Tomorrow will be waiting—
And I will go on . . .

—Lois I. Greenberg

❈❈❈❈❈❈❈❈❈❈❈❈❈

Death as the Final Stage of Growth

There is no need to be afraid of death. It is not the end of the physical body that should worry us. Rather, our concern must be to live while we're alive—to release our inner selves from the spiritual death that comes with living behind a facade designed to conform to external definitions of who and what we are. Every individual human being born on this earth has the capacity to become a unique and special person unlike any who has ever existed before or will ever exist again. But to the extent that we become captives of culturally defined role expectations and behaviors—stereotypes, not ourselves—we block our capacity for self-actualization. We interfere with our becoming all that we can be.

Death is the key to the door of life. It is through accepting the finiteness of our individual existences that we are enabled to find the strength and courage to reject those extrinsic roles and expectations and to devote each day of our lives—however long they may be—to growing as fully as we are able. We must learn to draw back on our inner resources, to define ourselves in terms of feedback we receive from our own internal valuing system rather than trying to fit ourselves into some illfitting stereotyped role.

It is the denial of death that is partially responsible for people living empty, purposeless lives; for when you live as if you'll live forever, it becomes too easy to postpone the things you know you must do. You live your life in preparation for tomorrow or in remembrance of yesterday, and meanwhile, each day is lost. In contrast, when you fully understand that each day you awaken could be the last you have, you take the time that day to grow, to become more of who you really are, to reach out to other human beings.

—Elisabeth Kübler-Ross
Death—The Final Stage of Growth

Death: A Haven to the Weary

What can we know of death, we who cannot understand life?
We study the seed and the cell, but the power deep within them will always elude us.

Though we cannot understand, we accept life as the gift of God.
Yet death, life's twin, we face with fear.

But why be afraid? Death is a haven to the weary, a relief for the sorely afflicted.
We are safe in death as in life.

There is no pain in death. There is only the pain of the living as they recall shared loves, and as they themselves fear to die.

Calm us, O Lord, when we cry out in our fear and grief. Turn us anew toward life and the world. Awaken us to the warmth of human love that speaks to us of You.

We shall fear no evil as we affirm Your Kingdom of life.

–Central Conference of American Rabbis
Gates of Prayer

On Death and Life

"Even though I walk through the valley of the shadow of death, I fear no evil." It is wonderful to be able to face death that honestly and openly with no fear. These great words come from one of the beloved chapters in the Bible, and is typical of the biblical attitude about death.

This ability has almost been lost in modern times. The unmentionable word today is *death.* We don't like to talk about it, or face it. In both practice and theory we attempt to hide from it. We use the phrase "passed away" instead of death. We artificially disguise death by making the body as lifelike as possible. We sometimes pretend and imagine that it is only a "nightmare" and really hasn't happened.

But death belongs to life as birth does. We must face it squarely and honestly—there is no hiding place.

In doing so, life becomes more precious. Until a person has faced the limitations of his mortal life, he cannot develop an authentic life. It is useless to pretend to ignore something as fundamental and certain as death.

The acceptance of the loss, loneliness, tears, alienation, and finality of death is the beginning of a deeper appreciation of life and of one another. We take as much for granted.

You and I will probably die sooner than we may wish. We should not take it lightly. It can make us more capable of an honest rearranging of our priorities. Perhaps we need to confront these basic questions: What is there that is sound? What is life all about? What rock is never washed away by the sea? What is the real foundation of human dignity? What is there that gives my life meaning? What can help me conquer emptiness? Is there anything I want to do? Is there anything I want to be? Is there anything I want to change? Is there any faith or love I want to express? I will do it now.

A friend was stricken with a heart attack in the midst of an active life. While recuperating he wrote, "The confrontation with death and the reprieve from it make everything look so precious, so sound, so beautiful that I feel more strongly than ever the impulse to love everything, to embrace it, to let myself be overwhelmed by it. Death and its everpresent possibility makes love—genuine love—more possible."

Without death to remind us, life would never be so precious, and love would never be deep.

—James L. Christensen
Creative Ways to Worship

✹✹✹✹✹✹✹✹✹✹✹✹✹

The Meaning of Kaddish

In the presence of death, we extol life—the creative force energizing each of us. In the presence of reality, we speak of mystery, of love stronger than death, of memories that turn each day into precious possibility. For lives gone from our midst, for tears shed in deepest affection, for what we have become and hope yet to be, we give assent. We affirm—and in that affirmation, we join with the fellowship of Israel and all humanity. Their loss is ours; ours is theirs. In seeking peace and understanding for ourselves, we promise our own understanding to bring peace to all we meet. And to this hope and promise we say, Amen.

—Author unknown

✹✹✹✹✹✹✹✹✹✹✹✹✹

Yizkor

These things are beautiful beyond belief:
The pleasant weakness that comes after pain;
The radiant greenness that comes after rain;
The deepened faith that follows after grief;
And the awakening to love again.

—Author unknown

The Goal of Life

The thought of death need not fill us with dark and despairing anxiety but rather with a creative determination to be for the little world of which we are a part at the center of the target toward which all the archers shall send the arrows of their aspiration; to be the oak tree, tall and stately, in the shelter of whose branches the young can sit and play and the old can find shade from the heat of the day. Let us live in such a way that our spirit shall be the rain causing the soil of other souls to grow moist and verdant; to be sunlight making chlorophyll in the filigree leaves of others' hearts and other minds; to be the star, the guiding North Star, by which the mariners and the navigators in our family and in our circle of friends can set their compass across the unchartered sea of being. This is the goal of life, so to live that others shall rehearse the story of our being with inspiration and with deep gratitude that we have walked the earth, rejoicing to tell of our strong youth, the power of our maturity, the wisdom of our old age. Then indeed our memory shall be a blessing.

—Author unknown

My Life Is Full

Many years ago, I saw a scene from a play on television, and I have never forgotten it. A young man and a young woman are standing at the railing of an ocean liner. They have just gotten married, and this cruise is their honeymoon. They are talking about how fulfilling their love and marriage have been, even beyond their expectations. The young man says, "If I were to die tomorrow, I would feel that my life had been full because I have known your love." His bride says, "Yes, I feel the same way." They kiss and move away from the rail, and now the audience can see the name of the ship on a life preserver: TITANIC.

–Author unknown

❈❈❈❈❈❈❈❈❈❈❈❈❈

Time Is Precious

Horace Mann, the great American educator, once put this announcement in a newspaper's lost-and-found column: "Lost somewhere between sunrise and sunset, two golden hours, each set with 60 diamond minutes. No reward is offered, for they are gone forever."

What can we do with time? Many things. We can kill it. We can waste it. The speeding motorist makes time. The prisoner does time. The idler passes time.

There is something else we can do with time. We can sanctify it. Certain days have been set aside as holy days.

How does time become holy? It becomes holy when we use it for holy purposes. Every religion sets aside such holy days. For the Jews the most important of these are the High Holy Days. They are a time to be reminded of the preciousness of every moment. They are a time to pause, to evaluate, to resolve; a time to forgive and to ask forgiveness; a time to remember things forgotten and to forget things too long remembered; a time to reclaim sacred things abandoned and to abandon unworthy things too highly cherished; a time to ask, "How are we using time?" Yes, time flies, but we are the navigators. More important than counting time is making time count.

There is a special urgency to the prayer of the Psalmist: "So teach us to count our days, that we may acquire a heart of wisdom."

–Sidney Greenberg
Say Yes To Life
Copyright © 1982, Crown Publishers

※※※※※※※※※※※※※※※

We Need Moments of Celebration

(The following was the last public statement of Rabbi Abraham Joshua Heschel before his death. Dr. Heschel is considered to be the greatest Jewish philosopher and theologian for this century and these final words spoken on "Meet The Press" speak directly to our community.)

I would say to young people a number of things. And we only have one minute. I would say let them remember that there is meaning beyond absurdity. Let them be sure that every little deed counts, that every word has power, and that we can, everyone, do our share to redeem the world in spite of all absurdities and all the frustrations and disappointments. And above all remember that the meaning of life is to build a life as if it were a work of art.

You are not a machine. And you are young. Start working on this great work of art called your own existence. And one of the ways of doing it – two ways of doing it – is one, remember the importance of self-discipline; second, study the great sources of wisdom. Don't read only the best-sellers. And third, remember that life is a celebration or can be a celebration. There's much entertainment in our life. And entertainment is destroying much of our initiative and weakens our imagination. What's really important is life as a celebration.

In a very deep sense, I would say that the addictions, the drug addiction from which so many people suffer, is due to the fact that man cannot live such a shallow life, stale. He needs moments of celebration. One of the most important things is to teach man how to celebrate.

– Rabbi Abraham Joshua Heschel

※※※※※※※※※※※※※※※

Joy and Sorrow Come Together

Then a woman said, "Speak to us of Joy and Sorrow."
And he answered:
Your joy is your sorrow unmasked.
And the selfsame well from which your laughter rises was oftentimes filled with your tears.
And how else can it be?

The deeper that sorrow carves into your being, the more joy you can contain.

Is not the cup that holds your wine the very cup that was burned in the potter's oven?

And is not the lute that soothes your spirit, the very wood that was hollowed with knives?

When you are joyous, look deep into your heart and you shall find it is only that which has given you sorrow that is giving you joy.

When you are sorrowful look again into your heart, and you shall see that in truth you are weeping for that which has been your delight.

Some of you say, "Joy is greater than sorrow," and others say, "Nay, sorrow is the greater."

But I say to you, they are inseparable.

Together they come, and when one sits alone with you at your board, remember that the other is asleep upon your bed.

Verily you are suspended like scales between your sorrow and your joy.

Only when you are empty are you at a standstill and balanced.

When the treasure-keeper lifts you to weigh his gold and his silver, needs must your joy or your sorrow rise or fall.

– Kahlil Gibran
The Prophet

❄❄❄❄❄❄❄❄❄❄❄❄❄

In Some Ways, However Small and Secret

In some ways, however small and secret
Each of us is a little mad.
Everyone is lonely at bottom,
And cries to be understood.
But we can never entirely understand someone else
And each of us remains part stranger.
Even to those who love us.

It is the weak who are cruel.
Gentleness can only be expected from the strong.
Those who don't know fear
Are not really brave,
For courage is the capacity to confront what
    can be imagined.

And you can understand people better
If you look at them,
No matter how old, or impressive they are
As if they are children.
For most of us never really mature,
We simply grow taller.
And happiness comes only when we push our heart
     and brains
To the farthest reaches of which we are capable.
For the purpose of life is to matter,
To count,
To stand for something,
To have it make some difference that you lived
At all.

– Leo Ralston

❈❈❈❈❈❈❈❈❈❈❈❈❈❈

Some Stars Shine after They Are Gone

The fact of life most conducive to living fully is an honest awareness and acceptance of death. Death tells us that we must live now and that tomorrow may never come. It tells us that it is not the length of our days, but rather the quality of our years that counts.

Shortly before her death, Hannah Senesh, the paratrooper who sacrificed her life in the attempt to save Jews in Hitler's Europe, gave tongue to those who fell for the love of Israel. She said: "There are stars whose light reaches the earth only after they themselves have disintegrated and are no more. And there are those whose scintillating memory lights up the world after they have passed from it. Those lights, which shine in the darkest night, are those which illumine for us the path."

In its totality, life continues even after death. A person dies but the race lives on, even as the train moves on. Passengers get off and passengers get on, and the train moves on. On a train journey, one knows at what hour the trip will end. But in the journey of life, we have no such forewarning. We know that at some time we must get off the train of life. Death will end life, but it will never end meaningful relationships. Therefore, we must establish meaningful attachments now.

– Rabbi Saul I. Teplitz
(from a forthcoming book)

All I Got Was Words

When I was young and fancy free,
My folks had no fine clothes for me–
    All I got was words:
        Got tzu danken
        Got vet geben
        Zol mir leben un zein gezunt.

When I was wont to travel far,
They didn't provide me with a car–
    All I got was words:
        Geh gezunt
        Geh pamelech
        Hub a glickliche reise.

I wanted to increase my knowledge,
But they couldn't send me to college–
    All I got was words:
        Hub saychel
        Zei nischt kein narr
        Torah iz di beste schorah.

The years have flown–the world has turned,
Things I've gotten; things I've learned–
    Yet I remember:
        Zog dem emes
        Gib Tzedakah
        Hub rachmonas
        Zei a mench!
All I got was words.

–Author unknown

Snowflake

We are each of us a snowflake
No two of us the same
Reflections of the ever loving source from which we came
Unique in form and beauty, crystallized at birth
Little flecks of heaven born to melt into the earth.

We are each of us a snowflake
Of infinite design
Transitory dancers on the window panes of time
Unique in form and beauty, no two of us the same
Reflections of the everloving source from which we came.

We are each of us a snowflake
A falling star in flight
A traveler through the universe in search of our own light
Unique in form and beauty, of infinite design
Transitory dancers on the window panes of time.

–Barbara Meislin
Association for Humanistic Psychology Newsletter

※※※※※※※※※※※※※

Out of the Ashes

There was a concert of extraordinary character here the other evening. It was painful, at time almost unbearable. But it was also uplifting, a testament to the power of the human spirit.

Theresienstadt was a Nazi concentration camp in Czechoslovakia. Jews were sent there beginning in November 1941. Among them were gifted musicians, composers, artists and writers.

The SS commanders at the camp allowed the camp to put on concerts and plays. The Nazis used them for propaganda, to show that Jews were not being ill treated. One concert was put on for representatives of the International Red Cross. The Nazis called Theresienstadt a "paradise ghetto," though in fact it was a place of starvation, torture and death.

In 1944 the inmates were forced to perform in a propaganda film called "The Fuhrer Presents the Jewish With a City." In order to create the impression in the film that Theresienstadt was home for the elderly, the Nazis first transported 7,500 young inmates and children to Auschwitz and the gas chambers.

Somehow, in that place, Jewish composers wrote music to be performed by the inmates. The composers died in Theresienstadt or other concentration camps. But miraculously, some of their compositions survived.

Mark Ludwig, a violinist in the Boston Symphony Orchestra, found the Theresienstadt music. He interviewed survivors of the camp who had performed it or heard it. And he prepared the compositions for fresh performance.

That was the music played in Boston the other evening. There were quartets and trios and other chamber works, performed by the Hawthorne String Quartet and Virginia Eskin, pianist.

First Mr. Ludwig and Marvin Kalb, the television correspondent, now a professor at Harvard, spoke about the historical setting: what the Nazis did. We know the facts. But hearing them again in detail – hearing individual stories – made the horror unbearably real.

Between November 1941 and May 1945, 140,000 people were sent to Theresienstadt. There 33,000 died of starvation, disease and mistreatment; 87,000 were sent on to be killed in Auschwitz and other death camps.

And there were children. Fifteen thousand entered Theresienstadt. Ninety-three survived.

Mr. Kalb spoke of the macabre circumstances of musical performance in Theresienstadt. Twice during performance of Verdi, singers in the chorus were taken away to trains for the death camps.

Mr. Ludwig talked about the composers. Gideon Klein, who wrote much chamber music, died in Furstengrubbe concentration camp in January 1945. (His sister, Eliska, survived the camps. Last year she gave Mr. Ludwig some earlier Klein works, hidden during the war and just rediscovered. One of these, a quartet, was also played in Boston.)

Hans Krasa wrote a children's opera that was used in the Nazi propaganda film. When the film was finished, he and many of the performers went to the gas chambers in Auschwitz. Viktor Ullman was also killed in Auschwitz. Robert Dauber, who was 19 in Theresienstadt, died in a place unknown.

And then the music was played. And the character of the evening – its point – seemed to change.

For what those composers wrote was not routine, was not mechanical. In a hell of inhumanity they created beauty: music of emotional and intellectual depth.

To hear it was heartbreaking at times. Gideon Klein wrote variations of the theme of a Moravian folk song that his nanny sang to him as a child: think of him remembering it in Theresienstadt. But in the end what one heard was a triumph of the spirit.

The concert was presented by the Walter Suskind Memorial Fund. And that was another moving aspect of the evening.

Walter Suskind was a Dutch Jew who saved 1,200 children from the Nazis. Night after night, over many months, he smuggled the children out of an Amsterdam theater where Jews were being held before being sent to concentration camps. He died in Auschwitz.

The world can never be the same after the Holocaust. It taught us that human beings can be irredeemably evil. But it also showed their capacity for goodness and courage against appalling odds, as this concert reminded us. Amid death, some could affirm life.

– Anthony Lewis
New York Times

※※※※※※※※※※※※

Native American Prayer

O Great Spirit, whose voice I hear in the winds,
and whose breath gives life to all the world, hear me.
I am small and weak. I need your strength and wisdom.

Let me walk in beauty and make my eyes ever
behold the red and purple sunset.

Make my hands respect the things you have made.

Make my ears sharp to hear your voice.

Make me wise so that I may understand
the things you have taught your people.

Let me learn the lessons you have hidden
in every leaf and rock.

I seek strength, not to be greater than my brother,
but to fight my greatest enemy – myself.

Make me always ready to come to you
with clean hands and straight eyes.

So when life fades, as the fading sunset,
my spirit may come to you without shame.

– Author unknown
from *A Garden of Prayer* (ed. Bassin and Lahr)

❈❈❈❈❈❈❈❈❈❈❈❈❈

As You Will . . .

A young man in a small village . . . was terribly envious of the revered sage of the community. He decided one day that he would demonstrate to the townspeople that he was wiser than the old man. Holding a sparrow in his hand, he challenged the sage saying, "Old man, is this bird dead or alive?" His intention was that if the wise one said "alive," he would crush the sparrow; if he said "dead," the young man would open his hand and allow the bird to fly away. The old man looked deeply into his eyes, saw the trickery there and replied, "It is as you will, my son; it is as you will." And so it is for each of us. To a great extent, at least, we choose what will be, and that choice is sometimes a matter of life or death. We decide whether we will wallow in "The Subtle Sin of Self-Pity" or respond more creatively to the disappointments and frustrations of life.

– Anthony Fries Perrino
Holyquest: The Search for Wholeness

❈❈❈❈❈❈❈❈❈❈❈❈❈

I Am Not Resigned

I am not resigned to the shutting away of loving hearts in
    the hard ground.
So it is, and so it will be, for so it has been, time out
    of mind:
Into the darkness they go, the wise and the lovely.
Now at rest, peaceful at last . . . but I am not resigned.

Lovers and thinkers, into the earth with you.
Be one with the dull, the indiscriminate dust.
A fragment of what you felt, of what you knew,
A formula, a phrase remains, – but the best is lost.

The answers quick and keen, the honest look, the laughter,
    the love, –
They are gone. They have gone to feed the roses.
So the flowers will grow. I know. But I do not approve.
More precious was the light in your eyes than all the roses
    in the world.

Down, down, down into the darkness of the grave
Their Torah, their Mitsvot, their memories,
they leave behind;
Quietly they go, the intelligent, the witty, the brave.
I know. But I do not approve. And I am not resigned.

– Author unknown

❋❋❋❋❋❋❋❋❋❋❋❋❋

To Accept with Equanimity

Apparently, nature does not have the power to create such marvelously sensitive organisms as we human beings are, and at the same time arrange for the durability in us of stone or mountain. This is a universe where everything has a price, and we cannot expect to purchase the fragile beauty of love and consciousness without the suffering of transiency and decay.

It is the part of wisdom to taste of the cup of joy and sorrow without inner rebelliousness, to accept with equanimity the inevitable fact that we and all we possess are transient just because we are such sensitive creatures.

– Rabbi Joshua Loth Liebman
Peace of Mind

❋❋❋❋❋❋❋❋❋❋❋❋❋

Where Will I Be?

Do not come when I am dead
To sit beside a low green mound,
or bring the first gay daffodils,
Because I love them so,
For I shall not be there.
You cannot find me there.
Where will I be?

I will be reflected from the bright eyes of little children;
In the smile of a bride under the chupah;
In the flames of Shabbat candles at the family simcha.
I will warm your hands through the glow
Of the winter fire;
I will soothe you with the drop
Of the rain on the roof;
I will speak to you out of the wisdom
Of the sages;
And make your heart leap with the
Rhythm of a hora;
I will flood your soul with the flaming radiance
Of the sunrise,
And bring you peace in the tender rose and gold
Of the after-sunset.
All these have made me happy.
They are a part of me;
I shall become a part of them.

–Author unknown

Next Time . . .

The following was written by a terminally ill young woman to her parents. She said: "Mom, Dad, it took this crazy disease to finally force us together. Before this we seemed so busy with our own silly things, that we forgot to get to know the most important people in our lives . . . each other. We wasted so much time in complaining . . . that we forgot to tell each other the crucial things about our lives. It took a calamity to finally make us sit down and talk to each other, and that, more than anything else has made the pain go away for a while. But . . . we never really said what I want to tell you right now. To say 'I love you' covers too large an area and is said too often to really be meaningful. Rather than telling you, I want to thank you for sharing your life with me . . . for making me your princess . . . that no matter what I have said or what I did to hurt you, I'm sorry and I promise you that next time, if I have more time, I'll care a lot more. Next time, if I have more time, I'll let you hear me laugh a lot more and yell a lot less.

Next time if I have more time, I won't be so embarrassed when you ask the waiter for an extra spoon so that we can share a dessert. . . . Next time, if I have more time, I'll let a lot more hurt pass me by before I get angry at you and give a little more kindness than criticism. Next time, if I have more time, I'll spend more of it trying to understand you. . . . Next time, if I have more time, I'll spend a lot more of it with you."

– The American Rabbi

�֎֎֎֎֎֎֎֎֎֎֎֎֎֎

Overcoming Defeat

History is replete with people who have overcome obstacles, always making the best out of the worst. Whistler failed at West Point. He was deeply humiliated, but it was not the worst thing that could have happened to him. Otherwise he would never have been an artist. After Daniel Defoe failed in business, he began writing "Robinson Crusoe." Beethoven composed some of the greatest symphonies of all time after he lost his hearing. Winston Churchill suffered chronic depression, yet led his nation to victory in its most desperate hour. Charles Darwin said, "If I had not been so great an invalid, I should not have done so much work as I have."

Michelangelo's statue of David is a masterpiece in marble. It stands nine feet high, with wonderful expressiveness of artistic genius. There's quite a story behind the statue. You notice that the young man David is slightly bent over, as if in the act of hurling the fatal stone. The reason is that Michelangelo carved the figure out of a block of marble ruined by the sculptor Baccellino, over a century before. Baccellino bungled his creation when he cut too large a slice out of the side. One hundred years later, the trained eye of Michelangelo saw the stone and caught the possibility that lay in it. The sliced out area of the marble block became the curve in the body of David which gives the appearance of his throwing the stone at Goliath. The same block of marble, ruined by one sculptor was redeemed by the other.

Failure to reach the goal is not the fault of something beyond ourselves as of something within ourselves. To succeed in life we must overcome the difficulties and not be overcome by them. This High Holyday season affords us an opportunity to look within ourselves.

–Rabbi Saul I. Teplitz
(from a forthcoming book)

❊❊❊❊❊❊❊❊❊❊❊❊❊❊❊

Live So You Have Enough Time

I went out, Lord
People were coming and going,
Walking and running.
Everything was rushing: cars, trucks, the
   street, the whole town.
People were rushing not to waste time,
To catch up with time, to gain time.

Good-bye, excuse me, I haven't time.
I'll come back, I can't wait, I haven't time.
I'd love to help you, but I haven't time.
I can't accept having no time.
I can't think, I can't read, I'm swamped,
   I haven't time.
I'd like to pray, but I haven't time.

   You understand, Lord, they simply haven't
   the time.

The children are playing, they haven't time
   right now . . . Later on . . .
The students have homework to do, they haven't
   time . . . Later on . . .
The young married have their house, they have
   to fix it up.
They haven't the time . . . Later on . . .
They are dying, they were going to give, but . . .
Too late! . . . They have no more time!

   And so, all people run after time, Lord.

They pass through life running, hurried,
   jostled, overburdened,
Frantic, and they never get there. They still
   haven't time.
In spite of all their efforts they're still
   short of time,

Lord, you must have made a mistake
There is a big mistake somewhere.

> The hours are too short,
> The days are too short.
> Our lives are too short,
> O Lord, why don't we have enough time.
> Time for our parents and our children.
> Time to study and learn.
> Time to think and to pray.
> Time to visit the sick and lonely.
> Time to do the Mitzvot we think of.
> Time to appreciate the blessings we have.

Lord, You who are beyond time, You smile to
    see us fighting it.
You know what You are doing.
You make no mistakes in Your distribution of
    time to people.
You give each one of us time to do what we
    really want to do.
So we must not deface time,
Waste time, kill time,

> For time is a gift that You give us,
> But a perishable gift,
> A gift that does not keep.
> Lord, I have time,

I have plenty of time,
The years of my life,
The days of my years,
The hours of my days
They are all mine, to use now in order to sanctify time.

> Mine to fill quietly with Shabbat and Yom Tov.
> Mine to fill completely with Torah and Mitzvot.
> So when the end of my time comes,
> I can say I did what I should have done,
> I had enough time.

—Author unknown

✻✻✻✻✻✻✻✻✻✻✻✻✻✻✻✻

We Need One Another

We need one another when we mourn and would be comforted.

> We need one another when we are in trouble and crave help, or when we are
> in the deep waters of temptation and a strong hand might pull us out.

We need one another when we would accomplish some great purpose and
cannot do this alone.

> We need one another in our defeats, when with encouragement we might
> strive again; and in the hours of success, when we look for someone to share
> our bliss.

And we need one another when we come to die, and would have gentle hands
prepare us for the journey.

> All our lives we are in need, and others are in need of us.

We best live when we bring to one another our understanding and our solace.

–Author unknown

✻✻✻✻✻✻✻✻✻✻✻✻✻✻✻✻

There Were Two Men

Once there were two men who ate exactly the same food, but the first had two
bowls, while the second had only one. The man with two bowls divided his food
into bitter and sweet, and put only the bitter in one bowl and only the sweet in
the other. When he would eat, he would make a great show of his pleasure and
delight over the sweetness of the contents of the one bowl; and over the latter's,
he would grimace and groan and complain. The man with only one bowl
naturally mixed the bitter and the sweet together.

As time passed, the first man grew thinner and thinner, and gradually wasted away. The second man, who ate the same food, grew healthier and stronger daily.

At last the first saw his death approaching. In desperation he asked the second to tell him the secret of his vitality and vigor. The second replied: "You having two bowls, divided the bitter from the sweet. Believing that taste is of paramount importance, you did not allow the food you took to sustain you with its own nourishment. But I had only one bowl, so I was forced to mix the bitter and the sweet, having not been seduced by the matter of taste. For whatever I have been given to eat I have taken simply as food, and it has yielded its nourishment to me, regardless of how it has tasted, thank God."

The first man stumbled from his death-bed and with great effort picked up one his bowls. He smashed it to the ground. Into the one bowl that remained he placed food that his friend gave him, both the bitter and the sweet, and ate. He became whole again.

Later, on the single bowl, he inscribed the phrase, *Gam zeh ya'avor: This, too shall pass.*

– Author unknown

9

MARTYROLOGY

The Example of the Martyrs

The purpose of the observance of Yom Kippur means more than to seek forgiveness for our sins. It means to rededicate our lives to all that makes life holy, to regard no sacrifice too great, if the welfare of humanity or the service of God requires it. To achieve that consecration of our lives, we need the inspiration which comes from the example of others who succeeded in achieving it.

We are especially inspired by the example of those who make the supreme sacrifice in order to hallow God's name. Israel has had many martyrs in every age who gave up their lives rather than be untrue to their deepest convictions.

The Martyrology readings are intended to convey to us something of that spirit of martyrdom, which asserted itself among our people whenever the occasion called for it.

–Author unknown

The Holocaust and Mazon

We hear so much about the Holocaust, the Shoah, as it is called in Hebrew. But we are not often encouraged to take action resulting from our raised consciousness.

As you know, our congregation has been encouraging people to make a contribution equal to 3% of the cost of every Bar or Bat Mitzvah, wedding, or other simcha, to Mazon, the Jewish Response to World Hunger. As part of their recent appeal letter, Mazon sent us a copy of a letter they received from someone who sent in his check:

Dear Mazon,

The enclosed check is contributed in memory of my brother, Michael Mittelman, whose last known communication was smuggled out of Buchenwald and forwarded to a former Christian neighbor (a baker) begging him for a loaf of bread because he was starving.

My thanks to Mazon for enabling me to do for my neighbors (wherever they are) what was not done for my brother!

The Mazon appeal letter then concludes, "This is not a Holocaust story as much as it's a story of choices that we are empowered to make.
"It is the best possible choices that Mazon, with your help, strives for."
The letter, I think, speaks for itself.

–Rabbi Dov Peretz Elkins

※※※※※※※※※※※※※※※

Remembering Martyrs from Our Own Time

As we have just read the martyrology on Yom Kippur, I have been realizing that in remembering the 10 great martyr rabbis of 1,800 years ago and the 6 million dead of 40 years ago, we may forget the martyrs of our own generation–people very much like us. I am thinking of several American Jews who took on themselves the obligation to affirm the holiness of God and of the Jewish path by working for *tikkun olam*–the healing of the world–and were killed because of their commitment.

The most recent was Ben Linder, a Jewishly conscious young Jew, an engineer from Portland, Oregon, who was murdered by a Contra terrorist attack in Nicaragua. He had gone there to help the poor by building dams for electric power and water supplies, and to delight children and adults as a juggler.

His sister Miriam's last letter to him, which arrived on the day he died but which he did not live to read, quoted Rabbi Nachman of Bratzlav, "All this life is a very narrow bridge, but above all is not to fear," and added, "If you're on a narrow bridge over a deep abyss, your safety comes in standing up straight."

The others that occur to me are:

- Gail Rubin, the American Jewish photographer–a "psalmist with a camera," as her book of photos calls her–who, also moved by Jewish ideals of social concern, went to Israel and was murdered on the Mediterranean coast near Tel Aviv, by terrorists from a Palestinian nationalist group.
- Ronni Karpen Moffitt, who was murdered in Washington, D.C., along with Orlando Letelier, a Chilean exile, when Letelier's car was fire-bombed on orders of the Chilean secret police. She and her husband had been doing research for Letelier on how to free the poor and desperate of Chile and Latin America.
- Alison Krause, who was killed by the National Guard at Kent State University in 1970 when they fired on her for taking part in a demonstration against the Viet Nam War.
- Michael Schwerner and Andrew Goodman, who were murdered along with James Chaney in Mississippi in 1964 for taking part in civil rights organizing and voter registration.
- Nana Freeman who was killed in an extremely suspicious auto accident while she was working for the United Farm Workers in Florida.

This and every Yom Kippur, we might well say aloud their names, to be remembered as a blessing, when we mention those who died for *kiddush hashem*– to affirm the holiness of God. And may we remember–that we must work to create a world in which martyrdom is unnecessary, a world in which everyone knows that human life is precious and those who work for life must be honored, not murdered.

–Arthur Waskow

❋❋❋❋❋❋❋❋❋❋❋❋❋❋❋

Martyrology

In his novel *1984*, George Orwell wrote that "whoever controls the present controls the past; whoever controls the past controls the future." When we listen to the reading of the Torah, when we extend its literal meaning by interpretation, it is not merely as an act of filial piety or an exercise in dutiful remembrance. By controlling the past, by understanding it, we can try to control the future; we are able to illuminate the present day and its events.

Several months ago, a new law was passed in California requiring high school students to study the four genocides of the 20th century: the mass killing of Armenians by Turks during World War II; Hitler's Holocaust; the famine forced upon the Ukrainians by the Soviet Russians; and the slaughter of Cambodians. Students learn not just about mass murder and human-rights violations but about how history is reported and interpreted. They learn that history is often manipulated for improper ends, and that our future depends on how we perceive the past.

I would like to make an observation on two of the unspeakable tragedies. How shocking it is that there are those who deny the Armenian massacre in 1915. I have a weighty tome in my study called *The Armenian File, The Myth of Innocence Exposed* that was given to me and a group of rabbis in Istanbul. The volume argues that the report of the Armenian massacre is a fabrication, a lie. The head of the Turkish historical society wrote, in essence, that the whole thing was a myth. The reason for the myth was that it served the interests of those countries that wanted to carve up the Turkish empire, "the sick man of Europe," after World War II. On another level, we remember that when Hitler was about to commence the Holocaust, some of his advisors urged against it for fear of its ultimate implications. He said to them, bluntly, "Who remembers the Armenians?"

Over and over again, we hear of people who deny that the Holocaust ever happened. Apparently these historical revisionists want to continue racism and Nazism. These latter-day Nazis try to control the future by misrepresenting the past. On several occasions during the past year, Kurt Waldheim attempted to deny his role in the Holocaust. It is painful to see the head of the world's largest church be the guest of Waldheim, and on other occasions Waldheim being his guest.

Let us study the past, let us understand its message. In that way, by controlling the past we can control, as best as we can, the future.

–Rabbi Seymour J. Cohen

❊❊❊❊❊❊❊❊❊❊❊❊❊

The Power of a Greeting

Near the city of Danzig lived a well-to-do Hasidic Rabbi, scion of prominent Hasidic dynasties. Dressed in a tailored black suit, wearing a top hat, and carrying a silver walking cane, the rabbi would take his daily morning stroll, accompanied by his tall, handsome son-in-law. During his morning walk, it was the rabbi's custom to greet every man, woman, and child whom he met on his way with a warm smile and a cordial "good morning." Over the years, the rabbi became acquainted with many of his fellow townspeople this way and would always greet them by their proper title and name. Near the outskirts of town, in the fields, he would exchange greetings with Herr Muller, a Polish Volksdeutsche (ethnic German): "Good morning, Herr Muller!" the rabbi would hasten to greet the man who worked in the field. "Good morning, Herr Rabbiner!" would come the response with a good natured smile.

Then the war began. The rabbi's stroll stopped abruptly. Herr Muller donned an SS uniform and disappeared from the fields. The fate of the rabbi was like that of much of the rest of Polish Jewry. He lost his family in the death camp of Treblinka and, after great suffering, was deported to Auschwitz.

One day, during a selection at Auschwitz, the rabbi stood on line with hundreds of other Jews awaiting the moment when their fates would be decided, for life or death. Dressed in a striped camp uniform, head and beard shaven and eyes feverish from starvation and disease, the rabbi looked like a walking skeleton. "Right! Left, left, left!" The voice in the distance grew near. Suddenly the rabbi had a great urge to see the face of the man with the snow white gloves, small baton, and steely voice, who played God and decided who should live and who should die. He lifted his eyes and heard his own voice speaking, "Good morning, Herr Muller!" "Good morning, Herr Rabbiner!" responded a human voice beneath the SS cap adorned with skull and bones. "What are you doing here?" A faint smile appeared on the rabbi's lips. The baton moved to the right – to life. The following day, the rabbi was transferred to a safer camp. The rabbi, now in his eighties, tells me in his gentle voice, "This is the power of a good-morning greeting. A man must always greet his fellow-man."

–Author unknown

✸✸✸✸✸✸✸✸✸✸✸✸✸

From Fire, Light

We are the generation that stands between the fires.
Behind us are the fires of Auschwitz and Hiroshima.
Before us is the nightmare of the Flood of Fire –
The thermonuclear holocaust that could burn the earth
And make each city a crematorium without a chimney.
The task for us is to turn fire into light:
Light to see each other with,
Light to see the Image of God in every human face.
The task for us is to live between the fires of Shabbat:
Behind us the candles that begin Shabbat;

Before us the candles that end it with Havdala.
Within us the pause of rest, of peace, of mystery: Shabbat.
We are the generation that must live between the fires:
Between the candles of Shabbat, or the flames of holocaust.
The flickering candle flames of Mystery,
Or the consuming flames of Mastery.

Blessed is the One Who creates from fire, light.

–Arthur Waskow
CCAR Yearbook, 1984

Kiddush over Tears

Elie Wiesel described a New Year's Eve in 1944, in a concentration camp. Services took place in the barracks. A cantor who knew the service by heart recited each line aloud, and then the congregation repeated it after him.

Wiesel says, "We felt like weeping, so great was our self-pity. It was hard, but we controlled ourselves until one of the men, at the end of his endurance, burst into sobs. A moment later everyone was weeping. . . . Together, we recalled family and friends, events dating to a time when Europe harbored rabbis and disciples, a thousand synagogues and millions of believers. We reminisced about a past when family meant presence, not separation. We mourned the dead and the living, the vanished homes and desecrated sanctuaries, we wept without shame or hope, and it seemed to us that we would go on weeping until the end of all exiles, until the last breath of the last survivor. . . .

"Suddenly, an inmate stepped forward and began to speak: 'Brothers, listen to me. Tonight is Rosh Hashanah, the threshold of a new year. And even though we are starved, in mourning and on the verge of insanity, let us continue our customs and our traditions of long ago. In those days, after services, we went up to our parents, our children and friends to wish them a good year. We don't know where they are now, or rather, we do know, which is worse. Let us, nevertheless, pronounce our good wishes–and leave God to transmit them to whomever they belong.'

"Whereupon the assembly cried out in unison and with all its might, as though wanting to shake heaven and earth, 'A good year! A good year.'

"And the speaker went on 'Before we part, we should make the customary Kiddush, bless the bread and sanctify the wine. But we have no bread; as for the wine, our enemies are getting drunk on it. Never mind, we'll take our tin cups

and fill them with our tears and that is how we will make Kiddush before
God. . . .' "

We are more fortunate. We don't have to fill our cups with tears. We can fill
them with our loyalty to Judaism. We can fill them with our hope for tomorrow.
We can fill them with our search for the presence of God. *A good year! A good year!*

–Author unknown

※※※※※※※※※※※※※※※

The Big Deportation
Kovno Ghetto, November 28, 1941

Early in the evening, notices were hung
Shrouding us in clouds of sorrow and pain.
Promptly at six the next morning
All were to report to the Assembly plant.

It did not matter–men, women, children
It did not matter–old, sick, or faint
Terror sat in every Jew's eye
At what might take place there today.

In the square the Jews assembled–
Each trying to ease his neighbor's fear.
Don't you worry; nothing will happen
It's nothing but a body count taking place.

The sun was already up, friend sought out friend.
What will happen here? The question blitzed through the crowd.
Suddenly, the Lithuanian mercenaries
Formed a ring around the square.

At ten o'clock the Germans appeared
Sauntering in and out of the crowd, casually inspecting.
Hearts beat fast in sweaty-cold fear
Eyes filled with fear, lips dry and sealed.

The ghetto police were dismissed
As were the labor supervisors and their cronies.
Separated and moved aside
To safety on Democrat Street.

And there, another group—
Women, children, aged and the like
But why were they weeded out?
And moved to Panirev Street?

Look out, Jews, it's an "action," they're sorting us out!
The German officer stood, unmoved, like a slave trader,
With one finger he coolly pointed right—or left—
Doling out their fate—with a wave of his hand.

And the mob, in fear and panic
Was driven like cattle, past his post
He moved only a finger—right or left—
His face betraying no wisp of concern.

And from right and left tears and wailing.
He has torn families in two
A mother sobs for her child, the child cries for her.
Will such a wound ever be healed?

And through the lucky side, the question runs:
What will happen to the others, on Panirev Street?
And for a moment a spark of hope flares
They're taking them to the Little Ghetto.*

At dusk, the lucky ones rushed like wild animals
Back to their homes, for which they had longed through the day.
But a few silhouettes remain motionless on the ground
Never again to rise.

The next morning and the square was again sunny, bright,
Here and there a corpse remained as it was;
And there to the hill—outside the city, the "chosen ones"
Were led, slaughtered and died.

O world, their blood calls to your conscience
The blood of men, women, children and the aged.
On the hill, appear now twin mass graves
Lonely, orphaned till the end of time.

—Translated by Samuel Rosenbaum

*A section of the ghetto which had been emptied some time earlier. The hope was that those on the unlucky side were being taken there for resettlement.

※※※※※※※※※※※※※

The New Anti-Semitism
Pull Up in Front of My House

JEWS GO HOME . . . Well, now, this is nothing new. Never in the past have you even taken this gentle suggestion to move on. But Heaven forbid, suppose just this once, you thought that expression of a few sick people actually expressed the conviction of all the people in this wonderful land of ours, and all of you started to pack your bags and leave for parts unknown.

Just before you leave, would you do me a favor? Would you leave your formula for the Salk Vaccine with me? You wouldn't be so heartless as to let my children contract polio?

And would you please leave your knack for government and politics and persuasion and literature and good food, fun and love, and all those things, and would you please leave with me the secret of your desire to succeed?

And please have pity on us, please show us the secret of how to develop such geniuses as Einstein and Steinmetz and oh, so many others who have helped us all. After all, we owe you most of the A-Bomb, most of our rocket research and perhaps the fact that we are alive today, instead of looking up from our chains and our graves to see an aging, happy Hitler drive slowly by in one of our Cadillacs.

On your way out, Jews, do me just one more favor. Will you please drive by my house and pick me up too? I'm just not sure I could live too well in a land where you weren't around to give as much as you have given us. If you ever have to leave, *Love* goes with you, *Democracy* goes with you, everything I and my buddies fought for in World War II goes with you. God goes with you. Just pull up in front of my house, slow down, and honk, because, so help me, I'm going with you, too.

– Author unknown

※※※※※※※※※※※※※

Chant for all the People on Earth

Not to forget, not to ever forget, so long as you live, so long as you love, so long as you breathe, eat, wash, walk, think, see, feel, read, touch, laugh.

Not to forget, not to ever forget, so long as you know the meaning of freedom, of what lonely nights are to torn lovers, so long as you retain the soul-heart of a man, so long as you resemble a man in any way, in any shape.

Not to forget, not to ever forget.

For many have already forgotten. Many have always planned to forget fire, fear, death, murder, injustice, hunger, gas, graves.

For they have already forgotten and want you to forget our beloved species.

Not to forget, not to ever forget. As long as you love, carry it with you. Let us see it, recognize it, in each other's face and eyes, taste it with each bite of bread each time we shake hands or use words for as long as we live.

Not to forget what happened to 6 million Jews, to living beings who looked just as we look – men – people – children – girls – women – young – old – good – bad – evil – profound – foolish – vain – happy – unhappy – sane – insane – mean – grand – joyous. All dead. Gone. Buried. Burned.

Not to forget, not to ever forget for as long as you live, for the earth will never be the same again. For each shred of sand cries with their cries and our lungs are full of their dying sounds.

For God was killed in each of them. In order to live as men, we must not forget. For if they are forgotten, O! if they are forgotten!, forget me also. Destroy me also, burn my books, my memory, and may everything I have ever said or done or written – may it be destroyed to nothing. May I become less than nothing, for then I do not want even one memory of me left alive on cold, killing Earth – for life would have no honor, for to be called a man would be an insult . . .

–Leslie Woolf Hedley

❊❊❊❊❊❊❊❊❊❊❊❊❊❊

The Soldier Weeping at the Western Wall

Asa, my uncle, died at the Wall –
In a village called Lublin, he died at the Wall,
With twenty six others; the SS shot them all.
For him and for them, I weep at the Wall.

Sarah, my cousin, died at the Wall,
In a chamber of Auschwitz, she died at the Wall.
With her child at her breast; so hungry, so small.
For her and her child, I weep at the Wall.

Shalom, my brother, died at the Wall,
On the Syrian border; he died at the Wall
Of the house he had built; he was rugged and tall.
For my brother, Shalom, I weep at the Wall.

O, God of my fathers, I fought for this Wall
for my uncle and those who fell with him, for all!
For my cousin, her baby, so hungry, so small.
For my brother, Shalom – rugged and tall.
Now, let my tears win the right, just to fall.

– Sister Felicia
Community of St. Mary's

✵✵✵✵✵✵✵✵✵✵✵✵✵✵

Feelings

I have always felt sorry for people afraid of feeling, of sentimentality, who are
unable to weep with their whole heart. Because those who do not know how to
weep do not know how to laugh either.

– Golda Meir

✵✵✵✵✵✵✵✵✵✵✵✵✵✵

A Parable

When the prophet Elijah knew that the time had come for him to ascend to
heaven on a fiery chariot, his disciples respectfully drew back and averted their
eyes. Only Elisha followed his master into the wilderness. "Turn back," pleaded
the prophet, "my road is hard; my task is never done; the prophet's mantle hangs
heavy on my shoulders; turn back." Elisha shook his head and followed his
master.

The time drew near.

"What is it that you want from me?" asked Elijah.

"A double portion of your spirit!" answered the disciple.

"Hard to give, hard to receive," said Elijah. "But if you see the fiery chariot, the
gift is yours."

Fire roared up into the sky, and Elijah's body ascended as smoke in air. The tree of time trembled, and a star stopped singing. Was it one chariot, or were there six million? Was there a witness? Elisha had not turned away. He saw. And his anguish screamed out into the night.

"My father, my father, the chariots of Israel and the horsemen thereof!" He tore his garments. He stumbled through the desert, falling over stones – or had it been a pile of children's shoes? He found a black cloak; it was the prophet's mantle.

And a terrible anger took hold of Elisha. He flailed the coat as though it were the staff of Moses, and the waters of the Jordan divided before him. He cried out the story. Blank disbelief: searching parties went out to seek the dust which trembled at the edges of the universe. They had not seen the chariot. They did not know. And it became the task of Elisha to tell them what had been lost and what had to be done. The salt of Elisha's tears fell into their springs of knowledge and purified the waters. Elisha replaced Elijah.

He was not a good prophet. Elijah had stood above the multitudes, had swept them along with his grandeur and power. Elisha was one of the crowd, and moved into their midst. Elijah's shadow hung over him. Elijah's cup was filled at every seder; his chair was occupied at every manchild's birth; his place was secure in the hopes of the people. They were sure Elijah would return before the coming of the Messiah.

But Elisha had seen him leave in the fiery chariot. And whenever he acknowledged that vision and accepted it, he gained the strength to wear the mantle. He would not be a great leader. But he could be one of the people, could be a witness in their midst. He spoke of the fiery chariot, he pointed up to the sky, he lived his testimony. "My father," he wept. "My father! Oh, the fiery chariot."

There are those who say that no Messiah can come until the world stops looking for Elijah and begins to listen to the testimony of Elisha. For the Messiah's pathway – once seen by the patriarch Jacob as a golden ladder – was seared and torn by the passing of the chariots. Once the ladder was built from heaven to earth; now it must reach from earth to heaven, and must be constructed by man. And this will only happen when the quiet testimony of an Elisha among the multitudes can get them to see the passing of the chariot. They must experience the terrible grief and loss. They must cry for the past turned to fire, for the future become ashes. Etched into their vision there must be the flaming path arching up into darkness. And from their lips, with reluctance and anguish, words must rise to form the threshold of the golden ladder:

Yitgadal v'yitkadash sh'mey rabah . . .

It is said that his prayer must be repeated six million times.

But people have forgotten why this should be so.

– Author unknown

Peace and Tranquility Will Return Again

That's the difficulty in these times: ideals, dreams and cherished hopes rise within us, only to meet the horrible truth and be shattered.

It's really a wonder that I haven't dropped all my ideals, because they seem so absurd and impossible to carry out. Yet I keep them because in spite of everything I still believe that people are really good at heart. I simply can't build up my hopes on a foundation consisting of confusion, misery, and death. I see the world gradually being turned into a wilderness. I hear the ever-approaching thunder, which will destroy us too. I can feel the sufferings of millions and yet, if I look up into the heavens, I think that it will all come right, that this cruelty too will end, and that peace and tranquility will return again.

In the meantime, I must uphold my ideals, for perhaps the time will come when I shall be able to carry them out.

–Anne Frank
The Diary of Anne Frank

A Prayer for Our Army

To all you who now find yourself in our army,
whether you are a son or a father,
may you be touched by peace and harmony.

Hear the core of our prayers.

May you believe in what you do
May you stand as one in purpose
In the battle, in the War,
may your hearts be filled with faith.

And my prayer for all of us and for all Israel,
that the bombs no longer fall
that we no longer in pain shed tears.

Dear God grant us
bring to us, fulfill for us our deepest prayer
a sense of peace, a sense of security.

And most of all,
may not even one more family be touched by bitter sadness.

— Einat Weiss

❊❊❊❊❊❊❊❊❊❊❊❊❊❊❊

In the Rising Sun

Permit the Sun to rise,
    Please let her shine
upon the faces of our sons, our fathers,
upon the faces of our mothers and so many others.

Permit the Sun to rise
wipe out all our doubts and fears
please erase all saddened faces, filled with tears.

Permit the Sun to rise,
silencing the rifle's cries
stopping the funerals before our eyes.

Permit the sun to rise
and just let our children live their lives
let them bloom and let them flower
let the growing rains upon them shower.

Permit the Sun to rise
Please just let her rise
and melt away the pain in all our lives.

    — Einat Weiss, an Israeli teenager
        Translated from the Hebrew by Rabbi Henry Schreibman

❋❋❋❋❋❋❋❋❋❋❋❋❋❋❋

Litany for Yom Kippur
In Remembrance of Yom Kippur, 5734/1973

FOR THESE I WEEP –

My heart aches . . .
For a Yom Kippur interrupted, and given to fighting and killing instead of to fasting and praying.

My heart aches . . .
For a time of quiet, six years of no war, shattered by blasphemy and treachery.

My heart aches . . .
For young boys and young men, whose strong bodies were massacred on their most solemn and sacred day of judgment.

My heart aches . . .
For families broken, lives ended, children orphaned, parents bereaved, wives widowed.

My heart aches . . .
For strong hearts that have been stilled, open smiles that have been closed, for the waste of life – young, promising, and beautiful.

My heart aches . . .
For the people of a young, new nation just a quarter century old, that has become old too soon – from the death of its young people.

My heart aches . . .
For searing photos of Israeli prisoners, and burning Stars of David in the sky, for a Sefer Torah in captivity.

My heart aches . . .
For hateful nations who applaud our enemies, who sit on the fence and pile guilt upon guilt to their already heavy burden.

My heart aches . . .
For a Jewish grandmother, born in Russia, reared in America, leader in Zion, whose reign and life were burdened with a new and heavy grief.

My heart aches . . .

For God. Once again God was hidden, concealed behind the tragic conver-
gence of violent lines. Is God angry, is God guilty, is God silent, is God? My
heart aches for you, God.

And my heart aches . . .

For me and my children. I want my children to believe that the world is good
and that humanity is kind. But this is our world – violent and painful and
something is wrong with humanity – and all we can do is pray, and give and
commit ourselves. So we shall commit ourselves, and give, and we shall
pray – if not to praise God then to seek Him.

–Rabbi Arnold Turetsky and Rabbi Dov Peretz Elkins

※※※※※※※※※※※※※※※

Stranger than Fiction

When the Old and New Cities of Jerusalem were reunited in 1967, a recently
widowed Arab woman, who had been living in Old Jerusalem since 1948,
wanted to see once more the house in which she formerly lived. Now that the
city was one, she searched for and found her old home. She knocked on the door
of the apartment, and a Jewish widow came to the door and greeted her. The
Arab woman explained that she had lived there until 1948 and wanted to look
around. She was invited in and offered coffee. The Arab woman said, "When I
lived here, I hid some valuables. If they are still here, I will share them with you
half and half."

The Jewish woman refused. "If they belong to you and are still here, they are
yours." After much discussion back and forth, they entered the bathroom,
loosened the floor planks, and found a hoard of gold coins. The Jewish woman
said, "I shall ask the government to let you keep them." She did and permission
was granted.

The two widows visited each other again and again, and one day the Arab
woman told her, "You know, in the 1948 fighting here, my husband and I were
so frightened that we ran away to escape. We grabbed our belongings, took the
children, and each fled separately. We had a three-month-old son. I thought my
husband had taken him, and he thought I had. Imagine our grief when we were
reunited in Old Jerusalem to find that neither of us had taken the child."

The Jewish woman turned pale, and asked the exact date. The Arab woman
named the date and the hour, and the Jewish woman told her: "My husband was
one of the Israeli troops that entered Jerusalem. He came into this house and

found a baby on the floor. He asked if he could keep the house and the baby, and permission was granted."

At that moment, a twenty-year-old Israeli soldier in uniform walked into the room, and the Jewish woman broke down in tears. "This is your son," she cried.

This is one of those incredible tales we hear. And the aftermath? The two women liked each other so much that the Jewish woman asked the Arab mother:

"Look, we are both widows living alone. Our children have grown up. This house has brought you luck. You have found your son, or our son. Why don't we live together?" And they do.

– Author unknown

✳✳✳✳✳✳✳✳✳✳✳✳✳✳

Side with the Humble

Creator of the world, we will renew our prayers even as You have renewed our hearts.

We know that a time will come when there will be no strong and no weak, no hunters and no hunted, no oppressors and no oppressed, no slayers and no slain, no masters and no servants, no rich and no poor.

For we know that this world is no waiting room for eternity. Eternity is here among us.

Therefore, we are bidden not to take thought for our own hereafter, but for our brothers' welfare in this world. And we know that this teaching will survive all its enemies and all our own.

Are our enemies more mighty than we? Torah is stronger than their might, and our dream is greater than their night.

The evil time is at an end. For redemption has begun.

But so long as evil still dwells in the world for the people of the world and, above all, for Your people, Creator of eternity, let us, while there still are oppressors and oppressed, be among the oppressed and not among the oppressors, among the hunted and not among the hunters, among the slain and not among the slayers.

Above all, Creator of the universe, let us continue to side with the humble and not with the arrogant.

We know that this world will be saved from evil. Should this not be true, may we know nothing further, for nothing will be worth knowing.

–Soma Morgenstern
The Third Pillar

✹✹✹✹✹✹✹✹✹✹✹✹✹✹

Jews Are Unique

Israel is not like the other nations.
Jews are different.
Our history
    written in martyr's blood
The nations rage against us
Our enemies cannot see our virtues.

Israel is not like the other nations.
Jews are different.
Our virtues
    mark our uniqueness
Jews are so creative
    So prominent in the causes that shape modern society
Our religion
    has given birth to two other
Our history
    is a barometer of human destiny

Israel is not like the other nations.
Jews are different.
We struggle with our uniqueness
    proud yet anguished
        special yet common
Our distinctiveness
    discomforts us as much as our suffering
Still we struggle with our unique fate
And with a sense of pride
We choose to affirm it

We have suffered
   but we have also survived.
Our enemies have cursed us
But we have lived to be a blessing
To their descendants.

Therefore we should thank God that
   Israel is not like the other nations.

—Rabbi Allen S. Maller

�֍✖✖✖✖✖✖✖✖✖✖✖✖✖

The Commanding Voice of Auschwitz

Jews are forbidden to hand Hitler posthumous victories. They are commanded to survive as Jews, lest the Jewish people perish. They are commanded to remember the victims of Auschwitz lest their memory perish. They are forbidden to despair of man and his world, and to escape into either cynicism or other-worldliness, lest they cooperate in delivering the world over to the forces of Auschwitz. Finally, they are forbidden to despair of the God of Israel, lest Judaism perish. A secularist Jew cannot make himself believe by a mere act of will, nor can he be commanded to do so. . . . And a religious Jew who has stayed with his God may be forced into new, possibly revolutionary relationships with Him. One possibility, however, is wholly unthinkable. A Jew may not respond to Hitler's attempt to destroy Judaism by himself cooperating in its destruction. In ancient times, the unthinkable Jewish sin was idolatry. Today, it is to respond to Hitler by doing his work.

– Rabbi Emil Fackenheim

✖✖✖✖✖✖✖✖✖✖✖✖✖✖

Life Is Not Fair

Life is not fair. The wrong people get sick and the wrong people get robbed and the wrong people get killed in war and in accidents. Some people see life's unfairness and decide: "There is no God; the world is nothing but chaos." Others see the same unfairness and ask themselves, "Where do I get my sense of what is fair and unfair? Where did I get my sense of outrage and indignation, my instinctive response of sympathy? Don't I get these things from God? Doesn't God plant in me a little bit of the divine outrage at my injustice and oppression, just as God did for the prophets of the Bible? Isn't my feeling of compassion for the afflicted just a reflection of the compassion God feels in seeing the suffering of God's creatures? Our responding to life's unfairness with sympathy and right-eous indignation, God's compassion and God's anger working through us, may be the surest proof of all of God's reality.

–Rabbi Harold S. Kushner
When Bad Things Happen to Good People

✖✖✖✖✖✖✖✖✖✖✖✖✖✖✖

The Righteous Gentiles – Who Are They to Me?

Who are "they" to me
I a child of Jewish Polish parents
whose memories are filled with ancestral
episodes of contempt for my people.

Eye-witnessed stories of ten decapitated Jewish heads placed upon
the S.S. desk shrunken heads upon which skull caps are
derisively displayed,
"This is your minyan, Jew."
Witnesses who saw green and yellow smoke
out of chimneys fueled by human bodies.

Who are "they" to me
the silent spectators who dare to deny
what "they" saw or heard.
"They," the collaborators,
the betrayers of sacred history.

Then I concluded in my heart
that "they" – all of them –
meant me and mine no good.
"They" are my enemies
if not overt then hidden foes.
No allies, no friends among "them."

Then as in a nightmare
within the evil heart rose
the cry of a sobbing infant.
How could innocence reside in that hellish heart?

Then I heard more of the others,
read of the others, met the others,
gentiles, Christians, believers, atheists
in every country Nazi tyranny controlled.

The others, non-Jews, not kith or kin, not fellow religionists
but those who danced to a different ritual
non-Jews from every walk of life
who turned themselves into hiding places
their sewers, stables, attics, basements
into sanctuaries.

They, not saints or supermen and superwomen
but persons of flesh and bone like yours and mine
who risked security, safety, life
to hide the hunted.

There were far more of the others who joined the enemy,
narrowed their heart to their parochial group.
But these valiant few transcended the boundaries
of their faith, their church
to enter the leprous circle of the condemned.

"They" are heroes from the other side,
whose decency and courage broke through the walls
designed to deny a common humanity.
"They," the healers of our disillusionment
set the brakes upon our generalizations.
"They" gave the lie to cynicism that
saw beneath the skin of all only
the implacable, eternal foe.

"They" are the ordinary men and women
who did what they did because
human decency and conscience demanded it.

And why? Why did they risk their lives?
They answer with a question
"And what else would you do?"

They hold up a mirror to my soul.
Would I let them in,
this hunted man,
this pregnant woman,
this trembling family.
Would I unlock the door?

Would I let them in
for days or weeks or months or years?
Would I scrounge for food to feed these strangers
when the offer of a loaf of bread
meant imprisonment and death?

Would I get hold of sleeping pills
to silence the cries of the infant
whose sobs might give away the hiding place?

Would I dispose of their excrement, bury their dead,
turn my home into whispers
lest the informants lurking about
sell hiders and hidden
for a carton of cigarettes or a bottle of vodka?

Would I falsify identity papers
forge baptismal certificates, visas
lie to the interrogators
seek out allies in a conspiracy of goodness?

"They" did, and theirs are lessons
that must not be lost to our children:
Know that there is always an alternative to passive complicity.
Know that knowing is no cognitive sport
to hear and see and then feign deafness, blindness, muteness.
Know such knowledge is evil,
a subterfuge for shedding the blood of innocence.

Know that there is goodness
even in hell.
Goodness precious, rare, but that must
be cultivated to resist evil.
Know that goodness must be recognized, searched out,
raised from the dust of amnesia,
Know that the good who protected the persecuted
must themselves be protected by us,
the family of the survivors.

We owe the world a double witness, double testimony
of those who slaughtered and of those who saved.
Know the darkness and know the light.
Know the evil and know, too, the good.
Remember the moral heroes for
a generation beyond the holocaust
enabling our children to hope again, to trust again,
to mend again the tattered fabric of our lives.

Breathe spirit into the smoldering ashes of the cremated past
that the sparks of decency may be fanned
to light the candle of many wicks,
to enlighten the future.
Bear witness to goodness that our hearts
and our children's hearts not fail.

—Rabbi Harold M. Schulweis

10

SERVICE – IN THE TEMPLE AND TODAY

The Meaning of Sacrifice

One of the popular illusions of our times views life as a giant commissary from which we are entitled to draw unlimited rations of food and clothing, power and privilege. That is a caricature of life. Life, the Torah would remind us, is an altar, and the things that go on an altar are sacrifices. Until we have learned that basic truth we are not yet ready for mature and meaningful living.

When Isaac Stern concluded a concert recital one evening, he was approached by an ardent admirer who exclaimed rapturously, "Oh Mr. Stern, I would give anything to be able to play the violin as magnificently as you do!" To which the maestro replied softly, "Would you give twelve hours a day?"

Genius has been defined as one percent inspiration and ninety-nine percent perspiration. This comment prompted my favorite cartoon friend, Ziggy, to boast, "I am ninety-nine percent genius."

Perhaps the percentages are not all that one-sided, but who will deny that genius is indeed the capacity for taking infinite pains, the capacity for doing without today so that you can do with tomorrow, the capacity to make demands of ourselves before we are entitled to expect anything from others.

A successful artist in a recent interview said that in order to be a good artist a person "must be willing to be ruthless with himself." Robert Frost was pointing in the same direction when he spoke of the "pain" of poetry: "Poetry, like all birth and creativity, is accompanied by pain and sacrifice."

Great character, great homes, great lives—all are built on sacrifice. And so is a vital, rewarding Jewish life.

"No religion is worth its salt," wrote Rabbi Abba Hillel Silver, "which does not make great demands upon its adherents. . . . Too many of our people want an easy-going religion, one which does not interfere with their leisure, their sleep, or their television, which calls for no study and no observance, which does not challenge or disturb them, a religion without any spiritual travail, without any stab of thought or conscience, without any sacrifices, the religion of a self-pampering people. No religion has ever survived in that kind of an emotional and intellectual vacuum. Judaism least of all."

Perhaps the time has come to go back to the first lesson.

—Rabbi Sidney Greenberg
Lessons for Living
Copyright © 1985, Hartmore House

※※※※※※※※※※※※※※※※

Service

※※

Strange is our situation here upon earth. Each of us comes for a short visit, not knowing why, yet sometimes seeming to devise a purpose. From the standpoint of daily life, however, there is one thing we know:

That Man is here for the sake of other Men . . . Above all, for those upon whose smile and well-being our own happiness depends, and also for the countless unknown souls with whose fate we are connected by a bond of sympathy.

Many times a day I realize how much my own outer and inner life is built upon the labors of my fellow men, both living and dead, and how earnestly I must exert myself in order to give in return as much as I have received.

—Albert Einstein

※※

This is the true joy in life, the being used for a purpose recognized by yourself as a mighty one; the being a force of nature instead of a feverish, selfish little clod of ailments and grievances complaining that the world will not devote itself to making you happy.

I am of the opinion that my life belongs to the whole community, and as long as I live it is my privilege to do for it whatever I can.

–Author unknown

The Arrogance of Self-Righteousness

And thus did the High Priest pray:

Oh, God, protect me from the arrogance of self-righteousness.

Let the pride of my office not ensnare me. Help me to realize that an elevated soul is exposed to greater temptations, and is more easily tarnished.

Commentary

The Rezhiner was fond of relating the following story:

A young Hasid of the great Rebbe of Mezeritch married the daughter of a fierce Mitnagged (an opponent to the Hasidic movement). The father-in-law made his son-in-law swear that he would never travel to Mezeritch to be with the Rebbe. After a few months, the son-in-law could not resist the urge to join his fellow Hasidim and their Rebbe. When the son-in-law returned home, his angry father-in-law dragged him to the local rabbi for a judgment for not having kept his oath.

The rabbi consulted the Shulchan Aruch and issued this verdict: Since the son-in-law had broken his promise, the young man was to give his wife a divorce at once. Overnight, the young man found himself on the street. He had no means of support and no relatives to whom to turn. Inconsolable, refusing all nourishment, the young Hasid fell sick. With no one to care for him, he died shortly thereafter.

After telling this story, the Rizhiner Rebbe then commented:

"When the Messiah will come, the young Hasid will file a complaint against his father-in-law and the local rabbi, both guilty of premature death. The father-in-law will say, 'I obeyed the local rabbi.' The rabbi will say, 'I obeyed the Shulchan Aruch.' And the Messiah will say, 'The father-in-law is right.' Then he will kiss the plaintiff and say, 'But, what do I have to do with them? I have come for those who are not right.' "

–Rabbi Morris Shapiro

✸✸✸✸✸✸✸✸✸✸✸✸✸✸

The Service of the Kohen Gadol

God's world is great and holy. Among the holy lands in the world is the Holy Land of Israel. In the Land of Israel, the holiest city is Jerusalem. In Jerusalem the holiest place was the Temple, and in the Temple the holiest spot was the Holy of Holies.

There are seventy peoples in the world. Among these holy peoples is the people of Israel. The holiest of the people of Israel is the tribe of Levi. In the tribe of Levi, the holiest are the priests. Among the priests, the holiest was the high priest.

There are 354 days in the year. Among these, the holidays are holy. Higher than these is the holiness of the Sabbath. Among Sabbaths is the Day of Atonement, the Sabbath of Sabbaths.

There are seventy languages in the world. Among the holy languages is the holy language of Hebrew. Holier than all else in this language is the holy Torah, and in the Torah, the holiest part is the Ten Commandments. In the Ten Commandments, the holiest of all words is the Name of God.

And once during the year, at a certain hour, these four supreme sanctities of the world were joined with one another. That was the Day of Atonement, when the high priest would enter the holy of holies and there utter the name of God. And because this hour was beyond measure holy and awesome, it was the time of utmost peril, not only for the high priest, but for the whole of Israel. For if, in this hour, there had, God forbid, entered the mind of the high priest a false or sinful thought, the entire world would have been destroyed.

Every spot where a man raises his eyes to heaven is a holy of holies. Every man, having been created by God in His own image and likeness, is a high priest. Every day of a man's life is a Day of Atonement, and every word that a man speaks with sincerity is the Name of the Lord.

–Folk Tale
Adapted from The Dybbuk (An-Ski)

※※※※※※※※※※※※※※※

A Prayer on the Meaning of These Days

As the High Holidays approach I always look for reading and materials to be used in the services. Often I feel myself overwhelmed with the meaning of those days and the significance of life. The other day I felt moved to write some of these feelings in a prayer using the thoughts of centuries and the intent of the Machzor:

Spirit of Life, who gives life and makes for goodness, we humbly present our selves before you. We pray for health for those who are dear to us, and the ability to do our duty to them. Let our eyes never be blind to the beauty of the world; let us feast our gaze upon the budding trees and flowers and may our spirits find delight as we see green leaves donning the multi-colored vestments of the fall season. Teach us to be patient and understanding in our dealing with our fellow men. Enlighten us so that we may comprehend the suffering of others and help to alleviate their pain and raise them up when they stumble.

Give us the ability to coax a smile to the face of the disheartened and to dry the tears of the bereaved. Attune our ears to the laughter and the prattle of little children so that we may through them, renew our youth.

Enable us to understand that the shortcomings we see in others exist, unobserved, in ourselves. As we want others to forgive us, so may we learn to forgive them and bear them no grudge.

May our hands be used to greet our fellow men, to confirm blessing upon him and never to grasp the tools of war or to strike at another human being. Endow us with the strength to fight bravely against the evils of ignorance, poverty and war.

May we find the power to face ourselves frankly, to cut through the superficialities of life, the conventional insecurities, and to reach the essential core of honest feeling. May we never succumb to the blandishments of material success and may we ever cherish the things which serve to enlarge and deepen our existence as creatures of your fashioning. We need help to find meaning in our life and purpose in the pursuit of our daily tasks.

May our attachments to our people remain strong within us and may we be able to help in the preservation of the priceless spiritual achievements which make the Jewish people great. Let there resolve within us to pursue our work and be strong, and hopefully we will feel to the end of life that our task is yet unfinished.

May our prayers be joined with those who supplicate for a world of peace and who work for it. And when our sad end comes, O Lord, let us leave behind some achievement in behalf of others which will serve as a token of appreciation and gratitude for having been allowed to live on earth.

–Rabbi Jeffrey A. Wohlberg

❋❋❋❋❋❋❋❋❋❋❋❋❋❋

Recalling the Ancient Temple Service

For our ancestors in ancient days, the Temple in Jerusalem was the symbol of God's presence. In the Temple sacrifices were offered daily in behalf of the entire nation. On the Sabbath and Festivals special sacrifices marked the holiness of the day. Thus did the Temple bear testimony to Israel's consecration to God.

The Temple has long since been destroyed; yet, the remembrance of it lives on in the heart of our people. The form of worship practiced there belongs to a bygone age; yet it continues to awaken solemn thoughts. When we recall the ancient Temple, we link ourselves to our past; we sense again that we are part of one people, dedicated to the service of God and His Torah of righteousness and truth.

Today our worship is one of prayer and praise. But when we think of the piety of our ancestors, who from their meager supply of cattle and grain offered their best possessions in the service of God, we feel called upon to devote not only our words but also our substance to God's service.

—Adapted from Rabbi Milton Steinberg
Reconstructionist Prayer Book

❋❋❋❋❋❋❋❋❋❋❋❋❋❋

A Preparation for the Avodah

When the great Rabbi Israel Baal Shem-Tov saw misfortune threatening the Jews, it was his custom to go into a certain part of the forest to meditate. There he would light a fire, say a special prayer, and the miracle would be accomplished and the misfortune averted.

Later, when his disciple, the celebrated Magid of Mezritch, had occasion, for the same reason, to intercede with heaven, he would go to the same place in the forest and say: "Master of the Universe, listen! I do not know how to light the fire, but I am still able to say a prayer."

And again, the miracle would be accomplished.

Still later, Rabbi Moshe-Leib of Sasov, in order to save his people once more, would go into the forest and say; "I do not know how to light the fire, I do not know the prayer, but I know the place and this must be sufficient."

It was sufficient and the miracle was accomplished.

Then it fell to Rabbi Israel of Rizhyn to overcome misfortune. Sitting in his armchair, his head in his hands, he spoke to God: "I am unable to light the fire and I do not know the prayer. I cannot even find the place in the forest. All I can do is to tell the story, and this must be sufficient."

And it was sufficient.

Listen, God. We are going to tell the story.

– Hasidic tale

✴✴✴✴✴✴✴✴✴✴✴✴✴

Picking Up Our Burdens

A Buddhist teaching story tells of a young monk seeking enlightenment traveling up on a mountain path looking for an old sage who lived high up on the mountain. On his way up the path, he met the old man coming down, and asked him to tell him about enlightenment. The old monk, who had been carrying a pack on his back, simply put down his burden for a moment. Then he picked up his burden again and resumed his journey down the path. The young monk understood and became enlightened.

– Frances Vaughan
The Inward Arc

✴✴✴✴✴✴✴✴✴✴✴✴✴

Light Is Sown for the Righteous
The Light of the Self

In the Upanishads there is a story about Yajnavalkya, the sage at a king's court. The king asked him one day, "By what light do human beings go out, do their work and return?" The sage answered, "By the light of the sun." The king then asked, "But when the light of the sun is extinguished, by what light do human beings go out, do their work and return?" The sage said, "By the light of the moon." And so question and answer went on. When the moon is extinguished, man works by the light of the stars; when they are quenched, by the light of fire. And when the light of the fire itself is put out, the king asked, "By what light then can they do their work and still live?" The sage replied, "By the light of the self."

– Laurens Van Der Post
The Heart of the Hunter

※※※※※※※※※※※※※※

World Server Vow

Having taken the Living Love Vow to infuse the Living Love Way into the wellsprings of my thought and action, I now wish to unfold the energy of my life beyond my own self. Having experienced my own growth in the Living Love Way, I am now rich enough to give myself to the world–generously, openly, and without expectation of return. My goal is no longer my own enlightenment; it is to do my part in helping to relieve the suffering and alienation in the world. By taking the World Server Vow, I am dedicating my life to serving my brothers and sisters on this earth who are suffering from the pain of negative, separating emotions and confusion caused by addictive programming.

I vow to put the well-being of others above my own. No longer working toward self-aggrandizement, I will surrender my time, my comfort, my privacy, and my other ego-defended spaces to people. I will relate to the world appropriately and generously, and will skillfully put loving energy into the situations around me. Having developed compassion and love for myself, I can now offer it to others. I will work to reduce the addictive separateness in myself and in the world.

I will give up my striving for a separate, private life hunting for my own security, pleasure, and success. I will continuously offer myself to the world– even though I may be unrewarded, unappreciated, or rejected. As a world server, I will love and serve people selflessly as though everyone were my guest. I can be both gentle and energetic when interacting with people. By relating to life intelligently, openly, compassionately, patiently, fearlessly, nonaggressively, warmly, and delightfully, I will exercise greater responsibility to the world.

Transcending my own paranoia, vulnerability, and hesitation, I will respond wakefully to situations as they arise. Trusting myself, I will learn to correct my errors in perception of action in the moment when things are happening. Since my ego is no longer concerned with protecting my addictive demands, I can serve the world patiently and peacefully, and will not feel threatened by the world. I thus will become increasingly skillful and helpful in adding positive energy to our world.

I will use my life situations to perfect my use of the Twelve Pathways. At all times I will flow my energy into loving everyone unconditionally–including myself. I will thus become a lighthouse that can help people through the sea of illusion, separation, and hostility.

I will avoid foolish compassion, which is a shortsighted and cowardly attempt to gloss over situations–instead of responding wisely in a way that is truly nurturing to people. When the situation calls for it, I will be courageously direct (or even cutting) to appropriately relate to people instead of being timidly kind or politely agreeable.

By taking the World Server Vow, I am allying myself with the immense energy of all men and women who love and serve the world. I am forever joined with all who devote themselves to the growth of the spirit of love throughout the earth – and the liberation of sentient beings from addictive bondage.

–Ken Keyes, Jr.
Discovering the Secrets of Happiness

11

YOM KIPPUR CUSTOMS

The Kittel

All who serve as officiants during the services on the High Festivals are also obliged to wear a white robe called a *kittel*. It is worn by the Synagogue Reader on three other occasions during the year: on Passover, when intoning a special prayer for the summer dew, on the seventh day of Tabernacles *(Hosha'na' Rabbah)*, which has the special character of a day of judgment; and, finally, on the eighth day of tabernacles when a special prayer is offered for winter rains to fall in the holy land.

The *kittel* calls to mind the white shrouds in which the dead are dressed before burial, an association which should prompt man to reflect upon the brevity of life and the final account he will be called upon to render when he departs this world. Since without rain life cannot exist, the *kittel* was also prescribed for those two occasions on which we pray for rain. It is hoped that the sight of Israel's spiritual representatives, clad in shrouds, will melt the divine heart and wrest His precious blessing from Him.

Another explanation of the *kittel*, taking into account its white colour, connects it with the prophetic promise: "Though your sins are like scarlet, they shall be white as snow" (Isaiah 1:18). Accordingly, the *kittel* is worn to symbolize the pure state that is attained through repentance.

Some see in the *kittel* a reflection of the angels, who are said to be clothed in white garments. The repentant souls, having received absolution, stand like the angels without sin.

–Rev. Dr. Jeffrey M. Cohen
Understanding the High Holyday Services

※※※※※※※※※※※※※※※

In What Language Should We Pray?

Is knowledge of the Hebrew language necessary for genuine prayer?

One of the many excuses modern man advances for not attending synagogue worship is: "I don't read, don't understand Hebrew, don't know what's going on."

There was a young shepherd who was unable to recite the Hebrew prayers. The only way in which he worshipped was, "Lord of the world it is apparent and known to you that if you had cattle and gave them to me to tend, though I take wages from all others, I would take nothing from you because I love you."

One day a learned man passing by heard the shepherd pronounce his offer and shouted at him, "Fool, do not pray thus!" The sheperd asked him, "How should I pray?" Thereupon, the learned man taught him the benedictions in order, the recitation of the Sh'ma and the silent prayer so that henceforth he would not say what he was accustomed to saying.

After the learned man went away, the shepherd forgot all that had been taught him and did not pray. And he was even afraid to say what he had been accustomed to saying, because the righteous man told him he must not pray thus.

One night, the learned man had a dream, and in it he heard a voice, "If you do not tell him to say what he was accustomed to saying before you came to him, know that misfortune will overtake you, for you have robbed me of one who belongs to the world to come."

At once the learned man went to the shepherd and asked him, "What prayers are you making?" The shepherd answered, "None, for I have forgotten what you taught me, and you forbade me to say, 'If You had cattle.' "

Then the learned man told him what he had dreamed and added, "Say what you used to say."

COMMENTARY

The Rabbi Bunam narrated this parable: A man of handsome raiment came into an institution to ask for charity, and was compelled to make considerable explanation as to the reason for his need.

Another man, poorly attired, entered, and he was given aid at once. In the same way a self-satisfied person who asks God for help needs to do much entreating. But one who is broken of heart and meek is answered at once.

We read: "But I am all prayer" (Psalm 109:4): My broken heart is in itself, and I hardly am required to entreat You.

Thus, the prerequisite for genuine prayer is not the knowledge of a language, but good deeds, compassion, and humility.

—Rabbi Morris Shapiro

※※※※※※※※※※※※※※※

Yom Kippur: The Jews Create a Day

On this awesome and joyful day of repentance, Jews gather in their Synagogues, their lives intermingled with the past of their people, re-living the tragedies of antiquity, re-enacting the ancient glories. During the long day the saints and martyrs, the poets and prophets of Israel come to life to sing again their song of triumph. Israel's sweet serenade to its God is heard above the strident noise of worldly pomp. Israel's spirit is vindicated before the world. The High Priest clad in white walks again in the Temple court to offer atonement for his people; Akiba repeats his defiance of the mighty Roman Emperor by teaching Torah to his faithful disciples; the power of the Crusaders is again set at naught as their victims recite the Shema with heads unbowed. On this day Israel draws inspiration from the past, looks toward its future and to the day the prophets dreamed when all men will worship the true God and his Kingdom will be established upon earth.

Other peoples have erected towering palaces, have built great bridges to span mighty rivers and wide roads to cross inhospitable deserts; they have produced fine art and moving music to stir the souls of men: the Jews created a day. A day of haunting beauty and power during which man is elevated far above his mundane concerns into the higher realms of the ideal. A day of peace and harmony and reconciliation, of prayer and reverence and awe when man comes face to face with God. A whimsical but profound Rabbinic calculation points out that the numerical value of the Hebrew letters of the word for Satan equals three hundred and sixty-four, one less than the number of days in the year. For on one day in the year the Satan of strife and contention, of coarseness and materialism, holds no sway over human affairs. On this day Israel is compared to the ministering angels in their sublime worship of the Lord of Hosts.

—Rabbi Louis Jacobs
A Guide to Yom Kippur

※※※※※※※※※※※※※※※

Petiychah – Opening of the Ark

In the practice of opening the Ark for particular compositions we again enter an area where considerable license was exercised throughout the centuries. Originally the Ark was opened during the course of a service only in order to take out the Torah scroll. This has remained the practice in all other rites except those of the Ashkenazim who, at a very early period, employed the practice of opening the Ark for particularly favoured compositions, in order to stress their importance and to stimulate a greater degree of concentration during their recitation.

In Franco-Germany, in the thirteenth century, some communities adopted the custom of opening the Ark for the whole of the repetition of the *Shacharith* and *Musaph' Amidahs,* closing it only for *Qedushah* and the Priestly Benediction. This did not win universal acceptance since many authorities preferred to open the Ark at intervals in order to highlight specific compositions. This had the added advantage of enabling the sacred honours to be distributed more widely among the members of the congregation. It was probably that consideration which accounted for the many compositions for which we, quite unaccountably, stand and honour with a *petiychah.*

– Rev. Dr. Jeffrey M. Cohen
Understanding the High Holyday Services

※※※※※※※※※※※※※※※

Liturgical Punctuation

L'eyla U'Le-eyla

The half-*Kaddish* is a kind of liturgical punctuation mark which serves to separate off certain parts of the service from other more important sections. Here it sets into sharper relief the *'Amidah,* the most important prayer. Its call, that God's name should be "magnified and sanctified," suggests that its purpose is also to serve as an exhortation to the congregation to recite the next section with particular devotion and concentration.

Ashkenazi tradition doubles the word *l'eyla'* in every *Kaddish* recited during *Rosh Hashanah* and throughout the Ten Days of Repentance. The repetition of the word *l'eyla'* ("exalted") is to convey the idea that God is never more exalted than at this time of the year when the thoughts and prayers of all Israel are directed towards Him.

The number of words in a particular prayer was regarded as mystically significant and not to be altered. Thus, because an additional *l'eyla'* was being inserted at this time, authorities suggested that we should compensate by taking out one word. The most convenient way was to contract the two words *min kol* (*birkhatha'*) to *mikkol*—a regular contraction which does not affect the meaning.

This practice of doubling the word *l'eyla'* is a comparatively late innovation, there being no reference to it in any source before the fifteenth century, where it is referred to for the first time in the note to the *Sepher Maharil* of R. Yaakov ben Mosheh of Moellin. There was, in fact, considerable variety of practice in this matter in Ashkenazi communities. In Posen they only doubled the word in the first *Kaddish* which preceded the *Selichoth* services. In Frankfort the extra *l'eyla'* was only inserted on *Rosh Hashanah* and *Yom Kippur*—not during the rest of the Ten Days of Penitence—and only during the *Kaddish* recited by the *Chazan*. Mourners did not include it.

–Rev. Dr. Jeffrey M. Cohen
Understanding the High Holyday Services

❋❋❋❋❋❋❋❋❋❋❋❋❋

Fasting

The most striking aspect of atonement in Judaism is fasting. . . . This rite was associated with both sacrifice and prayer. On Yom Kippur the fast consists of total abstinence from food for twenty-four hours at a time. The Hebrew terms *innuy nephesh* and *taanit* indicate that fasting has figured as a form of self-humiliation and self-mortification. In addition to Yom Kippur, Orthodox Jewry observes the four national fasts, commemorative of the fall of Jerusalem in 586 (Fast of Gedaliah, Tenth of Tebeth, Seventeenth of Tammuz, and Ninth of Ab) (see Zech. 8:19) and the Fast of Esther, preceding Purim. Pious individuals keep the three fasts of Monday, Thursday, and Monday in the months of Iyar and Heshvan, following the festive seasons of Passover and Tabernacles (cf. Job 1:5), Yom Kippur Katon (the day preceding the New Moon, introduced by the Cabbalist Moses Cordovero in the sixteenth century), and numerous other fasts on occasions of public calamity and private character, like Yahrzeit, etc.

While ascetics indulged in fasting to the extent of endangering their lives, the leaders of Hasidism discouraged excessive fasting and self-mortification as being contrary to the spirit of Judaism, which bids man to worship God in joy. . . . Secularistic influence in Jewish life threatens to do away with fasting on Yom

Kippur. . . . To abandon this hallowed practice would inflict irreparable loss to the already attenuated religious life of Jewry. A pampered generation like ours can ill afford to dispense with this sobering institution, which subjects the gratification of bodily appetites and cravings to the needs of the spirit, which forcibly brings home the truth that not by bread alone does man live, and which rouses the community to the fact that while some are sated with plenty, others are continually subjected to hunger and want. The fasting on Yom Kippur takes on the character of intense devotion and consecration to God. Coupled with repentance, prayer and charity, it vitally affects the currents of man's life and works miracles of spiritual regeneration.

–Rabbi Samuel S. Cohon
Judaism: A Way of Life

❊❊❊❊❊❊❊❊❊❊❊❊❊❊

Fasting: The Bible's Spiritual Diet

Almost all religions have special foods and diets for their sacred occasions. How, when, and what you eat has long been recognized to be filled with symbolic meanings as well as calories.

There are special Jewish foods for all the major holy days, with one exception: Yom Kippur, the Day of Atonement.

This day, according to the Bible, is a fast day. For 24 hours, Jews (in good health) are supposed to afflict their souls by abstaining from eating or drinking anything.

What is the Bible trying to teach us by decreeing a day of fasting? What spiritual benefits occur when we fast?

First of all, fasting teaches compassion. It is easy to talk about the world's hunger problem. We can feel sorry that millions of people go to bed hungry each day. But it isn't until one can really feel it in one's own body that the impact is truly there.

Compassion based on empathy is much stronger and more consistent than compassion based on pity. This feeling must lead to action.

Fasting is never an end in itself; that's why it has so many different outcomes. But all the other outcomes are amoral if compassion is not enlarged and extended through fasting.

As the prophet Isaiah said: "The truth is that at the same time you fast, you pursue your own interests and oppress workers. Your fasting makes you violent, and you quarrel and fight. The kind of fasting I want is this: remove the chains of oppression and the yoke of injustice, and let the oppressed go free. Share your food with the hungry and open your homes to the homeless poor."

Second, fasting is an exercise in will power. Most people think they can't fast because it's so hard. A headache, muscle pains from too much exercise, and most certainly a toothache are all more severe than hunger pangs.

I have on occasion fasted for three days, and I found that after the first 24 hours the pain decreases slightly as the stomach becomes numb. The reason it is so hard to fast is because it is so easy to stop. All you have to do is take a bite; and the food is all around, in easy reach.

Thus the key to fasting is the will power to decide again and again not to eat. Our society has become one of self-indulgence. We lack self-discipline. Fasting goes in direct opposition to our increasing "softness" in life.

When people exercise their will power and fast, they are affirming their mastery over themselves.

Thus, fasting serves as a penance. Self-inflicted pain alleviates guilt, although it is much better to reduce one's guilt with offsetting acts of righteousness to others. This is why contributing *tzedakah* is such an important part of Yom Kippur, and indeed fasting which doesn't increase compassion is ignored by God.

However, the concept of fasting as penance helps us understand that our suffering can be beneficial. Contemporary culture desires happiness above all else. Any suffering is seen as unnecessary and indeed evil.

While we occasionally hear people echo values from the past that suffering can help one grow, or that a life unalloyed with pain would lack in the qualities of greatness, the dominant attitude among people today is that the most important thing is "you should only be happy."

Thus the satisfaction one can derive from the self-induced pain of fasting provides insight into a better way of reacting to the externally caused suffering we have to experience anyway.

Taking a pill is not always the best way to alleviate pain, especially if by doing so we eliminate the symptoms without reaching the root cause.

Fourth in our list of outcomes, fasting is a denial of dependencies.

We live in a consumer society. We are constantly bombarded by advertising that tells us we must have this thing or that to be healthy, happy, popular, or wise. By fasting we assert that we do not need to be dependent on external things, even such an essential thing as food.

If our most basic need for food and drink can be suspended for 24 hours, how much more can our needs for all the non-essentials be ignored?

Judaism doesn't advocate asceticism. In fact it is against Jewish law to deny one's self normal pleasures. But in our over-heated consumer society, it is necessary to periodically turn ourselves off to the constant pressure to consume, and forcibly remind ourselves that "man does not live by bread alone."

The fifth outcome of fasting is improved physical health. Of course, one 24-hour fast will not have any more effect than one day of exercise. Only prolonged and regular fasting promotes health. The annual fast on Yom Kippur, however, can awaken us to the importance of how much, and how often, we eat.

For many years, research has shown that when animals are underfed, receiving a balanced diet that in quantity was below the norm for maximum physical health, their life spans were prolonged from 50 to 100 per cent.

Other studies indicate that people with a below average caloric intake are less susceptible to cancer.

It was common in Kabalistic and Chassidic circles to fast every Monday and Thursday. If one eats normal meals the other five days, this would result in a decrease of 25 per cent in caloric intake. Over the years this could add years to one's life span.

Sixth, fasting is good for the soul. It is an aid for spiritual experiences. For most people, especially those who have not fasted regularly before, the hunger pains are a distraction. People who are not by nature spiritual/emotional individuals will probably find that a one-day fast is insufficient to help induce an altered state of consciousness.

Those who have fasted regularly on Yom Kippur might like to try a two or three day fast (liquids permitted). It is best to go about your daily activities and devote your late evening to meditation and prayer. Since you have already fasted for Yom Kippur, the easiest way is to simply extend the fast another 36–48 hours.

We are prohibited to fast prior to Yom Kippur (eating a good meal prior to Kol Nidre is a *mitzvah*). This is because Judaism opposes excessive asceticism.

The seventh outcome of fasting is the performance of a *mitzvah*. We do not do *mitzvot* in order to benefit ourselves. We do *mitzvot* because our duty as Jews requires that we do them.

Fasting is a very personal *mitzvah*. Its effects are primarily personal. Fasting on Yom Kippur is a personal offering to the God of Israel from each member of the family of Israel.

For more than 100 generations, Jews have fasted on Yom Kippur. Your personal act of fasting is part of the Jewish people's covenant with God. The only real reason to fast is to fulfill a *mitzvah*.

The outcome of your fast can be any of a half-dozen paths to self-fulfillment. Simply knowing that you have done one of your duties as an adult Jew is the most basic and primary outcome of all.

Finally, fasting should be combined with the study of Torah. Indeed, the more one studies, the less one has need of fasting.

A medieval text states: "Better eat a little and study twice as much, for the study of Torah is superior to fasting."

12

JONAH AND HUMAN RESPONSIBILITY

Jonah and Jewish Responsibility

The story of Jonah read on Yom Kippur is a subject which has inspired many speakers.

I refer to a thought expressed by the late Rabbi Louis Rabinowitz of South Africa who was a master preacher.

It is thought that Jonah may have lived during the reign of Jeroboam II, the last king of the Northern Kingdom of Israel. Certainly, he is remembered as an exceedingly wicked king, but he is also recognized as a great nationalist who extended the borders of Israel (see II Kings 14:24, 25), and in speaking of Jeroboam's conquests, the Book of Kings adds, "according to the word of the Lord which he spoke by the hand of his servant Jonah the son of Amittai the Gath-Hepher."

Thus we know when Jonah lived and we also know that the great enemy of Israel was Assyria with its capital city Nineveh!

Why then should Jonah go and preach to that city and save it? God did indeed command him to do so, but Jonah as a Jewish patriot understandably refuses the command. It would be as if today someone went to save Mr. Assad in Damascus or Kadafi in Tripoli – why should a Jew do this?

Possibly the answer is that admirable enough though it may be to constantly proclaim *Avdi Anochi,* we also have to bear in mind that God is telling Jonah that although we may have a different agenda, the people of Nineveh are also human beings. "Should I not have pity on Nineveh that great city, wherein are more than 120,000 people . . . and also much cattle?" (Jonah 4:11). For God and seemingly the Jews there is a dual responsibility – we think of the words of Ecclesiastes (4:1) "the tears of all the oppressed under the sun which have none to comfort them."

– Rabbi David H. Lincoln

✖✖✖✖✖✖✖✖✖✖✖✖✖✖

The Healing Powers of Repentance and Renewal

Rend your hearts, not your garments, and turn back to the Lord your God, for He is gracious and compassionate, patient and abounding in kindness, renouncing punishment (Joel 2:13).

When you hear the name Jonah, do you think of a whale? According to the Bible, Jonah was swallowed not by a whale, but by a big fish.

Mistaking a big fish for a whale is no misfortune. But it is a misfortune to treat the Book of Jonah as a fish story.

God told Jonah to go to Nineveh and warn its people to turn from their evil ways.

Yet Jonah took the first ship in the opposite direction.

The real question is not whether Jonah could survive three days in the belly of a fish, but

Why did Jonah run away?

Jonah refused to help the people of Nineveh because he judged them unworthy.

He wanted to see the wicked punished. As God's prophet, he knew that they would not be destroyed if they really changed.

Jonah fled not only his duty, he fled God's compassion.

Jonah was inflexible. He preferred the punishment of the wicked to the possibility that they could change. He wanted God's decrees to be final, not influenced by human endeavors. He resisted the reality of a basic principle of faith:

It is never too late to turn from evil to good.

Ultimately, Jonah realized he could not run away. When he was released from the big fish, the reluctant prophet did go to Nineveh, accepting his mission.

As Jonah had feared, the people of Nineveh heeded his warning. They fasted and put on sack-cloth. The king himself fasted and sat in ashes, declaring:

> "Let everyone turn from his evil ways and from the injustice of which he is guilty. Perhaps God will relent, and we shall not perish."

Because its people turned from evil ways to good, in true repentance, Nineveh was saved.

That is why the Book of Jonah is read in the synagogue on Yom Kippur, the most sacred day of the Jewish year, climaxing the ten days of repentance, of turning.

It is a tale for our time, about us. Nineveh and Jonah are alive.

Injustice is everywhere. Many try to run away from God and from compassion. Many judge others as being inexorably doomed.

Like Jonah in flight, some would rather see the corrupt trapped forever than absolved and rehabilitated.

They would rather wallow in anger or succumb to despair than reach for and celebrate the healing powers of repentance and renewal.

They resent the truth that God's justice includes compassion.

As the people of Nineveh perceived, compassion is not easy. It is more than remorse.

They were not saved because they *said* they were sorry, nor were they saved because they wore sack-cloth and fasted. Rather,

> "God saw what they *did,* how they *turned* from their evil ways . . ."

In the liturgy of Yom Kippur, we affirm each year:

> **"God extends a welcome to all transgressors, ready to embrace those who turn in repentance."**

With the Book of Jonah, we also reaffirm the powers of repentance and compassion.

We embrace the possibility of renewal, not the inevitability of destruction.

We exchange cynical despair for resolute hope, as we pray for ourselves, and for all the Ninevehs of this world.

We celebrate the glory that we are human,
that we are *not* robots,
that we *can* turn in repentance,
that we can *cleanse* our souls,
that it is *never too late* for us to change.

Consider the words of the prophet Ezekiel, recited in the Yom Kippur service:

> "As I live, says the Lord God, I do not desire the death of the wicked, but that he abandon his ways and live."

–High Holiday Message, Jewish Theological Seminary

Jonah and God's Repentance

> O Lord, this is precisely what I predicted when I was still in my own land; I therefore hastened to run away to Tarshish, for I knew that Thou art a gracious and merciful God, patient, abundant in kindness, and relenting of evil. – Jonah 4:2

> The Lord, the Lord is a merciful God, slow to anger and abounding in kindness and truth; He keeps mercy for thousands of generations, forgiving iniquity and transgression and sin, and pardoning. – Exodus 34: 6–7

The Book of Jonah has been assigned a climactic role in the liturgy of the Days of Awe by being selected as the Haftarah for the afternoon service of Yom Kippur. In other words, it is the final biblical reading of the Ten Days of Penitence. Why?

Jonah is commanded by God to go to Nineveh, the capital of Assyria, and to proclaim judgment upon it because of Nineveh's wickedness. But Jonah boards a ship and flees westward to Tarshish, in the opposite direction. God thwarts his escape by whipping up a violent storm which threatens the boat. When the passengers cast lots to discover on whose account the storm has arisen, Jonah owns up that he is fleeing from the service of the God of Heaven and suggests that they throw him overboard in order to quiet the storm. They finally comply and there follows the famous episode of Jonah's survival in the belly of the Big Fish.

Having learned the lesson that he cannot avoid the Lord, Jonah arrives in the city of Nineveh and proclaims: "Forty days more and Nineveh shall be overturned." When he is no more than a third of the way through the city, the people believe God's word and go into mourning. The king himself proclaims comprehensive rites of penitence and commands all to turn back from their evil ways and the injustice of which they are guilty.

The Ninevites' reform works: the human turning produces a divine turning. When God sees that they have abandoned their evil ways he renounces their punishment. This repentance of God distresses Jonah greatly, and he expresses himself: "That is why I ran away the first time. For I know that You are a merciful and gracious God, slow to anger and abounding in kindness, and renouncing punishment."

Why did Jonah flee from the mission God had given him? Jonah says he knew God would forgive the Ninevites and cancel their punishment. But what objection could Jonah possibly have to the forgiveness of the truly penitent? The oldest Jewish interpretation of the book holds that Jonah fled because he wished to protect his credibility. Since the Ninevites were sure to be forgiven, Jonah who was to predict their doom, would look like a false prophet. A variation on this view holds that it was *God's* credibility that Jonah sought to protect. God's willingness to forgive and forget would destroy the fear of God; His word would become a mockery and men's trust in Him would be shaken if His threats were so easily evaded.

It is not clear from the book itself whether Jonah is really concerned about credibility, but it is clear that God is not. God is willing to risk humiliation, to allow His word to be discredited, for the sake of compassion. Seen from this perspective, the Book of Jonah teaches that God is able and willing and even desirous of annulling His own word.

This new concept, opposed by Jonah but advocated by his biographer, has gained a foothold in Judaism. "God wants not the death of the sinner, but that he turn away from evil and live," as the High Holiday prayer book, quoting Ezekiel (18:23), puts it. Further, Judaism has gone so far as to twist the words of the Torah itself in order to make the point. The list of God's merciful qualities that is recited at almost every opportunity in the liturgy of the Days of Awe is highly reassuring to the Jew facing the Heavenly Court in this season of judgment. To anyone who knows his Bible, however, the list must appear downright scandalous. It is a blatant example of a quotation lifted out of context, interrupting a sentence of Exodus in the middle of a phrase for the sake of omitting the inconvenient sequel. For the last word on the list, "pardoning," is actually part of a phrase that reads in full, "but He does *not* pardon absolutely."

The rabbis have given the Book of Jonah prominence among the biblical readings of the Days of Awe to emphasize that at times God does pardon absolutely. It is an attribute of both God and man to repent.

– Dr. Jeffrey H. Tigay

✻✻✻✻✻✻✻✻✻✻✻✻✻✻

Human Choice and Action

Jonah's laconic message was (3:4): "Forty days more, and Nineveh shall be overthrown!" The Ninevites amended their ways; their city was spared. Prophecy is not pre-prediction, but diagnosis and warning. Jonah's concise verdict was fulfilled, his mission successfully accomplished. Even in its literal ("predictive") sense, Jonah's prophecy came true. The Hebrew word for "overthrown" (*nehepakhet*) means to turn down, to undergo drastic change . . . either physically, by violent destruction ("upside down"), or spiritually by moral revolution ("from evil to good"). What was the divinely ordained fate of Nineveh – death and doom, or life and revitalization? The Ninevites themselves would decide the meaning of the Divine Word. Prophecy aims to direct and inspire human choice, not forecast and seal human destiny. The Divine Word is forever true; its real meaning and application is ultimately deciphered and decided by human choice and action.

– Rabbi Zvi Yehuda
Cleveland Jewish News

✻✻✻✻✻✻✻✻✻✻✻✻✻✻

On Imaging God

Our recent re-encounter with the Book of Jonah on Yom Kippur provided me with a renewed appreciation of what a remarkable and complex document it is, despite its apparent simplicity.

The main point of the book, of course, is not the story of the fish. Nor is it a lesson on the power of repentance. If it were the latter, the book would end with Chapter 3 when God responds to Nineveh's repentance and determines not to destroy the city. But the book continues into a fourth chapter which describes

Jonah's fury at being made to look like a fool, and God's ensuing lesson about what kind of God He truly is. The paradox of the book is that Jonah is the only successful prophet that we know of, yet he felt himself to be a failure until God set him right.

The true climax of the book is the second verse in chapter 4. Jonah rages against God, "That is why I fled beforehand to Tarshish," he exclaims, "for I know that you are a compassionate and gracious God, slow to anger, abounding in kindness, renouncing punishment." Jonah knew that he would be an effective prophet. He also knew that God was a "soft touch." Nineveh would repent, and he, Jonah, would look like a fool – prophesying a disaster that would never come.

But Jonah's description of God as "compassionate and gracious, slow to anger, abounding in kindness" should strike us as familiar. Where did Jonah learn this? Clearly from Exodus 34:7, where God reveals Himself to Moses with what has come to be known as the "Thirteen Attributes." That passage, in full, reads as follows: "The Lord! the Lord! a God compassionate and gracious, slow to anger, rich in steadfast kindness, extending kindness, extending kindness to the thousandth generation, forgiving iniquity, transgression, and sin; yet He does not remit all punishment, but visits the iniquity of fathers upon children and children's children, upon the third and fourth generation."

Jonah clearly knows the passage and quotes it verbatim – up to a point. The Exodus passage is, in fact, a mixed bag. God does portray Himself as compassionate and forgiving. But as the passage continues, God notes that human sinfulness is never fully cleansed. Punishment may be mitigated, may be held in abeyance, but eventually it must be meted out. There is no room for repentance here. The possibility of repentance as powerful enough to cancel punishment doesn't enter into biblical religion until the emergence of the classical prophets. At this stage, sin must be punished, if not immediately, then eventually.

Jonah, then, quotes God's word back to God, but what he quotes is heavily edited in the process. In fact, he only quotes that part of God's self-image that he agrees with – God as compassionate, gracious, and slow to anger. The latter portion of the passage – the portion about the inevitability of punishment for sin – he ignores, and replaces it with the very opposite: "renouncing punishment"!

Jonah's statement, then, is scandalous. Did God not remember what He originally said? Did Jonah not know that he was standing God's self-description on its head? The answer is the conclusion of the chapter. God not only knows, He even confirms Jonah's new characterization. He is indeed a fully compassionate God and does renounce punishment completely – as a response to genuine human repentance.

What changed, of course, was not God Himself, but our ancestors' perception of God – which is all we human beings can ever have. None of us can know God in His essence. Our task is to construct images of God – not plastic images which are forbidden–but conceptual images, metaphors, or symbols which are indispensable. These images are human creations and they change with the inevitable changes that occur as civilization evolves.

The Book of Jonah catches one of these crucial changes. Its message is that God's power and divinity do not demand that He be a punishing God. In fact, the book tells us, He is even more divine and powerful because He can conquer His wrath in response to genuine human repentance.

This last claim is, of course, mere speculation. But the broader issue is the significance of the human enterprise of imaging God in conceptual terms. That enterprise is tension-ridden. On one hand, our images must be faithful to God's total otherness, to what makes Him God in the first place. On the other hand, they must also be concrete enough to enable this "other" God to enter our theological and religious belief. The balance between these two imperatives is precarious–but it is the only course available to us.

Above all, we must never forget that we are always dealing with human images of God, not objectively true "photographs." To do otherwise is to slip into idolatry in its classic definition which is to substitute images of God for God Himself. That, of course, is the cardinal Jewish sin!

–Rabbi Neil Gillman

❈❈❈❈❈❈❈❈❈❈❈❈❈

In Defense of Jonah

1. Every age interprets the Bible in its own light, in terms of its peculiar problems, anxieties and hopes.

   In this hour, the Book of Jonah takes on an entirely different meaning to the point where I begin to doubt some of the past interpretations.

   The story of Jonah is set in the time of Jeroboam II in the eighth century. It is usually interpreted as a rebuke to Jonah's narrow chauvinism. Hardly a contemporary commentator fails to mention that the great biblical scholar, Cornill, considers Jonah the noblest book in the Bible because of its wide humanity and deep compassion. Poor Jonah, he is pictured and condemned as a clannish isolationist and maybe even a segregationist.

2. Is Jonah so deserving of our condemnation? Was Jonah altogether wrong?

3. The speculations of the scholars on the date of the composition of the Book of Jonah range from the eighth century BCE to the end of the Ezra period in fifth century BCE. Preponderance of opinion is that the Book was written in the Ezra period.

   In Judea intermarriage with the local natives and absorption of the pagan ways of neighboring people had taken their toll of the Jewish people. Jewish loyalty was at its lowest ebb.

   Ezra introduced some drastic changes, both social and religious, among them being the ban on Gentile wives. He reconstituted thereby a part of the people that became the nucleus of a revitalized nation.

   As we know from our own experiences, such a movement must have generated some extremists who exaggerated the doctrines of Ezra and taught total exclusivism and rejection of any involvement with the Gentile world. The inspired author of Jonah seeks to reject this extremist teaching, that the God of Israel is the God of Mankind. He seeks the repentance of Jews and Gentiles alike.

4. But was *Jonah rebuked for placing his Jewish loyalties first?* Did his protective zeal for the Jew overwhelm any concern for humanity? So this book was interpreted by many.

5. But Jonah was a *prophet* of the Jews placed among Amos, Hosea, and Isaiah. Could he have been so wrong to deserve *total rebuke?*

6. In Yalkut Shimoni an ancient sage rises to answer those who would altogether condemn Jonah.

   Amar Reb Natan lo halach Yonah ela l'abaid atzmo bayam v'chen ata motzai b'avot u'banviim shenatnu nafsham al Yisrael.

   He goes on to equate Jonah with Moses and with David. Jonah emerges then as a national hero. The implication being that in his anger and passion his vision of human justice was momentarily obscured. This was Jonah's sin. But in no way are his passionate Jewish loyalties subject to rebuke. On the contrary, he is the model of genuine loyalties.

7. Isaiah rose to the heights of the concept of a universal God, but at the same time he proclaimed:

   L'maan Tziyon lo echesheh u'lemaan Yerushalayim lo eshkot.

   For Zion's sake I will not keep silent.
   And for Jerusalem's sake I will not rest
   Until her vindication comes forth clear as light
   And her salvation as a burning torch.

   For Isaiah and for Jonah, to be a Jew is to advance the redemption of man.

8. The new left and the new liberals give this mistaken reading of Jonah.
   Jewish loyalty is an obstacle to the advancement of man. They fight for
   ethnic and religious rights of the Catholics in Northern Ireland, the
   Palestinian Arabs and the Black Panthers, but Jewish self-determination
   is condemned as narrow chauvinism.

9. This Yom Kippur we need affirm that the true idealism for us comes
   through the path of our Jewish loyalties.

–Rabbi Benjamin Z. Kreitman
The Rabbis Speak (ed. Teplitz)

※※※※※※※※※※※※※

Jonah and the Jews of Today

Jonah has had the unhappy fate of having his biography – or at least one detail of
it – survive, and his message ignored. People generally have but one association
with the book of Jonah – a man who flees God and is swallowed by a fish, in
whose belly he survives for three days. Like Ms. Lot, forever frozen into a salt
statue just outside of Sodom, Jonah's story generally stimulates more merriment
than reflection, and leaves many Jews wondering why the rabbis chose the book
as the central prophetic reading on Yom Kippur.

The overriding reason for the rabbinic choice is of course due to the central
theme of the book: repentance. After the prophet warns the citizens of Nineveh
that God will destroy them for their wickedness, they do three things. They
fast – as we do on Yom Kippur, they pray – as we do on Yom Kippur, and they
turn from their evil ways – as we are expected to do on Yom Kippur. "The
repentance of the people of Nineveh," Bible scholar Uriel Simon has noted, "can
be considered a model of what repentance is to be." What is remarkable, though,
and less frequently commented upon, is that the biblical model chosen to show
us how to repent on Yom Kippur is the *non-Jewish* city of Nineveh.

The book of Jonah makes yet another significant point about repentance.
That the central issue involved in repentance is an *ethical*, not a *ritual* transformation. "God saw what they [the people of Nineveh] did, how they were turning
from their evil ways" (3:10). The Talmud comments: "The verse does not read,
and God saw their sackcloth and their fasting, but God saw what they did, how
they were turning back from their evil ways" (*Ta'anit* 16a). This biblical and

talmudic emphasis on ethical transformation might come as a surprise, for nowadays when we hear that someone has become religious our sole assumption is that the person has started observing more Jewish rituals.

These two teachings of the book of Jonah are perhaps the more obvious reasons the rabbis chose it as the Yom Kippur haftorah.

But Jonah has more lessons to yield, ones which are even less frequently acknowledged.

1. *Jonah* underscores that the Jewish people have a universal mission. God has commanded us to go into the world and bring the message of God and of ethical monotheism. This is what we were *chosen* to do. And however one regards the issue of Jewish chosenness, it is historically indisputable that it is through the Jews that God has become known to the world. Given the history of anti-Semitism, our impulse might be to resist this obligation of spreading the news about God and His demands, and to flee like Jonah. But historical experience reveals that just as God did not allow Jonah to evade his task, so too will He not allow us. Repeatedly, whether we have wanted to or not, we have found ourselves playing the often dangerous role of being God's messengers. I remember dancing with Jews in Moscow on Simhat Torah, 1973 and singing with them:

> "Nye byusa nikavo,
> Krome boga odnavo –
> I fear no one
> Except God, the only one."

The KGB was monitoring our dancing, and the Kremlin itself was a mere ten minutes away.

Hermann Rauschning, an early associate of Hitler who later broke with him, reports that the Nazi leader saw the very existence of the Jews as a challenge to his message of atheist moral nihilism. His mission in life, Hitler declared, was to destroy "the tyrannical God of the Jews," and His "life-denying Ten Commandments."

Strangely too, even at the very moment Jonah was refusing to carry out God's mission to Nineveh, his very being was bearing testimony to God's rulership over the world. "Then they [the sailors] took Jonah and threw him overboard," the book reports. And when the raging seas calmed down, "the crew were filled with the fear of the Lord and offered sacrifices and made vows to Him." A non-Jewish Bible scholar, John Watts, has noted: ". . . despite his firm intention, [Jonah] is forced to fulfill a prophetic role in identifying the Lord as the source of the storm, in interpreting what He is doing, and instructing the sailors how they can do His will."

2. The book conveys that Judaism's central wish from non-Jews is ethical behavior. While this might seem trite and obvious, think how differently the

book would have been written had it appeared in either the New Testament or the Quran. Would not the proof of the repentance of the Ninevites have been their conversion to either Christianity or Islam? Throughout most of Christian history – and among Fundamentalist Christians to this day – God's central demand of non-Christians has been that they become Christians, and express faith in Jesus who died for their sins. Indeed, it is this issue, of emphasis on faith vs. emphasis on deeds, that has been the central dividing issue between Judaism and Christianity – and not whether or not Jesus was the Messiah.

Over the years, while studying various commentaries and essays on Jonah, I have been pointed to several other unusual features of the book. Let me touch on just a few of them.

The book opens, of course, with God commanding Jonah to arise and deliver a message to the sinful city of Nineveh. The prophet doesn't want to do so, presumably because he is afraid the message will be heeded, and he would prefer to see the Ninevites punished. It would appear that while both God and Jonah want to see an end to Ninevite evil, the prophet wants this to come about through an end to Nineveh, while God wishes to see an end to its evil. It is this desire to see punishment inflicted that distinguishes Jonah from other prophets. As Elie Wiesel writes: "A strange character, he resembles no one in Scripture . . . A man who argues with God not to save men but to punish them – what kind of prophet is that anyway?" (*Five Biblical Portraits,* p. 129).

Wiesel notes yet another incongruity in Jonah's behavior. "He does precisely what he has been ordered to tell Nineveh not to do; he resists God's will" (p. 129).

Rabbi David Shapiro points out a literary device through which the Bible shows that fleeing from God inevitably leads man into descent. "Instead of heeding the divine call to *arise* and go to Nineveh (1:2), Jonah rather *goes down* to Jaffa, *goes down* to the ship, and finally *goes down* to the innermost part of the ship, fleeing from God in a continuous state of descent" (*Studies in Judaism,* p. 236).

Strangely enough, though both a religious Jew and a prophet, Jonah needs a lesson in religion from the non-Jewish captain of the ship on which he flees. When the ship starts to be buffeted by stormy waters, Jonah goes down into its hull and falls into a deep sleep. Chapter 1 verse 6 reports: "And the captain went over to him and cried out, How can you be sleeping so soundly? Get up and call upon your God . . ."

"What a scene," non-Jewish Bible scholar Julius Bewer writes. "The heathen sailor admonishes the Hebrew prophet to pray."

That God can indeed choose anyone, including a heathen ship captain, as his messenger is emphasized by yet another Christian commentator, Leslie Allen. "*Kum Lekh* – Get up and call upon your God," the captain yells at the prophet. "Jonah must have thought he was having a nightmare; these were the very words with which God had disturbed his pleasant life a few days earlier."

The forty-eight verses of Jonah both remind and teach us many things; most importantly, what God wants of human beings. But it also reminds us that we Jews have a mission to the word, *l'take'n olam b'malkhut Shaddai*—to perfect the world under the rule of God.

—Rabbi Joseph Telushkin
CLAL—*News and Perspectives*

❊❊❊❊❊❊❊❊❊❊❊❊❊

God and Humans as Partners

A story is told about a tailor who worked very hard but never succeeded. He turned to the rabbi and asked, "Rabbi why is it that I work hard, do everything right, and yet have never been able to make an adequate living?"

The rabbi answered, "Mr. Tailor, your problem is that you must make God your partner. You must work closely with God—with faith and trust in Him. Make God your partner."

Five years later, the rabbi was walking down the street, and saw his friend the tailor, this time driving a fancy, expensive Rolls Royce, with a chauffeur, obviously extremely successful. The rabbi asked, "How has such success come to you, Mr. Tailor?"

The tailor explained, "You see, Rabbi, I took your advice. I made God my partner, and now I am very rich and successful. In fact, there goes one of my thousands of delivery trucks driving by right now."

The rabbi looked on the truck and saw a sign that read "Lord and Taylor."

In all seriousness, this significant philosophical idea, that we as humans are partners with God in the daily creation of the world, goes back to the Talmud. Everything constructive and worthwhile which we do to improve ourselves and society is considered as a divine act, working in partnership with God.

—Author unknown

❊❊❊❊❊❊❊❊❊❊❊❊❊

If I Can Stop One Heart from Breaking

If I can stop one heart from breaking,
I shall not live in vain;
If I can ease one life the aching,
Or cool one pain,
Or help one fainting robin
Unto his nest again,
I shall not live in vain.

–Emily Dickinson

❋❋❋❋❋❋❋❋❋❋❋❋❋❋

The Jonah Syndrome: Fulfilling Human Potential

The Book of Jonah, which we study each year on Yom Kippur, is pregnant with rich meaning to the discerning reader. It is a study of a human being who went astray and makes a good object lesson for the Day of Atonement. Jonah sinned and repented and thus became the model for all of us. He is the epitome of the fallible human being, who, nevertheless, learns from his errors and from them emerges into a better person.

What exactly was Jonah's sin? The biblical book explains that he did not fulfill God's charge to go and speak to the people of Nineveh, that great Assyrian capital, and warn them to repent. He failed to carry out God's mission.

The late Dr. Abraham Maslow, of Brandeis University, whom I consider one of the most revolutionary minds of the twentieth century, recorded his own interpretation of Jonah's sin (Maslow, 1967, pages 162f). In a piece called "The Jonah Syndrome," Maslow explained that what Jonah did is what we all do— namely, we evade our highest destiny, we fear our own greatness, we run away from our own best talents.

Jonah was selected by God, just as dozens of prophets before him were singled out, because of his unique ability, his charismatic leadership qualities, his exemplary conduct in human affairs. He was singularly qualified to undertake a mission of education and indoctrination to the teeming metropolis of Nineveh and impart to them of God's teachings of justice, equality, compassion, brotherhood, and human understanding.

And yet he paralyzed himself by fear, awe, and weakness. He felt himself unequal to God's task. He considered his shortcomings and inadequacies, and decided they were too great, that he was unworthy of this sacred mission.

Maslow explains that this pattern is a very human and widespread one, but one which prevents most of us from growing into the bigger and more highly evolved human beings we have the potential of becoming. In his words: "We fear our highest possibilities. . . . We are generally afraid to become that which we can glimpse in our most perfect moments. . . . We enjoy and even thrill to the godlike possibilities we see in ourselves in such peak moments. And yet we simultaneously shiver with weakness, awe, and fear before these very same possibilities."

He tells of saying to his students at the university, "Which of you in this class hopes to write the great American novel, or to be a Senator, or Governor, or President? . . . Or a great composer? Who aspires to be a saint, like Schweitzer, perhaps? . . . Generally," he explains, "everybody starts giggling, blushing, and squirming until I ask, 'If not you, then who else?' " He then recalls a picture he once saw in a psychology textbook, divided into two parts. "The lower half was a picture of a line of babies, pink, sweet, delightful, innocent, and lovable. Above that was a picture of a lot of passengers in a subway train, glum, gray, sullen, and sour. The caption underneath was very simply, 'What happened?' This is what I'm talking about."

One of the first people to recognize the fact that human beings were only living up to a fraction of their potential was Harvard professor William James, some three-quarters of a century ago. He made this observation: "I have no doubt whatever, that most people live whether physically, intellectually, or morally, in a very restricted circle of their potential being. . . . The so-called 'normal man' of commerce, so to speak . . . is a mere extract from the potentially realizable individual he represents, and we all have reservoirs of life to draw upon which we do not dream." (Goble, 1971, page 155).

I recall reading once that the sculptor who carved out of Mt. Rushmore the faces of four of our country's leading presidents was asked how he could accomplish such an enormous feat. He replied: "The figures were right there in the mountain. All I had to do was uncover the rock surrounding them." That, in a way, summarizes my message this evening. We all have within us marvelously etched features of brilliance and spiritual greatness. All we need do is get through the covers, to bore through the hard surface of fear and awe and trepidation and let it be seen before the world.

Jewish tradition has for millennia presented an image of man that was far higher than any other known conception among the religions, philosophies, and psychologies of the people of the world. Man was made but little lower than the angels (Psalm 8) in the image of God himself (Genesis 1:27).

The implications of this view of man are enormous! They have been read and taught for centuries, and yet only today are we beginning to fully realize the far-reaching consequences of seeing man as made in the image of God.

Dr. W. Ross Adey, of the Brain Research Institute at UCLA's Space Biology Laboratory, recently stated that "The ultimate creative capacity of the brain may be, for all practical purposes, infinite."

of the human limitations. You must be able simultaneously to laugh at yourself and at all human pretensions (Maslow, 1967, page 166).

I am reminded of the Hasidic admonition that a person must have two pockets in his coat, and in each carry a slip of paper containing an ancient Hebrew quotation. In one pocket the slip reads "For my sake the world was created" (Mishna Sanhedrin 4:5). In the other pocket it says: "I am but dust and ashes" (Genesis 3:19).

Another fear which prevents us from realizing our best selves is that we will have reached the climax of life too soon, we will have peaked out, done too much, reached too far beyond our time. We need something to hold out which is still not done, so we cripple ourselves, and hold back, and don't give our all.

But the truth is that we can stretch ourselves anew each time we reach a new and higher stage of accomplishment and being. The ultimate capabilities which we can reach are so far beyond us that instead of holding back, we ought to be stretching as high as we can, and then, reaching that new plateau, remain only until an even higher goal begins to beckon to us.

In George Bernard Shaw's words, "To have succeeded is to have finished one's business on earth, like the male spider, who is killed by the female the moment he has succeeded in his courtship. I like a state of continual *becoming*, with a goal in front and not behind."

We need never worry that if we reach too far, our business on earth will be finished. There is more in us than that. There is always another goal farther out, in the farthest reaches of human nature, which we can aspire to when we achieve the stage we thought would be the highest.

Sources:

Buber, Martin. *Hasidism and Modern Man.* New York: Harper, 1958.

Coleman, Lyman. *Serendipity Frog Kissin' Workshops.* Scottsdale, PA: Serendipity House, 1974.

Goble, Frank G. *The Third Force: The Psychology of Abraham Maslow.* New York: Pocket Books, 1971.

Jourard, Sidney M. *Healthy Personality: An Approach From the Viewpoint of Humanistic Psychology.* New York: Macmillan, 1974.

Lamm, Norman. *The Royal Reach.* New York: Philip Feldheim, 1970.

Maslow, Abraham H. "Neurosis a Failure of Personal Growth," from *Humanitas,* 1967, pp. 153–169.

                                                                                  –Rabbi Dov Peretz Elkins

13

CLOSING THE GATES

N'eelah – An Army of Good Deeds

During the High Holy Day service, it is told that Reb Levi Yitzchok of Berditchev once mounted the pulpit in fear and trembling. He wanted to find a way to convince God to grant his people a year of blessing and happiness. So he did three things.

First, he pleaded with God, "Lord of the universe, a plain Jew, if his tfillin fall from his hand, he bends down and picks them up. But you, dear God, you have let your tfillin the Jewish people, fall from your hand to the earth. For two thousand years your people have groveled in the dust of exile and you haven't bent down to lift them up! Is it too much to ask that you act like a simple Jew acts?" Reb Levi Yitzchok saw his words mount heavenward and the very gates of Heaven began to open, just a little.

What more could Reb Levi do? If pleading opened the gates part way, perhaps repentance would open them up the rest of the way. So, when Reb Levi reached the confessional, he began to weep, "Woe upon us. We live in a mixed up world. It used to be that, in the streets, people told the truth while only in the synagogue did they speak falsehood. Since people carried on their business affairs in truth and honesty, when they came to the synagogue on High Holidays and said, 'We have sinned,' they were really lying. But now, the opposite is the case. Falsehood reigns in the street and truth only in the synagogue. For now when people come to the synagogue and confess that they have sinned, how true it is." As he spoke, a bitter cry of remorse and repentance was heard throughout the synagogue. The cry mounted heavenward and opened the gates a little bit wider – but not yet completely.

There was only one thing left for Reb Levi Yitzchok to do – wage war. Now, a saint doesn't wage war like a king or a general, nor does he use the same weapons. A saint uses an army of the righteous whose weapons are good deeds. In his last desperate attempt to open wide the gates of heaven, Reb Levi Yitzchok lifted his eyes heavenward and declared, "Let them speak and not I. Remember, God, the two rubles that the widow Sarah paid her son's teacher, denying herself the dress she longed for; remember too, the bowl of soup that the Yeshiva student gave his hungry classmate when he was hungry himself, and the strip of forest that Reb Hayim lost because he refused to go back on his word." And on and on, cataloguing, one by one, the simple, kindly deeds of ordinary men and women – deeds of loving kindness and mercy. And suddenly, as the congregation raised their eyes, they could see not only the gates of heaven open completely, but the Holy One, blessed be He, descend from the seat of judgment and mount the seat of mercy, even as their prayers became a garland and rested upon his head.

The calamities threatening our people and the world are no less severe than those in the days of Reb Levi Yitzchok. We fervently hope that the gates of heaven will open wide for us and that the coming year will be a year of goodness and blessing. What then shall we do? Plead before God? Of course, but that alone is not sufficient. Confess? Also terribly important, but still not enough.

For us, as for Reb Levi Yitzchok, the third and most potent weapons are the good deeds of simple, ordinary people, an army of righteousness, performing deeds of goodness and truth. If we create such an army, next year will be indeed a good year.

– Rabbi Abraham J. Karp

※※※※※※※※※※※※※※

Passing through the Gates

"With each passage (each hallway between doors), some magic must be given up, some cherished illusion of safety and comfortably familiar sense of self must be cast off to allow greater expansion of our own distinctiveness" (Gail Sheehy: *Passages: Predictable Crises of Adult Life*). Our task, therefore, is to acknowledge at each stage of life that one passage has come to an end.

– Author unknown

※※※※※※※※※※※※※※※

As Yom Kippur Comes to a Close

We have not succeeded in answering all your problems. The answers we have found only serve to raise a whole set of new questions. In some ways we feel we are as confused as ever, but we believe we are confused on a higher level and about more important things.

—A poster, author unknown

※※※※※※※※※※※※※※

God's Thirteen Attributes
Four Kinds of Love

Levi Yitzchak teaches us of four kinds of love: unconditional one-way love (grace), compassionate empathetic compelling love, love which cherishes being for its own sake, and love which purposely blinds itself to the faults of the other. It is a very profound analysis.

First, think of the people we know. Some of them we love because they are part of humanity. We need not even know them—the unknown children starving and abused, the poor and oppressed, Jews we don't know in Russia, the sick. These are all part of the broad family of humanity and the entire Jewish people. We love them even if they do not know of it. Sometimes we even love family members and friends, even if they don't know it, because they are fellow living creatures.

Some of the people we know we love because we have empathy with them. We know them, we feel their specific pain, we sense their specific distress. We cannot stand to see them suffer and we long to help them in any way. Their concrete being compels us. Our empathy binds us.

Some of the people we know we simply like. We may not even know why. It's chemistry, or instinct, or very finely tuned training, or the subconscious. But we know we like them. We cherish their presence.

And for some people, we know we have a great deal of patience. We know their faults yet we accept them. We know their shortcomings, yet we love them.

Second, think of ourselves. We all want to be loved unconditionally; to be loved compassionately, to be cherished for ourselves; and to have others ultimately be patient with us, accepting us in spite of our faults. As a matter of reflection, each of us really should ask, Which type of love do I need most? And which type of love can I give best?

So it is with God, says Levi Yitzchak. God loves each one of us in grace, compassion, in cherishing, and in patience. But which is the most important, the most powerful? We need only consult God's own prayer to see the order in which He puts them: it is compassionate love. Why is compassionate love first? Precisely because it is *engaged,* involved, bonded; it is covenantal. We have a moral claim on God's compassionate love. We have a right to His empathy, as a child has the right to the bonded love of a parent. And the reverse is true too: God has a moral claim on our compassionate love, a right to our empathy; as a parent has a claim on the compassionate love of a child. As it is with God, so it is with humanity. Each of us has a moral claim on the compassionate love of the other, a right to the empathy of the other. And others have a claim on our compassionate love and empathy. Compassionate love is not the easiest kind of love; indeed, it may be the most difficult, the most demanding. But it is the most profound, the most spiritually resilient. This is a very powerful lesson for the Day of Judgment.

Complete and true love encompasses all four types. It belongs to God, though it can be ours fleetingly. This is the love for which we can only pray. This, too, is a powerful lesson for the Day of Judgment.

-Rabbi David R. Blumenthal
God at the Center—Meditations on Jewish Spirituality

☀☀☀☀☀☀☀☀☀☀☀☀☀

The Day Is Fading, the Sun Setting

The day is fading, the sun is setting, the silence and peace of night descend upon the earth. Vouchsafe rest, O God, unto our disquieted hearts; lift up the soul that is cast down. Turn, in Your all-forgiving love, to Your children who yearn for Your mercy; turn, O Father, to all fainting hearts, to all heavy-laden souls. Let this hour bring us the assurance that You have forgiven, that we have found favor in Your sight. Consecrate our hearts unto Thee, and make them Your living altars, whereupon shall burn the holy flame of devotion to Thee.

From Your house, O merciful Father, we are about to return to our homes, to seek shelter in the communion of our family life. Open unto us the gates of Your love! Enter with us into our home so that it may become Your sanctuary, and Your spirit may abide within its walls. Then will our habitation stand firm amidst the storms of life, a refuge from evil, a bulwark against temptation.

And still another dwelling You have destined for us, O Source of life; an eternal abode to which we shall go after our brief day on earth has closed. Open unto us the gates of Your grace; unlock for us the portals of eternal peace when the gates of our earthly home shall have closed behind us. Be our guiding star on our homeward journey. Let Your light shine in the night of our death as the dawn of a new morning, that from our graves may sprout not the barren thistle but the fragrant myrtle, a blessed memory redounding to Your honor and glory.

This twilight hour reminds us also of the eventide when, according to Your gracious promise, Your light will arise over all the children of men, and Israel's spiritual descendants will be as numerous as the stars in heaven. Endow us, our Guardian, with strength and patience for our holy mission. Grant that all the children of Israel may recognize the goal of their changeful career, so that they may exemplify by their zeal and love for humanity the truth of Israel's message: One humanity on earth even as there is but one God in heaven.

You alone know when this work of reconciliation shall be fulfilled; when the day shall dawn on which the light of Your truth shall illumine the whole earth. But the great day shall come, as surely as none of Your words returns void. Then joy will thrill all hearts, and from one end of the earth to the other will echo the gladsome cry: The Lord our God, the Lord is One! Then Your house shall be called a house of prayer for all peoples, and all nations shall flow unto it. And in triumphant joy shall they cry out: Lift up your heads, O ye gates, and be ye lifted up, ye everlasting doors, that the King of glory may come in. Who is the King of glory? The Lord of Hosts, He is the King of glory.

–Adapted from *New Union Prayerbook for Jewish Worship, Part II*

Havdalah

We kids would gather in a dark room, like this, while Zaida, our grandfather, would light the Havdalah candle. Zaida couldn't stand to say Havdalah right away; he wanted Shabbos to stay as long as possible, so we would stand in the dark while he talked to us. He liked to say, "You know why this candle melts? Because it's more than a candle; it's the heart of Shabbos. You see, just like we don't want to leave it, it doesn't want to leave us. So it cries and melts tears. I don't want to go, it says. I've been your queen, your bride for one whole glorious day. If only I could stay with you the other six days." And then Zaida would say very sadly, "If only she could; if only we had her the other six days of the week. If only her happiness and peace could live in people's hearts the whole week long."

Once, after hearing this, I looked up at Zaida and said, "Don't cry, Zaida, see the melted tears? They're all over your hands. If you don't wash the wax off your fingers, Shabbos will be with you all week long. You can have Shabbos with you every single day, if you just decide to."

Zaida smiled at me and sighed, "If only we could decide not to wash the wax off our fingers . . . if only we could decide that."

–Philip Arian
He Kindled a Light: A Philosophy of Jewish Education

❊❊❊❊❊❊❊❊❊❊❊❊❊

Havdalah after Yom Kippur

Why are no spices (besamim) used in Havdalah?

"Now the reason why the benediction over spices is recited after the close of the Sabbath is because the soul is in pain at the close of the Sabbath and is therefore rejoiced and comforted with a goodly odor (Rambam, Hilkot Shabbat 29). But on Yom Kippur, when the soul is not in pain at the end of the day, for Yom Kippur makes atonement at nightfall and the soul is at ease, there is no need for spices. . . ."

If Yom Kippur falls on Shabbat, add the bracha for spices, since Rabbenu Gershom, Meor HaGola, holds that blessing over spices is recited EVERY Yom Kippur, even when it does not fall on the Sabbath.

–Adapted from *Days of Awe*

❊❊❊❊❊❊❊❊❊❊❊❊❊

A Plea for Adult Education in the New Year

A man went to Israel and bought a mezuzah for the first time in his life. He brought it back and showed it to the rabbi. "Rabbi," he said, "I bought this beautiful mezuzah; I'm so excited! But, I don't know what to do with it."

The rabbi looked at it–it was a gorgeous mezuzah with beautiful silver filigree. He said to the man, "But it's empty! There's nothing in it!" The man said, "Oh, when I bought it there was a sheet with instructions on it, but it was in Hebrew and I couldn't understand it, so I threw it away."

–Author unknown

※※※※※※※※※※※※※※※

Taste Everything: Swallow Only That Which Fits

Let your beautiful eyes close. Be aware that your eyelids did what you asked. If you can, notice that it is possible for you to be in touch with all of your body in much the same way. Now, as you're in touch with your eyelids and your body, let your attention go to your breathing. Your breathing depends on you and your awareness, and no one else.

Perhaps as you're in touch with your breathing you can feel it fill your body even more fully. . . .

Perhaps at this moment you can give yourself a message that at the time when your body feels stressed, whether there are tears flowing or not, you can remember to be in touch with your breathing. It will allow nurturing in your body, and it will allow you to be in touch with both your humanness and your divinity.

While your eyes are still closed, I'd like you to be aware of the significance of your life, and of the life-force we all have.

> Become aware that the ever-present life-force
> does not determine what we are to do with life.
> We determine that.

> When we are children, the people around us are our main teachers.
> Then when we learn
> that some of the things our teachers taught us
> no longer fit
> we can honor our teachers for what they gave us
> and go ahead
> and learn that which we still need.

> We are capable of infinite possibilities and
> become limited only when we shut the door on new ones
> or when we are not aware
> that there are doors we haven't seen.

> —Virginia Satir
> *Meditations and Inspirations*

※※※※※※※※※※※※※※※

Closing Prayer

We have shared many words together. That we could speak them and hear them spoken, means that there is a place in the world for them, that our songs of praise and prayers of hope have not gone empty from our mouths, but still remain in the air, waiting for other words to join them. Too often they are not joined, rhetoric propounded but not meant, accents without acts. If the hopes that we have shared tonight are not to have been shared in vain, we must not leave our words here in our seats neatly folded in our books. Our words must leave with us, go streaming out the doors of this New Year, accompany us as we walk on the road, when we sit in our homes, when we lie down and when we rise up. They must emblazon the doorposts of our house, and seal themselves into our hands before our eyes, that the world might remember the words it has so long forgotten, and compose from them a new song which all might sing in celebration of the world we all desire.

–Rabbi Richard N. Levy
On Wings of Awe

❉❉❉❉❉❉❉❉❉❉❉❉❉

When the Gates Are Closed

We are taught by our Rabbis that the "gates of tears are not closed"; namely that tearful pleas to God for mercy are acceptable by Him. It may be asked, since they are not closed, of what use are gates? The answer is: if one begs tearfully but without intelligence, the gates are then closed.

–Medzibozer Rabbi
Butzina De-Nehorah

❉❉❉❉❉❉❉❉❉❉❉❉❉

Starting Again

Two men come to a rabbi asking for help to settle a problem. Both are angry at each other, and neither will apologize.

The rabbi says: OK, at the count of 3, both of you extend your hands and shake. OK, 1, 2, 3.

Very good, says the rabbi but now you have to say something. In Judaism it's not enough to just shake. Now which one of you will say something to the other?

OK, said one man, I'll start. I wish for you everything in the new year that you wish for me.

The other man responds: You see, Rabbi, he's starting up again.

– Author unknown

※※※※※※※※※※※※※※

Closing Prayer

O Lord, our God and God of our ancestors, grant us of Your spirit, that we may be cleansed of the jealousy and hatred, the haughtiness and pettiness, the treachery and prejudice which befoul life and poison happiness.

May the New Year bring to all people and to all nations the ability to live justly and to walk humbly with You. May our hearts be open with generosity, and our hands ready with kindness.

May the words of our mouths and the meditations of our hearts find expression in our lives day by day, that we may bridge the gap between our conscience and our conduct, between what we believe and what we do.

May all our inspirations for good soon be fulfilled. Amen.

– Author unknown

14

NEXT YEAR IN JERUSALEM

We Pray for Jerusalem

Bless this land, and bless the State of Israel. We wear coats of many colors. Many loves and many loyalties are spun into the fabric of our lives. We are patriotic citizens of the lands of the dispersion, and we order our day according to the lunar calendar. We pray for the peace of Jerusalem, and we work for the betterment of our neighborhood and nation. Said Philo, domiciled in Alexandria, Egypt, some nineteen hundred years ago, "We who live throughout the world all owe a debt of loyalty to our fatherland. But we also have a motherland which is the holy city of Jerusalem."

—Rachel Rabinowicz
The Rabbinical Assembly Haggadah

✴✴✴✴✴✴✴✴✴✴✴✴✴

The Wall

Jerusalem, at Rosh Hashanah, is a city for dreamers. I climb the walls and watch the sun set over the ancient city, heightening the magical golden splendor of the panorama. It is a sight that seems always new, yet thoroughly familiar.

The Wall stands free again in a place of freedom, under the sunlight of emancipation. Blow the shofar at the Western Wall and it echoes on Mt. Zion. Blow the shofar on Mt. Zion and it is heard at the Western Wall. Mountain and Wall ascent and defense.

The story of our people is in these three words and in that mountaintop and Wall. We are a mountain people whose life began at Mt. Sinai, a mountain people who built their Holy City on a mountain aspiration. We are an upward toiling people, not satisfied with the valleys and the lower slopes. We seek the heights. Our faith needs eminence. We are a defending people, the protectors of Sinai and the rebuilders of Zion. We see the celestial fire and we protect it against those who would extinguish it.

May we be reckoned among those who make the ascent, among those who in our day defend the highway from earth to heaven.

—Rabbi Jacob Philip Rudin
Very Truly Yours

✼✼✼✼✼✼✼✼✼✼✼✼✼✼

A Parable Explaining Why We Say "Next Year in Jerusalem" at the End of Yom Kippur

There once was a king who had a very beautiful daughter, and since she had come of age, he sought to marry her off. Royal Ministers and noblemen came to seek her hand, but she refused them all, saying, "This one is a glutton," "This one a drunkard." Her father then pledged that he would give her to the first person that happened along. It happened that a simple peasant came by and her father married her off to him.

The peasant took her and brought her to his farm, treating her as a peasant would. The face of the princess became blackened with soot, and the local peasants mocked her. Understandably, she wrote woeful letters to her father.

Moved by what he heard from his beloved daughter, the king fixed a time to visit her. However, when it became known that the king was planning to come, the peasants panicked, cleaned house, and showered her with dainties. Soon runners came, announcing that the king was drawing near. The peasants welcomed them with great honor and invited them into their homes.

Before long, word came that the king was about to arrive. Immediately they dressed the daughter in white lovely garments and they lit many candles until the whole farm was illuminated. The king came and saw the honorable way in which his daughter seemed to be treated and was pleased. He stayed with her, and they had pleasant times together.

When the time came for the king to leave, his daughter fell on his neck and wept uncontrollably, crying, "Father, father, how can you leave your daughter in such a way?" He replied, "What's wrong, dear daughter? Behold—have I not seen you treated with great honor?" She wept more loudly and said, "All the honor which you see was contrived only for today, because they knew that you were coming. On account of that, everyone took fright and treated me with great respect. Now that you are leaving, they will return to mocking me." Said the king to his daughter's husband, "Is it possible that you could treat my daughter in such a way, don't you realize that she is the king's daughter?" The husband burst into tears and said, "Of course I realize that, but what can I do; for I am but a poor man, and it is difficult for me to eke out a living. I am not able to treat your daughter in a suitable way. And moreover, I live among people who don't recognize your daughter's qualities. But you, my Lord, are a great king. Since we have become related by your giving me your daughter, please lift me up and bring me to your dwelling place; give me a portion and an inheritance in your estate in order that your daughter and I may dwell there. Then I will be able to conduct myself with great honor and respect towards her as befitting a king's daughter."

The king in the parable is the King of Kings, the Holy One, Blessed be He, who wanted to give his daughter, the Torah and its teachings, to the first man, Adam. Said the Torah, "He is a glutton, for he ate of the fruit of the Tree of Knowledge." The Lord wanted to give the Torah to Noah but she said, "He is a drunkard," for the Bible tells us that he drank much wine. Then the Holy One, Blessed be He, decided to give the Torah to us, the Jewish people.

But we make light of her and pay her not the respect due to her. Thus she writes woeful letters each day to her father. When the days of Elul before the High Holidays approach, (the King's runners announcing His imminent arrival), we greet them with study, prayer, and good deeds. Then the sound of the shofar on Rosh Hashanah is heard. We come out to greet the King; in our prayers we proclaim His sovereignty and we are reminded that He is King, for He is in our midst and as we walk in the light of His countenance, we repent. When Yom Kippur arrives, the Holy King, may His Name be blessed, dwells with us and sees Israel as pure as the heavenly angels. They wear white garments and are wrapped in white taleisim from the evening of Kol Nidre to the time of Neilah. They stand in holiness and purity paying respect to the Torah. The Lord, as it were, derives satisfaction from the scene and is exceedingly pleased and full of joy at the state of the Torah.

When the time arrives for the parting of the Divine Presence after the Neilah prayer, the Torah bursts into tears and says, "Father, Father, how can you leave me? They shall immediately strip me of all the honor with which they have today clothed me!" Says the Holy One, Blessed be He, to the Jewish people, "Is it possible that you could treat my daughter in such a way? Don't you realize that she is the daughter of the King?" And the Jewish people say to the Holy One blessed be He, "Oh Lord of the World, we realize this. What are we to do, for we are but poor men. We lack a place for ourselves where we may dwell with your daughter in due honor. We live amidst nations who do not recognize the qualities and values of the Torah and we cannot honor her as she deserves. You are a great King, about whom it is written, 'The earth is the Lord's and the fullness of it.' Lift us up and bring us to Your land, the land of Israel. Give us a place in that, your true estate, so that we may truly honor the Torah with all the respect due to her."

And so, at the time that the Holy Presence departs at the end of this Yom Kippur day, we pray that Next Year We Shall be in Jerusalem.

L'Shana Haba'ah B'Yerushalayim.

– The Dubner Maggid
Yamim Noraim (Agnon, trans. Wechsler)

❋❋❋❋❋❋❋❋❋❋❋❋❋

In Moscow

A visitor to the USSR tells this story about the close of the Yom Kippur service in a Moscow synagogue.

"Then the old sexton brought out the shofar. 'Tekiah gedolah,' sang out the rabbi. And as the long blast of the shofar pierced the stillness, the hushed congregation held its breath.

"And then it happened! As if in response to a mysterious command from some unknown source, some 3,000 Jews turned as one body toward the visitors' section where the members of the Israeli consulate stationed in Moscow had been worshipping throughout the day. Six thousand Russian Jewish eyes stared directly into the Israeli eyes as if trying to read in them their past, their future, and the secret of their existence. It lasted but a moment, but it seemed like an hour.

"Then, shattering the awful, mounting silence, the 3,000 worshippers suddenly burst into a wild, spontaneous cry which came as if from a single throat.

Leshanah haba'ah b'Yerushalayim!
Next Year in Jerusalem!"

– Rabbi Alfred Kolatch
Sermons for the Seventies

❋❋❋❋❋❋❋❋❋❋❋❋❋

A Letter to the World from Jerusalem

I am not a creature from another planet, as you seem to believe. I am a Jerusalemite – like yourselves, a man of flesh and blood. I am a citizen of my city, an integral part of my people.

I have a few things to get off my chest. Because I am not a diplomat, I do not have to mince words. I do not have to please you, or even persuade you. I owe you nothing. You did not build this city; you do not live in it: you did not defend it when they came to destroy it. And we will be damned if we will let you take it away.

There was a Jerusalem before there was a New York. When Berlin, Moscow, London, and Paris were miasmal forest and swamp, there was a thriving Jewish community here. It gave something to the world which you nations have rejected ever since you established yourselves – a human moral code.

Here the prophets walked, their words flashing like forked lightning. Here a people who wanted nothing more than to be left alone, fought off waves of heathen would-be conquerors, bled and died on the battlements, hurled themselves into the flames of their burning Temple rather than surrender; and when finally overwhelmed by sheer numbers and led away into captivity, swore that before they forgot Jerusalem, they would see their tongues cleave to their palates, their right arm wither.

For two pain filled millennia, while we were your unwelcome guests, we prayed daily to return to this city. Three times a day we petitioned the Almighty: "Gather us from the four corners of the world, bring us upright to our land; return in mercy to Jerusalem, Thy city, and dwell in it as Thou promised."

On every Yom Kippur and Passover we fervently voiced the hope that next year would find us in Jerusalem. Your inquisitions, pogroms, expulsions, the ghettos into which you jammed us, your forcible baptisms, your quota systems, your genteel anti-Semitism, and the final unspeakable horror, the Holocaust (and worse, your terrifying disinterest in it) – all these have not broken us. They may have sapped what little moral strength you still possessed, but they forged us into steel. Do you think you can break us now, after all we have been through? Do you really believe that after Dachau and Auschwitz we are frightened by your threats of blockades and sanctions? We have been to Hell and back – a Hell of your making. What more could you have in your arsenal that could scare us?

I have watched this city bombarded twice by nations calling themselves civilized. In 1948, while you looked on apathetically, I saw women and children blown to smithereens, this after we had agreed to your request to internationalize the city. It was a deadly combination that did the job: British officers, Arab gunners and American-made cannons.

And then the savage sacking of the Old City: the willful slaughter, the wanton destruction of every synagogue and religious school; the desecration of Jewish cemeteries; the sale by a ghoulish government of tomb stones for building materials, for poultry runs, army camps – even latrines.

And you never said a word.

You never breathed the slightest protest when the Jordanians shut off the holiest of our holy places, the Western Wall, in violation of the pledges they had made after the war – a war they waged, incidentally, against a decision of the UN.

Not a murmur came from you whenever legionnaires in their spiked helmets casually opened fire upon our citizens from behind the walls.

Your hearts bled when Berlin came under siege. You rushed your airlift "to save the gallant Berliners." But you did not send one ounce of food when Jews starved in besieged Jerusalem. You thundered against the wall which the East Germans ran through the middle of the German capital – but not one peep out of you about the other wall, the one that tore through the heart of Jerusalem.

And when the same thing happened 20 years later, and the Arabs unleashed a savage, unprovoked bombardment of the Holy City again, did any of you do anything? The only thing that brought you to life was when the city was at last re-united. Then you wrung your hands and spoke loftily of "justice" and the need for the "Christian" quality of turning the other cheek.

The truth is – and you know it deep inside your gut – you would prefer the city to be destroyed rather than have it governed by Jews. No matter how diplomatically you phrase it, the age old prejudices seep out of every word.

If our return to the city has tied your theology in knots, perhaps you had better re-examine your catechism. After what we have been through, we are not passively going to accommodate ourselves to the twisted idea that we are to suffer eternal homelessness until we accept your Saviour.

For the first time since the year 70 there is now complete religious freedom for all in Jerusalem. For the first time since the Romans put the torch to the Temple everyone has equal rights. (You preferred to have some more equal than others.) We loathe the sword – but it was you who forced us to take it up. We crave peace – but we are not going back to the peace of 1948 as you would like us to.

We are home. It has a lovely sound for a nation you have willed to wander over the face of the globe. We are not leaving. We have redeemed the pledge made by our forefathers: Jerusalem is being rebuilt. "Next year" – and the year after, and after, and after, until the end of time – "in Jerusalem!"

– Eliezer Whartman

※※※※※※※※※※※※※※

This Christmas Spend Chanukah in Israel

People have died just to live in Israel. And people have lived just to die in Israel. Why? Why Israel? Why here, in such a little place?

You can drive over it in a day or fly over it in an hour. In it are a sea where nothing swims and a desert where nothing grows. As real estate, it's nothing much. But here, in this little place, every ethic of Western man was born.

The Bible was written here, and every man has a root here, deep in Israel's stubborn soil. Come to Jerusalem, to Bethlehem, to Nazareth, to the Galilee. Follow the course of a life that changed the course of a billion lives.

Come to the same Jerusalem, to the wall of Solomon's Temple. For 1900 years, men have vowed, "Next year in Jerusalem." Solomon's wall is only one reason why.

Mount Moriah, where Abraham offered Isaac in sacrifice, is in Jerusalem. This is the city of David and David is buried here. Mount Zion is here, and the Dome of the Rock. Gethsemane is here, the Mount of Olives is here, the Church of the Holy Sepulchre is here. All here.

Yet if Israel is only a dot on the map of the world, Jerusalem is only a dot on the map of Israel. And wander where you will, every inch is history. (The Bible is still the best guidebook to Israel.) Hear the names: Acre, the Crusader city. Beersheba. Eilat. Sodom. Massada.

Even as you land at our airport, you're a stone's throw from Modi'in, the birthplace of the Maccabees.

Here, in 165 B.C.E., Judah Maccabee led a victorious Jewish army to dramatic victory against overwhelming Roman force.

Chanukah, the 8-day Festival of Lights, celebrates that victory. And that victory is still celebrated here every year.

You are most welcome to join our celebration this winter.

And you are most welcome to explore all of the modern Israel as well as the ancient Israel.

In a land of miracles, miracles are to be expected. And so you will see us harvest chemicals from the Dead Sea where nothing swims, and oranges from the desert where nothing grows.

You will find our cities sprawling, our people vital, our night life hectic, our weather mild, our beaches uncrowded, our hotels superb, our mood elated.

You will find that Israel has no beginnings or endings. Time collapses utterly; you can touch the past and present with one hand. You will find a new sense of history here, perhaps even a new sense of yourself.

And you will never, ever forget.

—EL AL Advertisement

※※※※※※※※※※※※※※

The Shofar at the Western Wall

※※

The Western Wall of the Temple in Jerusalem was the object of friction between Arabs and Jews for many years. In 1929, as a gesture of appeasement to the Arabs, the British Mandatory government forbade the sounding of the shofar at the Western Wall at the conclusion of Yom Kippur, but the Jewish underground decided to ignore this prohibition.

As the *Neilah* service was being concluded with the cantor chanting the *Avinu Malkenu,* he interpolated the Hebrew verse, "Our Father, our King, we have the shofar; draw a circle around us." There was a momentary deep hush when suddenly, from one end of the wall, a tremulous but clear shofar sound clarioned from a child's voice. As the British police converged upon the child, a *tekiah gedolah* reverberated from the other end of the wall. Whereupon the assembled worshippers united in a spontaneous cry "Next year in Jerusalem rebuilt," and then burst out singing *Hatikvah.*

The following year, Moshe Segal, watchman in the Galil, came to spend Yom Kippur in Jerusalem and to pray at the Western Wall. When the fast day ended he blew a shofar and was immediately arrested by the British. They held him at the police station without food until midnight, when he was released. Only then did he learn how his release was effected. The late chief rabbi of Palestine, Abraham Isaac Kook, when informed that Segal was arrested, phoned the secretary of the British administration and told him, "I have fasted all day but I will not eat until you free the man who blew the shofar." "But the man violated a government order," the secretary replied. To which Rabbi Kook retorted: "He fulfilled a religious commandment." The rabbi's moral persuasion prevailed, and the secretary promised to release Segal.

Year after year, despite the arrest of Jews, many of whom were disciples of Segal, ways were devised to outwit the British police and to conclude Yom Kippur according to tradition. When the Old City of Jerusalem became part of Jordan in 1948, Jews ascended Mount Zion and facing the Western Wall, they sounded the shofar to conclude the ritual of the holiest day of the year.

On June 7, 1967, when the Israel Defense Forces recaptured the Old City of Jerusalem, the shofar was again sounded to proclaim the victory and to reassert the right of the Jews to worship in freedom at their most sacred site. At the end of Yom Kippur that year, Moshe Segal, at the request of Minister Menahem Begin, was given the distinction of being the first to sound the shofar.

–Tuvia Preshel
High Holiday Bible Themes (ed. Greenberg)
Copyright © 1973, Hartmore House

✳✳

Rabbi Shlomoh Goren, chief of chaplains of the Israel Defense Forces, advised soldiers near enemy bases that they were exempt from listening to the sounds of the *shofar,* so that their locations might not be betrayed.

–Rabbi Sidney Greenberg
High Holiday Bible Themes
Copyright © 1973, Hartmore House

✳✳✳✳✳✳✳✳✳✳✳✳✳

Jerusalem – Never to Be Lost

There is an old legend concerning a Jew who was very pious. His children were hungry and poorly clothed. He continually prayed to God for help. One day an angel appeared and informed him that God had heard his prayers. He will receive a great sum of money on one condition – that he keep it for ten years and at the expiration of that period give it back without complaint. The man accepted. He walked into his little kitchen and on the table was a bag of gold. He soon became a prosperous businessman and gave much charity to the poor. Every man who needed help could come to him. He became known as a doer of good deeds and a friend of the poor. In this manner ten years passed. The angel then reappeared and said: "Are you ready?" The man replied: "I have the bag of gold prepared. Before you take it, I have only one request to make. Promise me that you will give it to a person who will use the money better than I did." The angel reflected, and then announced: "I know of no one who could have used the gold better. Keep it and continue your good works."

I would say to our president and to all who protest: Show me another people who will keep Jerusalem open, who will continue to make it a center of spirituality, culture, and brotherhood, and who will with our assistance – through the United Jewish Appeal – resettle Russians, Ethiopians, Romanians, all who enter its gates and seek shelter within its walls. The reestablishment of Jerusalem as an undivided city under Israel must never be lost.

–Rabbi Matthew H. Simon

✳✳✳✳✳✳✳✳✳✳✳✳✳

Jerusalem
A Review of Literary History

The most direct route seemed along a road once named Street of the Military Police. Today it was named after Benjamin Disraeli. My wandering had disoriented me slightly, and for a moment I was unsure whether I was indeed on the right block. The municipal authorities often hid street signs on the corners of buildings, and if you were at the wrong corner or a sign had fallen off or somehow become covered, only the help of a local could help you find your way.

"Can you tell me where Disraeli is?" I asked a white-haired woman who walked nearby.

"Buried in England," she said with a laugh, and then added, "It's on the next block. Come – if you carry this package for me, I'll show you the way. I'm going there myself."

She handed me her groceries.

"Do you live here?" I asked.

"Almost thirty-eight years. And you – where are you from?"

The American accent in my Hebrew must have given me away.

"New York."

"Ah, there you only have to know the numbers to find your way around. Fifty-sixth Street is after Fifty-fifth and before Fifty-seventh. Here in Jerusalem, you have to know history," she said, still smiling.

Like other neighborhoods of the city, Talbieh was oriented around themes which determined the names of streets.

"A walk through Talbieh," my guide continued, "is a review of the literary history of Zionism. Nahum Sokolov, Yosef Hayim Brenner, Leon Pinsker, Simon Dubnov – these are the great writers of our people."

Others, she explained, were memorialized by their *noms-de-plume:* Shalom Aleichem, Mendele Mocher Seforim, Ahad Ha-am. And still others were remembered by the books they wrote: Ha-Lev Ha'ivri (*The Hebrew Heart* by the Zionist writer Akiva Schlesinger), Dor V'Dorshov (*Each Generation and Its Seekers* by Rabbi Isaac Weiss).

"And Disraeli?"

"Ah, he and Marcus are great Jewish foreigners."

"You see," she added, "here in Jerusalem, asking for directions is no simple matter."

She was right. Inquiries like "Can you tell me the way to The Hebrew Heart?" or "How far am I from Mendel?" have the unexpected effect of exciting the collective consciousness of the Jews who ask and answer them. Can those speakers, who understand the meaning of what they say, be totally oblivious to the *double-entendres* in their conversation?

"Turn here," the old woman said as we walked into Hovevei Zion (the Lovers of Zion) Street. "Are you a tourist?"

"Yes, more or less."

"More or less?"

"Well, I have come here for the time being to write a book about Jerusalem."

"What sort of book?"

"One that will explain what it means to live here."

"That's quite ambitious. How much time do you give yourself?"

"As long as it takes."

"Ah, good," she said, a teasing smile crossing her face. "You have come on *aliyah* [to immigrate], then." Both of us laughed.

"If you are interested in this neighborhood, you should look on this block. I can recall," she continued, "when Martin Buber moved into Number 3." She pointed toward a large stone house, now nearly covered by creeping ivy and wreathed in sweet-smelling jasmine.

"In 1948, during the heaviest battles, Buber ran away from his home in the eastern sector, in Abu Tor. This house had been vacated, and so he moved in here. He was not very happy in those days. Of course, the street was not like it is today. Then it was hardly more than a dirt path. But the house, abandoned by its former inhabitants, was fine. Still, Buber was inconsolable because he had fled without his books, which were still in the east."

"What happened?" I asked.

"What happened? He said that he could not go on living without his books."

"Was there anything to be done about it?"

"What do you think? A great philosopher without his books. Would we Jews allow that?" A tinge of sarcasm colored her voice. "A group of graduate students from the university took time out from defending the city and dragged cartons of his books over to here.

"But I suppose it was worth it, because later, after the war, on Friday evenings, Buber gave wonderful Bible classes in that building." She pointed to Mo'adon Ha-Oleh.

–Samuel Heilman
A Walker in Jerusalem

�֍✶✶✶✶✶✶✶✶✶✶✶✶✶✶✶✶

The Plazas Shall Be Filled with Children

I walked toward the engraving, recalling the story in the Talmud. I wondered what Ricarda would have thought of it, and for a moment I imagined myself repeating it to her:

"Shortly after the destruction of the Second Temple, Rabbi Akiva, the man who learned to read only in his fortieth year of life but ultimately became among the greatest scholars Jewry has ever known, was walking atop Mount Scopus, along with other equally great rabbis. From their viewpoint his companions believed they could still see the smoke rising from the heaps of ashes and destruction atop the Temple Mount, and so in mourning for the loss of majesty at this most holy of sites, they rent their clothing.

"When they reached the point closest to the Temple Mount, they suddenly saw a jackal run out of the place that had once been the Holy of Holies – the most sacred spot of the Temple, where the High Priest alone could enter and then only once a year on the Day of Atonement. Seeing this, they all began to weep in despair – all except Rabbi Akiva, who smiled.

"Stunned at his reaction, his companions asked the reason for his smile and he answered – you know we Jews have always liked answering questions with a question – he answered: 'And why do you cry?'

"So, rabbis and scholars that they were, they began to quote verses from the sources. Pointing to the spot from which the jackal had come, one of them – I think it was Rabban Gamliel, but I'm not certain – said: 'This is the place of which the Holy Scriptures warned that the common man who even so much as dared to draw near it would be put to death, and now jackals stroll upon it. How can we not weep?'

"To the rabbis, the jackal was visible proof of the denial of all God's promises to His people, a portent of worse things to come, the end of hope, proof that the glories of the past were gone. But for Akiva, who continued to smile, it was quite the opposite. Turning to his companions, he said: 'Why, that jackal is precisely the reason I can smile. Do those very same Scriptures not tell us through the mouth of Isaiah that God shall take as witness of His deeds Uriah the priest and Zechariah, the son of Berechiah?

" 'Now,' continued Akiva, we have always been troubled by this verse.' The other, happy to be swept up in Talmudic dialogue, nodded. 'What, we wondered, could Uriah, who comes from a far earlier period of history, have to do with Zechariah, who comes much later? And yet the word of God had coupled their prophecies.

" 'And what had each one seen? Through Uriah, the Almighty had promised that Zion shall be plowed like a field and Jerusalem be in heaps; and the Temple Mount deserted as a wooded hilltop.

" 'And,' Akiva added, 'so it is now, as jackals wander among the heaps on what is only a wooded hilltop.

" 'But in the book of Zechariah we find the prophet speaks otherwise.' "

The quotation from Zechariah was the lines engraved on the wall. I walked over to read them. In the bright afternoon light of the plaza, children, already home from school, ran everywhere. Some were playing soccer, the most popular game of the season. A few were riding bicycles and playing tag. A small group of tourists was shuffling into a cafe at the far end of the square. On one of the benches, near a small playground set up in another of the corners of the place, an old man sat reading the afternoon paper and holding a cane between his legs.

I turned to read the writing on the wall.

THUS SAYS THE LORD OF HOSTS: "THERE SHALL YET SIT OLD MEN AND OLD WOMEN IN THE SQUARES OF JERUSALEM, AND A MAN LEANING ON HIS STAFF BECAUSE OF HIS MANY YEARS. AND THE PLAZAS SHALL BE FILLED WITH BOYS AND GIRLS PLAYING IN THEM."

Turning to look again at the fulfillment of Zechariah's prophecy, I imagined concluding Akiva's story for Ricarda: " 'Until the prophecy of Uriah had been fulfilled, I feared that the prophecy of Zechariah might not come to be. Now that we see that Uriah's prophecy has been fulfilled, we may be certain that Zechariah's promise will also come to be.'

" 'You have comforted us, Akiva,' the others said. 'You have comforted us.' "

I turned to watch an old woman walk a little girl to the slide in the playground across the square. Jerusalem was a place where history is not a one-way street; here the resurrection of old glories still seemed possible.

–Samuel Heilman
A Walker in Jerusalem

ACKNOWLEDGMENTS

Special appreciation is expressed to my devoted and efficient secretary, Audrey Katzman, of The Park Synagogue, Cleveland, Ohio, who oversaw the acknowledgments and many other aspects of the preparation of this volume. Spending hours before and after work and during lunch hour enabled her to be of major assistance to me. Both her administrative and editorial acumen were of incalculable value.

Below we acknowledge the authors, publishers, and other copyright holders who have kindly extended permission to us to reprint their materials in *Moments of Transcendence*. Several persons and publishers deserve special mention for the extent and quality of pages they permitted us to reprint:

Rabbi Jonathan Levine, Editor, Media Judaica/Hartmore House/Prayer Book Press
Rabbi Sidney Greenberg
Rev. Dr. Jeffrey M. Cohen and Routledge, Chapman & Hall, Ltd.
Rabbi Yosef Goldman
Rabbi Morris Shapiro
Rabbi Saul I. Teplitz
New York Board of Rabbis

The following selections are reprinted from: Rabbi Saul I. Teplitz, ed. *The Rabbis Speak: A Quarter Century of Sermons for the High Holy Days*. New York: New York

Board of Rabbis, 1986. Titles in parentheses refer to the readings as named in *Moments*.

Rabbi Max Arzt. "Kippurim" ("The Highest Level of Insensitivity to Injustice").

Rabbi Philip S. Bernstein. "How to Face Death" ("In Old Age, Cast Us Not Out").

Rabbi Isaac Klein. "The Sins of Civilization" ("Responsibility for Each Individual").

Rabbi Benjamin Z. Kreitman. "The Day Yom Kippur Became Simchat Torah" ("Kol Nidre – Once a Time for Joy?"); "Was Jonah Altogether Wrong? Or In Defense of Jonah" ("In Defense of Jonah").

Selections from the following books are reprinted with permission of Media Judaica/Hartmore House/Prayer Book Press.

Rabbi Sidney Greenberg. *Contemporary Prayers and Readings for the High Holidays, Sabbaths, and Special Occasions.* Copyright © 1972, Prayer Book Press, Bridgeport, CT, and New York City, pp. 1, 40. Reprinted by permission of Media Judaica and Sidney Greenberg.

Rabbi Sidney Greenberg. *High Holiday Bible Themes.* Copyright © 1973 by Hartmore House, Bridgeport, CT, and New York City. Reprinted by permission of Hartmore House and Rabbi Sidney Greenberg.

Rabbi Sidney Greenberg. *Lessons For Living.* Copyright © 1985 by Hartmore House, Bridgeport, CT, and New York City, pp. 44–45, 82, 98, 112. Reprinted by permission of Hartmore House and Rabbi Sidney Greenberg.

Rabbi Sidney Greenberg. *Say Yes To Life.* Copyright © 1982 by Crown Publishers, pp. 6–7, 44–45, 76–77, 68, 88–89, 116–117. Reprinted by permission of Sidney Greenberg.

Rabbi Michael Hecht. *The Fire Waits.* Copyright © 1972 by Media Judaica, Bridgeport, CT, and New York City. Reprinted by permission of Media Judaica and Rabbi Michael Hecht.

Rabbi Harold S. Kushner. *For Modern Minds and Hearts,* ed. Rabbi Abraham Karp. Copyright © 1971 by Media Judaica, Bridgeport, CT, and New York City, p. 25. Reprinted by permission of Media Judaica.

Tuvia Preshel. "The Shofar at the Western Wall," in *High Holiday Bible Themes,* ed. Rabbi Sidney Greenberg. Copyright © 1973 by Hartmore House, Bridgeport, CT, and New York City, pp. 184–185.

Rabbi Nahum Waldman. "Let Us Commit," in *Likrat Shabbat,* ed. Rabbi Sidney Greenberg. Copyright © 1987 by Media Judaica, Bridgeport, CT, and New York City.

Acknowledgment is accorded to the following authors and sources of publications with reference to material included in this volume:

Rabbis Eliezer Berkovits, Seymour J. Cohen, Wayne D. Dosick, Abraham J. Karp, Simcha Kling, David Lincoln, Stephen Chaim Listfield, Allen S. Maller, Arthur Oleisky, Jonathan Perlman, Stanley Platek, Stanley Rabinowitz, Bernard Raskas, Daniel A. Roberts, James S. Rosen, Gilbert Rosenthal, Elijah J. Schochet, Harold Schulweis, Morris Shapiro, Richard Sherwin, Matthew H. Simon, Samuel Stahl, Dr. Jeffrey Tigay, Arnold Turetsky, Jeffrey Wohlberg, Zvi Yehuda, Joel Zion.

Rabbi Morris Adler. From *May I Have a Word With You?* by Morris Adler, compiled by Goldie Adler and Lily Edelman. Copyright © 1967 by B'nai B'rith. Reprinted by permission of Crown Publishers, Inc.

S. Y. Agnon. From *Days of Awe,* by S. Y. Agnon. Copyright © 1948, 1965 by Schocken Books Inc. Copyright renewed 1975 by Schocken Books Inc. Reprinted by permission of Schocken Books, published by Pantheon Books, a division of Random House, Inc.

S. Y. Agnon. *Yamim Noraim.* Copyright © by Schocken Books Inc. Reprinted by permission of Schocken Books Inc.

Rabbi Philip (Shragai) Arian. From *He Kindled A Light: A Philosophy of Jewish Education,* edited by Chaim Picker from speeches and writings of Shragai Arian (New York, 1976). Reprinted with permission of the publisher, United Synagogue Commission on Jewish Education.

Shirley Barish. *Bikurim,* Vol. #8, No. 2, Spring, 1991. Coalition for the Advancement of Jewish Education (CAJE) Curriculum Bank. Reprinted by permission of CAJE and the author.

Jenna Bassin and Jane Lahr. *A Garden of Prayer.* New York: Philosophical Library, 1989.

Leonard Bernstein. "Kaddish." Copyright © 1963, 1965, 1983 by Amberson, Inc.; Copyright Renewed. Reprinted by permission of Jalni Publications, Inc., Publisher, and Boosey & Hawkes, Inc., Agent.

David R. Blumenthal. Excerpt from *God at the Center: Meditations on Jewish Spirituality* by David R. Blumenthal. Copyright © 1988 by David R. Blumenthal. Reprinted by permission of HarperCollins Publishers Inc.

Rabbi Ben Zion Bokser, ed. *Hamachzor: The High Holyday Prayer Book.* Reprinted by permission of the publishers, Hebrew Publishing Company, P.O. Box 157, Rockaway Beach, NY 11693. Copyright © 1959. All rights reserved.

Joan Borysenko. Reprinted by permission of Warner Books, Inc. from *Guilt is the Teacher, Love is the Lesson.* Copyright © 1990 by Joan Borysenko.

Joan Borysenko. *Minding the Body, Mending the Mind.* Reprinted by permission of Addison Wesley Publishing Co., Inc., Reading, MA; pp. 176–177.

Central Conference of American Rabbis. CCAR Press: "The Day is Fading, The Sun Setting," from *The Union Prayerbook for Jewish Worship.* Copyright © 1948 by Central Conference of American Rabbis.

Central Conference of American Rabbis. Excerpts from *Gates of Prayer: The New Union Prayerbook.* Copyright © 1975 by Central Conference of American Rabbis and Union of Liberal and Progressive Synagogues (London) and used by permission.

James Christensen. From *Creative Way to Worship,* by James Christensen. Copyright © 1974 by Fleming H. Revell Company. Used by permission of Fleming H. Revell Company.

Rev. Dr. Jeffrey M. Cohen. *Understanding the High Holy Day Services.* Copyright © 1983 by Routledge Publishers. Reprinted by permission of Routledge.

Rabbi Samuel S. Cohon. *Judaism: A Way of Life.* Copyright © 1948 by Union of American Hebrew Congregations. Reprinted by permission of Union of American Hebrew Congregations.

Norman Cousins. *The Nature of a Humane Society.* Copyright © 1976 by Fortress Press. Published by Augsburg Fortress, 1976. Reprinted by permission of Augsburg Fortress Publishers.

Kahlil Gibran. From *The Prophet,* by Kahlil Gibran. Copyright © 1923 by Kahlil Gibran and renewed 1951 by Administrators C.T.A. of Kahlil Gibran Estate and Mary G. Gibran. Reprinted by permission of Alfred A. Knopf, Inc.

Rabbi Neil Gillman. "On Imaging God," in *Ometz Shaliach,* Vol. 4, No. 1, Winter 1986–87. Reprinted with permission of the Jewish Theological Seminary of America.

Frank G. Goble. From *The Third Force: The Psychology of Abraham Maslow,* by Frank Goble. Copyright © 1970 by the Thomas Jefferson Research Center. Reprinted by permission of Viking Penguin, a division of Penguin Books USA Inc.

Allan R. Gold. "Dukakis Learned Lesson as Teacher." *The New York Times,* August 31, 1988. Copyright © 1988 by The New York Times Company. Reprinted by permission.

Rabbi Arnold M. Goodman. "A Near-Death Experience." Cong. Ahavath Achim Bulletin, November 1990. Reprinted by permission.

Rabbi Robert Gordis. *Leave a Little To God.* Copyright © 1967 by Bloch Publishing Co., pp. 83–86, 185–186, 202–203. Reprinted by permission of Bloch Publishing Co.

Rabbi Morris A. Gutstein. *Frontiers of Faith.* Copyright © 1967 by Bloch Publishing Co., p. 143. Reprinted by permission of Bloch Publishing Co.

Anthony Hecht. *Collected Earlier Poems (The Hard Hours).* Copyright © 1990 by Anthony E. Hecht. Reprinted by permission of Alfred A. Knopf, Inc.

Samuel C. Heilman. *A Walker in Jerusalem.* New York: Summit Books, 1986, pp. 31–33, 44–45, 242–243. Reprinted by permission of Samuel C. Heilman.

William Herberg. *Judaism and Modern Man.* Copyright © 1951 by The Jewish Publication Society. Reprinted by permission of The Jewish Publication Society.

Rabbi Abraham Joshua Heschel. "Should We Forgive the Nazis?" From a speech given at Dartmouth College. Used with permission of Sylvia Heschel.

Gene Knudsen Hoffman. "Listening With Our Spiritual Ear," from *Fellowship,* Vol. 56, No. 6, June 1990. Reprinted with permission from *Fellowship,* June 1990.

Ina J. Hughes. "A Prayer of Responsibility for Children." Columnist, *Knoxville News-Sentinel,* Knoxville, TN.

Ann Landers. Permission granted by Ann Landers and Creators Syndicate.

Rabbi Richard N. Levy. *On Wings of Awe: A Machzor for Rosh Hashanah,* edited and translated by Rabbi Richard N. Levy. Copyright © 1985 by B'nai B'rith Hillel Foundation, by permission of Rabbi Levy.

Anthony Lewis. "Abroad at Home; Out of the Ashes," in *The New York Times,* March 22, 1991. Copyright © 1991 by The New York Times Company. Reprinted by permission.

Rabbi Joshua Loth Liebman. *Peace of Mind.* Copyright © 1946 by Joshua Loth Liebman, renewed © 1975 by Fran Liebman. Reprinted by permission of Simon & Schuster, Inc.

Mark Link, S.J. From *In The Stillness Is The Dancing,* by Mark Link, S.J. Copyright © 1972 by Mark Link, S.J. Published by Tabor Publishing, a division of DLM, Inc., Allen, TX 75002.

Rabbi Allen S. Maller. From *Tikkun Nefashot: A High Holiday Mahzor,* edited by Rabbi Allen S. Maller.

Rabbi Bernard Martin. From *Prayer in Judaism,* by Bernard Martin. Copyright © 1968 by Basic Books, Inc., Publishers, New York. Reprinted by permission of Basic Books, a division of HarperCollins Publishers.

Abraham Maslow. *Toward a Psychology of Being.* Copyright © 1968 by Van Nostrand Reinhold. Reprinted by permission of Van Nostrand Reinhold.

Barbara Meislin. "Snowflake," in *Association for Humanistic Psychology Perspectives,* Oct. 1983. Reprinted by permission of Barbara Meislin [The Purple Lady].

Soma Morgenstern. *The Third Pillar.* New York: Farrar, Straus, & Giroux, 1977. Reprinted by permission of Literary Estate of Soma Morgenstern; Dan Morgenstern, executor.

Anthony Fries Perrino. *Holyquest: The Search for Wholeness.* Carmel, CA: Sunflower Ink, 1988, pp. 43–44, 50–51, 54–55, 82–85, 147.

Rabbi Lawrence M. Pinsker. *Lawrence M. Pinsker's High Holiday Supplement,* West End Synagogue, New York City. Adapted from a traditional folktale.

Laurens Van Der Post. *The Heart of the Hunter.* Text Copyright © 1961 by Laurens Van Der Post. By permission of William Morrow and Co., Inc.

Dennis Prager. From *Ultimate Issues,* a quarterly journal by Dennis Prager, 6020 Washington Boulevard, Culver City, CA 90232.

Rachel Rabinowicz. From "A Haggadah Born of Paradox," by George Vecsey, *New York Times,* March 30, 1988.

Rachel Rabinowicz, ed. *The Feast of Freedom.* Copyright © 1982 by The Rabbinical Assembly. Reprinted by permission of the Rabbinical Assembly.

Rev. Robert A. Raines. *The Ridgeleaf,* March 1988, and September 1988. Copyright © 1988 by Rev. Robert A. Raines, *The Ridgeleaf,* Kirkridge Retreat and Study Center, Bangor, PA.

Carl R. Rogers. *A Way of Being.* Copyright © 1960 by Houghton Mifflin Company. Used by permission.

Rabbi Jacob Philip Rudin. *Very Truly Yours.* Copyright © 1971 by Bloch Publishing Co., p. 82. Reprinted by permission of Bloch Publishing Co.

Virginia Satir. Reprinted from *Meditations and Inspirations.* Copyright © 1985 by Virginia Satir, with permission from Celestial Arts, Berkeley, CA.

Rabbi Philip Scheim. "Hide and Seek," from the Rabbinical Assembly Homiletics Service/Yamim Noraim, 5751. Copyright © 1991 by the Rabbinical Assembly. Reprinted by permission of the Rabbinical Assembly.

Irmgard Schloegl. *Wisdom of the Zen Masters.* Copyright © 1975 by Irmgard Schloegl. Reprinted by permission of New Directions Publishing Corp.

Jeff Schwaber. "Jerusalem," in *Near East Report,* 10–15–84. Reprinted with permission from *Near East Report.*

Rabbi Daniel Jeremy Silver. The Temple, Cleveland, Ohio, Yom Kippur, 1989. Reprinted by permission of Adele Silver.

Rabbi William Silverman. From The Temple Congregation Bnai Jehuda (Kansas City, MO) *Bulletin.* Reprinted by permission of Rabbi Michael Zedek. From *Orchard,* UJA Rabbinic Advisory Council, Sept. 1988.

Barbara Silverstone and Helen Kandel Hyman. *You and Your Aging Parent.* Copyright © 1976 by Pantheon Books. Reprinted by permission of Random House, Inc.

Theo Sommer. From *Newsweek,* 7–9–90. Reprinted by permission of *Newsweek.*

Rabbi Milton Steinberg. *The Reconstructionist Prayer Book,* ed. by Rabbi Milton Steinberg. Reprinted by permission of Drs. Jonathan and David Steinberg and the Reconstructionist Foundation.

Peter Steinfels. "Lent's Start Finds Fasting Still Has a Religious Role," in *The New York Times,* February 8, 1989. Copyright © 1986 by The New York Times Company. Reprinted by permission.

Rabbi Joseph Telushkin. "Jonah and the Jews of Today," in *CLAL News and Perspectives,* July 1988. Reprinted by permission from CLAL–The National Jewish Center for Learning and Leadership *News and Perspectives,* July 1988.

Temple Emanu-El Bulletin (9–21–90). "Most Dramatic Moment." Reprinted by permission of Rabbi Ronald Sobel.

John Marks Templeton. Excerpt from *Riches For the Mind and Spirit,* by John Marks Templeton. Copyright © 1990 by K.S. Giniger Company, Inc. Reprinted by permission of HarperCollins Publishers Inc.

UJA Rabbinic Cabinet. "Stranger Than Fiction" (author unknown) in *The Orchard,* September 1988. *The Orchard,* published by the UJA Rabbinic Cabinet. Reprinted by permission of the UJA Rabbinic Cabinet.

Robert Vallett. "Prescriptions for Happiness." Reprinted by permission of Robert Vallett.

Frances Vaughan. From *The Inward Arc,* by Frances Vaughan, Copyright © 1985. Reprinted by arrangement with Shambhala Publications, Inc., 300 Massachusetts Ave., Boston, MA 02115.

Rabbi Nahum M. Waldman. "Lt. William Calley and Others," in *Jewish Exponent,* 5–21–71. Reprinted with permission of the author and the *Jewish Exponent.*

Washington Jewish Week, 3–6–88. Reprinted by permission of *Washington Jewish Week.*

Dr. Arthur Waskow. "From Fire, Light," and "Martyrology." Copyright © by Arthur Waskow; used by permission.

Rabbi Harlan J. Wechsler. "The Dubner Maggid," in *Yamim Noraim,* by S. Y. Agnon. Reprinted by permission of Harlan J. Wechsler and Schocken Books.

Rabbi Eliezer Whartman. "A Letter to the World From Jerusalem." Copyright © 1967. Used by permission of Eliezer Whartman.

INDEX

About the Editor

Nationally known lecturer, educator, author, and book critic, Rabbi Dov Peretz Elkins is spiritual leader of Princeton Jewish Center, Princeton, New Jersey. He has written widely for the Jewish and general press and is the author of twenty books, including *Humanizing Jewish Life: Judaism and the Human Potential Movement*, *My Seventy-Two Friends: Encounters with Refuseniks in the U.S.S.R.*, and a series of handbooks for Jewish group leaders. Rabbi Elkins is a member of the Committee on Jewish Law and Standards of the Rabbinical Assembly, the Council for Jewish Education, and the Association for Humanistic Psychology. He was one of three rabbis selected nationally for a mission to the Jewish community in Addis Ababa, Ethiopia. Rabbi Elkins and his family live in Princeton.